ONE SIGNAL
PUBLISHERS

ATRIA

NETWORK OF LIES

THE EPIC SAGA OF FOX NEWS, DONALD TRUMP, AND THE BATTLE FOR AMERICA

BRIAN STELTER

ONE SIGNAL
PUBLISHERS

ATRIA

New York ■ London ■ Toronto ■ Sydney ■ New Delhi

ONE SIGNAL
PUBLISHERS

ATRIA

An Imprint of Simon & Schuster, LLC.
1230 Avenue of the Americas
New York, NY 10020

First One Signal Publishers/Atria Paperback edition September 2024

ONE SIGNAL PUBLISHERS / ATRIA PAPERBACK and colophon are trademarks of Simon & Schuster, LLC.

Simon & Schuster: Celebrating 100 Years of Publishing in 2024

For information about special discounts for bulk purchases, please contact Simon & Schuster Special Sales at 1-866-506-1949 or business@simonandschuster.com.

The Simon & Schuster Speakers Bureau can bring authors to your live event. For more information or to book an event, contact the Simon & Schuster Speakers Bureau at 1-866-248-3049 or visit our website at www.simonspeakers.com.

Interior design by Dana Sloan

Manufactured in the United States of America

1 3 5 7 9 10 8 6 4 2

Library of Congress Cataloging-in-Publication Data has been applied for.

ISBN 978-1-6680-4690-6
ISBN 978-1-6680-4691-3 (pbk)
ISBN 978-1-6680-4692-0 (ebook)

To Jamie, the love of my life

CONTENTS

"Is the Fox News Channel news, or is it entertainment?"
Rupert Murdoch: *"Oh, it is news."*

"Does Fox have a responsibility to tell the truth, even when its viewers don't want to hear it?"
Rupert Murdoch: *"Yes."*

"Do you think it is acceptable to bury the truth?"
Rupert Murdoch: *"No. Of course not."*

"Do you think it's healthy for democracy when millions of people believe a falsehood about whether an election was rigged?"
Rupert Murdoch: *"It is not good for any country if masses of people believe in falsehoods."*

PROLOGUE

The indictments of Donald Trump are also a trial for the nation he once led—a stress test of American democracy, the rule of law, and the very notion of a shared political reality. Can we achieve accountability for assaults on democracy? What forms can accountability take?

That's what this book is about.

In America we have the courts of law, of politics, of public opinion, of the press. The nation is shaped by them all. When Trump and his network of lies claimed he won an election he lost in 2020, he failed in court but prevailed in the court of public opinion he cared about most: the opinion of his loyal voters. Then, special counsel Jack Smith alleged, Trump perpetrated three criminal conspiracies, each one "built on the widespread mistrust the Defendant was creating through pervasive and destabilizing lies about election fraud."

The conspiracies sought to overturn the results of a free and fair election in a brazen attempt to retain power. In other words, a coup. We watched some of it happen on live TV on January 6, 2021, but the plans for a "cloud of confusion" were secretly seeded months earlier. The coup attempt could not have happened without the help of Fox News, the cable network controlled by Rupert Murdoch and his son Lachlan.

All of the indictments Trump faced in 2023 and 2024 related, in one way or another, to the misguided advice, misinformation, and mendacity of the Fox machine. So it was apropos that, on the evening of August 1, 2023, when the special counsel indicted Trump in the historic January 6 conspiracy case, the former president's companions were Fox News Media CEO Suzanne Scott and Fox News Media president Jay Wallace.

Scott and Wallace were at Trump's summer home in Bedminster, New Jersey, for a dinner that doubled as a rapprochement. The two executives asked to see Trump so that they could lobby him to attend the first Republican Party debate of the 2024 season, set for August 23 in Milwaukee. Trump was going to skip it; he was so far ahead in GOP primary polls that he said "it would be foolish." Plus, he said, Fox News was "hostile" toward him. Scott and Wallace tried to disabuse him of that notion; they wanted him to see Fox as the heavyweight fighter in the arena defeating the liberal media and defending Trump's America. In their telling, Fox was, to reprise the network's founding lie, the only "fair and balanced" one out there. But Trump didn't want "fair." He certainly didn't want "balanced." He wanted complete and total control.

Rupert recalled that Trump once told him, of Fox, "You're 90 percent good. That's not enough. I need you 100 percent." Rupert claimed that he replied, "Well, you can't have it."

What a self-aggrandizing story for Rupert to tell—a multinational media mogul rebuffing an American president. But it masked a much less flattering truth. For four years, Fox and Trump were partners in propaganda. Trump needed Fox for access to his rabid followers; Fox needed Trump for popularity and enormous profits. They benefited one another enormously, but, as with other self-absorbed codependents, the situation made them both vulnerable, because they knew each other so well. Fox could hurt Trump by puncturing his force field of audacious lying. Trump could hurt Fox by directing his legions of acolytes elsewhere.

The alliance broke down after January 6; Rupert said "we want to make Trump a non person," and Scott told him that Fox's Trumpiest host, Sean Hannity, wanted "to help lead the 75 million forward away from Trump." But the relationship was not irreparably damaged; far from it. When GOP voters lifted Trump back to the top of the 2024 heap, Fox meekly followed along. The Bedminster dinner was proof. So was Rupert's late-2023 transition to a new role, chairman emeritus, which his aides depicted as "semi-retirement." It meant that the loudest Trump critic inside Fox was shifting into a lower, less influential gear. Lachlan, Rupert's chosen successor, was more tolerant of Trump and more blasé about the GOP's capitulation to the man. Lachlan cared more about campaign ad spending at his stations than antidemocratic conduct by his favorite candidate. Maybe Fox would now be "100 percent good" as Trump faced four criminal cases.

■

Trump was the only defendant named in Jack Smith's indictment. But in the detailed account of actions taken to subvert the election—and American democracy itself—the prosecution team cited the participation of six unindicted co-conspirators. Two of the six, Rudy Giuliani and Sidney Powell, had been regulars on Fox when the Big Lie was born. The indictment's description of the lie—"dozens of specific claims that there had been substantial fraud in certain states, such as that large numbers of dead, non-resident, non-citizen, or otherwise ineligible voters had cast ballots, or that voting machines had changed votes for the Defendant to votes for Biden"—was also a painstaking summary of Fox's opinion programming from November 2020.

After telling Trump supporters to ignore "fake news" from real news outlets, Fox stars rolled out the ultimate fake story, injecting false hope of a second Trump term into millions of people like it was ivermectin. They cheered on Trump's pitiful legal losing streak and offered up the fanciful promise that he'd win before the Supreme Court. They did it to keep the fans happy, to keep the applause coming; in other words, to juice their ratings, as they sometimes admitted to each other.

It was grotesque. And it led some to picture Fox as the seventh unindicted co-conspirator in the January 6 criminal case. There would never be charges to that effect, of course, but there was already a legal squabble over Fox's culpability. When a website in Rupert's native Australia published a story headlined "Trump is a confirmed unhinged traitor. And Murdoch is his unindicted co-conspirator," Lachlan sued the site, alleging defamation. He withdrew the thin-skinned lawsuit shortly after he approved Fox's $787.5 million settlement with Dominion Voting Systems.

Of all the efforts at Big Lie accountability—like the House select committee that probed January 6 and handed a road map to Smith—Dominion's lawsuit against Fox was the costliest. At first Fox's executive team dismissed Dominion's chances ("it's a slam-dunk First Amendment case," lawyers told producer Abby Grossberg) with the same language that Trump's lawyers used to defend him. Some Fox insiders mocked the suit by likening Dominion to a nuisance fly on the back of the Fox elephant. But they wised up once deposed. The 8 p.m. host Tucker Carlson recoiled at the thought of his day-long deposition in late 2022. The Dominion lawyer was a "slimy little motherfucker," he told a colleague afterward. "That guy, he triggered the shit out of me." Carlson had wanted to preface all his answers with "fuck you," to which the appropriate retort would have been, "Tucker, you already fucked yourself."

Because Fox was subject to the pretrial discovery process, it was forced to give Dominion years of emails, texts, chats, and memos, including Carlson's highly offensive messages to his friends at Fox. Through court filings, Dominion ensured that thousands of the documents were exposed to the public. For the first time in the network's history, outsiders were able to see how it worked on the inside.

However, some of the ugliest texts were still under seal on the eve of the expected trial in Wilmington, Delaware. There was a palpable fear, on the Fox side, and excitement, among the network's critics, that the rest of Fox's secrets would be laid bare in the courtroom. And Carlson was expected to be the first Fox host to take the stand because Dominion thought he would help them win their case.

With all that in mind, it is little wonder why Fox authorized a staggering self-imposed fine of $787.5 million to avert the trial. Carlson would not have to go through the wringer of testifying—and neither would Rupert or Lachlan. (Some of Carlson's terrible texts still came out, though.)

As is the case with most court proceedings, the material in *Dominion v. Fox* was hard to find and harder to digest. A handful of embarrassing emails and hypocritical texts became national news, but the full treasure trove of information was mostly inaccessible. That's the problem I wanted to solve by writing this book.

I drilled into the court documents—more than two gigabytes' worth—and found nuggets of gold. In reconstructing the pivotal post-election period, I saw that Fox was more directly responsible for the chaos than anyone realized at the time. "It's getting too crazy," Carlson texted fellow prime-time star Laura Ingraham in the middle of November 2020. "We're becoming the left." They both knew that Trump had lost and talked about ways he could have won:

"If Trump had run on law and order and re-opening the schools, he would have won in a landslide," Carlson wrote. They privately recognized that Trump's narcissism ruined him. "He's always on a grievance loop that is focused on him," Ingraham texted, sounding more like an MSNBC host than a Fox personality.

At the same time, the Dominion case also revealed that other Fox hosts were so under Trump's spell that they actually believed the election was stolen. Maria Bartiromo said, "I want to see massive fraud exposed." Lou Dobbs said, "We know Joe Biden didn't persuade 80 million people to vote for him—how many did?" Dobbs still claimed to feel the same way years later. Rupert Murdoch thought this undying loyalty to Trump was nuts: Under oath with Dominion's lawyers, when asked about people who still believed Trump won in 2020, Rupert said "they are crazy."

What Rupert and his hosts all had in common was selfishness and greed. By protecting their own personal brands, political futures, and self-interests, they put profits over patriotism and the public interest. Fox was far from alone on this count, but the network was a critically important nexus. When Trump was indicted on racketeering charges by the district attorney of Fulton County, Georgia, I studied the documents and saw that five of the codefendants and at least two of the unindicted co-conspirators were regular guests on Fox at the time of the alleged crimes. The consequences of their lies are going to be litigated for years to come.

◼

Lies are—or ought to be—uncomfortable to think about. Journalists and researchers and analysts and scientists are trained to focus on what's true, not what's invented or imagined or twisted beyond recognition. But I will tell you this: Studying the liars has dramatically improved my understanding of the political universe. Anne Applebaum, the Pulitzer Prize–winning historian, was right when she said that "sometimes the point isn't to make people believe a lie—it's to make people fear the liar." Other times, the point is, in the immortal words of Trump adviser Steve Bannon, to "flood the zone with shit"—to overwhelm the press and the public with so much misinformation and disinformation that democracy can't function.

None of this is by accident. It's not a natural phenomenon. It is a network, a system, a construction of conservative billionaires and activists. Surveying the network of lies up close has taught me about the dangerous excesses of egotism and greed; the human capacity for self-rationalization and bullheaded denialism; and the sheer limits of facts and logic. As the historian Jon Meacham put it, "the American Right has become unmoored from reality because of their devotion to this singular figure."

But reality has a tendency to reassert itself: Witness the prosecutions of January 6 insurrectionists, the criminal charges against Trump, and the thicket of Big Lie civil lawsuits.

For Fox, Dominion was just the beginning. Another voting technology company, Smartmatic, demanded $2.7 billion in damages. One of the men smeared by Carlson after the election, Ray Epps, drew up his own defamation suit. One of Fox's own Capitol Hill reporters sued for illegal discrimination and retaliation. And the former head of booking at Carlson's show, Abby Grossberg, pursued twin lawsuits against Fox, Carlson, and several members of Carlson's production staff. Grossberg alleged a "sexist and hostile" workplace where "distaste and disdain for women infiltrated almost every workday decision." She said Carlson made her life "a living hell."

Grossberg eventually settled, but the other cases continued well into 2024, and formed the backbone of this book. I relied on dozens of primary sources, almost all of them on the record. In addition to court filings, the raw transcripts of depositions by the House's January 6 committee were particularly helpful. I also reviewed internal slideshows and presentations from Fox Corp; Chartbeat data showing the guts of Fox's web traffic; dozens of Carlson's public speeches and podcast appearances; and some of his more private moments, like video clips of him riffing during commercial breaks of his show. I also spoke with some of the same Fox and GOP sources who helped inform my 2020 book *Hoax*, and dozens of new sources who emerged in the years since. Some of these insiders showed me highly sensitive emails, texts, and spreadsheets. I owe every source a debt of gratitude.

■

Accountability comes in many shapes and speeds. Therefore so do these chapters. Here's what to expect in this updated fall 2024 edition.

Part One introduces the main characters in the Fox saga and travels back in time to the creation of Rupert's modern media empire;

Part Two uses the Dominion revelations to reconstruct November and December 2020, the same months that are dissected in Smith's January 6 indictment;

Part Three details the failed coup, the cover-up, and the first three years of the Biden administration;

Part Four explores what Dominion learned by deposing Rupert, how Fox decided to settle, and why Lachlan finally decided to hold Carlson accountable;

And Part Five, brand-new to this edition, reveals how Fox and Trump reached an uneasy truce for the 2024 election.

So let's journey back in time a little bit, with the promise that you won't end up like Carlson, radicalized and remanded to the fringes of the media. Hopefully you'll come away feeling the way I do: empowered and equipped to tell the truth more loudly than ever.

PART ONE

"The purge"

The firing of Tucker Carlson was the type of genuine bombshell that almost never happens in the television business because it is, unavoidably, disruptive to the bottom line.

Television, and cable news in particular, is all about consistency. Fans expect to see the same faces night after night, year after year, decade after decade. Steve Doocy and Brian Kilmeade have been cohosting Fox's morning show for more than a quarter century. Sean Hannity has been a fixture of Fox's prime-time lineup since the day the network was founded, October 7, 1996. The shows are, if nothing else, dependable. The fear-stoking topics are predictable.

But in April 2023, less than a week after Fox settled with Dominion, Carlson was fired. Deep-sixed. Shit-canned. The most popular host on Fox was marched off the plank and into the stormy seas of "independent" media.

People inside and outside Fox struggled to make sense of it. Theories about his sacking sprouted like ragweed. One of his producers was convinced the cancellation was tied to the Dominion settlement. Another producer thought it was triggered by Abby Grossberg's lawsuits. A third wondered if it was related to Ray Epps's interview on *60 Minutes* the night before, when Epps said Carlson was "going to any means possible to destroy my life."

Through several months of reporting, I figured out why Carlson was defenestrated. But I'm going to save the details for the later chapters (in TV we call that a "tease") because there was another, earlier firing that revealed what Fox has become.

The staffer's name was Jason Donner. He was a producer on Capitol Hill. The average Fox viewer never heard from or about Donner, which was part of the problem; the network usually prioritized remote talking heads over real reporters. But he was content working behind the scenes until he was fired in September 2022. Fox said Donner's policy violations and unspecified "antagonistic conduct" led to his termination, but he hired a lawyer and sued in late 2023, alleging discrimination and retaliation. "Ultimately," Donner's complaint said, "Fox News wanted to purge the news division of any staff that would not get in line with the directive to only report information that [appeased] Trump supporters and former President Trump."

■

Until 2020, Donner led a charmed existence at Fox. He worked his way up in the same manner so many broadcast journalism majors do, by first landing a job as a desk assistant in Fox's D.C. bureau in 2010, then winning multiple promotions, including a stint as a so-called "campaign embed," tracking multiple candidates during Trump's run for president in 2016.

Fox invests mostly in ranters and ravers, not reporters; its news-gathering operation is puny compared to CNN and NBC. But Capitol Hill was one of the few areas where Fox was competitive. Donner ensured that Fox stayed on top of every House and Senate storyline. But "after the 2020 election," his lawsuit charged, "something changed at Fox News."

Donner was right. The network's right-wing bent was obvious from the very beginning, but the programming was "reality-based," relatively speaking, until Trump came along. Trump radicalized both the GOP and its media systems. Trump's loss in 2020 intensified everything. Donner cast himself as a victim of "the purge in the news division."

"To win back viewership and pledge its loyalty to President Trump, Fox's corporate leadership purged the news division and those reporters who spoke out against claims of election fraud," Donner's suit claimed. (The following chapters contain some of the same examples the suit cited.)

"This toxic environment for Fox News' reporters attempting to report truthfully reached its peak after the insurrection," the suit continued. But Donner alleged that he felt the chill a month and a half earlier, when he covered Rudy Giuliani's sweaty, stultifying press conference in support of Trump's fraud lies. Donner tweeted, "At the presser, Rudy Giuliani keeps claiming voter fraud in Philadelphia, but he said this to a Pennsylvania court: 'This is not a fraud case.' "

Donner's tweet was straightforward and perfectly true. But his boss, Anita Siegfriedt, reprimanded him, according to his complaint. She said he wasn't allowed to post his "opinions." His tweet wasn't an opinion, and Siegfriedt said she'd "let it go," but Donner said he believed that he "had a target on his back" from that point on.

In more ways than one. Late on the evening of January 5, 2021, Donner's father texted him, knowing Donner would be at the Capitol for the certification of the Electoral College ballots the next day. Fears of violence were pronounced since Trump had urged his fans to descend on Washington.

"Be safe," his dad wrote.

"I'll be fine," Donner replied, in a too-dismissive tone.

Donner realized his dad was onto something when he was working in Fox's office nook near the Senate chamber and he saw a text from a colleague on the House side of the Capitol saying that some protesters had penetrated the building. "Then the video feed from the Senate floor abruptly stopped," he recalled in an essay for Fox's website a few days later. Everyone was told to shelter in place. "Our evacuation point was supposed to be the Senate chamber, but it was too late," Donner wrote. "We had to lock the doors and hunker down in our offices."

Donner and two of his Fox colleagues turned off the lights and continued to work. They could hear a loud commotion nearby. And they could see, on social media, that rioters were wandering the Senate floor and stealing documents from senators' desks. Donner began to plan an escape route. He wondered if he could use a monopod, a portable stand for a camera, as a weapon. But thankfully the Capitol Police came knocking before the Trumpers. The police escorted the journalists to the Capitol basement. "They told us not to touch anything because pepper spray and tear gas residue blanketed the halls of Congress," Donner wrote. "It covered everything: floors, railings, statues, walls, and more. There were also broken glass, furniture and garbage strewn about inside the Capitol."

His account was harrowing—but Donner left one shocking detail out of his essay. Two years later, when he sued Fox, he said that he was watching Fox's "false reporting" while hiding from the rioters. The lawsuit pointed to one particular remark by Fox anchor Martha MacCallum as being particularly offensive. MacCallum said on the air at 2:51 p.m., "you can understand why" the protesters "are severely disappointed."

Donner alleged that he heard voices like MacCallum's and felt compelled to grab the phone in Fox's broadcasting booth. He called the Fox control room. "I'm your Capitol Hill Producer," he said, according to his complaint. "Tear gas is going off on the second floor in the Ohio Clock corridor, rioters are storming the building, reports of shots fired outside the House Chamber. I don't want to hear any of this fucking shit on our air ever again because you're gonna get us all killed."

Donner's lawsuit didn't reveal what the person on the other end of the phone said. And Donner declined my interview requests in 2024, citing the pending litigation. But his description of the phone call is extraordinary in and of itself. Barely one hour into the insurrection, a ten-year veteran of Fox News was self-aware that his network was culpable. He blasted "this fucking shit," meaning two straight months of televised lies about the election outcome, and said "you're gonna get us all killed," recognizing the connection between TV tirades and real-world threats.

MacCallum alluded to it, as well, during the live segment that Donner lamented. Here is the full context of what she said: The MAGA fanatics who showed up in D.C. "were promised something. These people were told that today was going to overturn the election. And when you hear the passion in their voices, you can understand why they are severely disappointed. Now, we're going to talk a lot about whether those ideas ever should have been elevated for them."

Other media outlets did exactly what she predicted—at CNN, for instance, we talked a whole lot about who concocted the Big Lie, how it spread, and "whether those ideas ever should have been elevated." But Fox overwhelmingly shied away from that sort of introspection. Some of its own stars were implicated.

■

After Donner sued, Fox lawyers argued that he was just trying to "monetize his disagreement" with the network's "opinion commentary and editorial decisions." Their lawyers noted that Donner, once fired, "left the news business entirely and instead went into

Republican politics"—as if there is a big, beautiful wall between news and politics. Fox is living proof that there isn't. And Donner's suit contained even more data points to that effect. He claimed that he told Fox managers that the network's lack of support after January 6 was "demoralizing," but was ignored. He also said that the D.C. bureau's VP of editorial, Doug Rohrbeck, "circulated far-right-wing opinion articles to shape the stories reported on by the news division."

In mid-2022, after he was criticized by a supervisor for creating a "toxic environment" at work, Donner wrote to the HR department and described what was actually toxic about Fox, namely, Tucker Carlson et al.'s conspiracy-theorizing about the causes of the riot and their minimizing of the violence.

"Fox," he wrote in his HR memo, "has not supported its journalists since the January 6, 2021, attack on the Capitol. . . . Allowing highly paid hosts and contributors to make factually false statements about that day is not only demoralizing but creates a hostile work environment. I barely watch our programming or read our website anymore because it's hard to stomach these untruths being aired and written."

Donner put an even finer point on it later: "Our lives were endangered that day. My colleagues and I put our lives at risk covering the story and yet my employer continually allows these lawbreakers to continually be portrayed as victims."

The reframing of January 6 criminals as victims began at the grassroots level, among obscure Republican activists, worked its way up to TV shows like *Tucker Carlson Tonight,* and quickly influenced, or intimidated, many GOP lawmakers. As a former high-ranking aide told *The Washington Post,* most Republican House members "knew exactly what happened, knew how wrong it was, and knew that Donald Trump was responsible," but some succumbed to the anti-police, pro-rioter feedback from constituents. This rewriting of history enabled Trump to re-exert control over the GOP after leaving office in disgrace. By the end of 2023, he was referring to people who committed criminal acts of violence against law enforcement as "hostages." "More than just continuing to feed denialism and conspiracies about the 2020 election, he is constantly distorting the reality of what happened that day, preaching vindication to his base of voters," a team of CNN reporters wrote in March 2024. They observed that Trump "glosses over the violence" and "promises pardons for the people who committed it."

None of this happened in a vacuum. It happened because Fox hosts like Carlson created a permission structure for Trump. Some Fox staffers tried to object at the time, but were overruled.

Donner's lawsuit alleged that he complained in late October 2021 to D.C. bureau chief Bryan Boughton that Fox was letting Carlson "gaslight the country with false information, especially in light of the fact that Fox News reporters were present in the Capitol on January 6th, witnessed what happened at the Capitol, and were endangered by the insurrectionists." Donner had the moral high ground in the conversation, to be sure. But Boughton had nothing but hollow words to offer in response. According to Donner, Boughton said there was "nothing they could do because Tucker had gotten bigger than the network and was out of control. The executives could not stop him."

That is, until Lachlan Murdoch made a very expensive bet.

"Hurting America"

Tucker Carlson was on an island. Literally.

His show, *Tucker Carlson Tonight,* was based at the Fox D.C. bureau on North Capitol Street when it launched in 2016. He still retained a prized corner office for those precious few occasions when he dropped by for a visit. But Carlson fled D.C. during Trump's presidency and used his burgeoning star power to set up a whole new life for himself. While the Capitol dome still sparkled above his right shoulder on air, the fabulously rich, wildly famous purveyor of right-wing grievance spoke from remote TV studios near his winter compound along the Gulf Coast of Florida and his summer retreat in bucolic Bryant Pond, Maine. Fox outfitted him with all the gear he needed; most viewers never guessed that he was hundreds of miles from D.C., and he wanted it to stay that way, one of many secrets he kept from the viewing public.

Carlson's remoteness mattered because it changed him, separated him from people and events, from the diversity of the real world. He rarely talked with his show team in person. He was isolated in almost every sense of the word. "His whole world really shrank," an ex-colleague told me. "And he started to believe his own bullshit."

Carlson was not an innocent victim of the actually-fake-news age. He was a top perpetrator. He reveled in the power he acquired. (In June 2019, for instance, Carlson passionately cautioned against a spiraling conflict with Iran, and within days Trump signaled de-escalation. Weeks later, Carlson traveled with Trump to the G20 summit in Osaka, Japan, and they taped an interview together.) His professed beliefs became so extreme, so unglued, that Carlson circa 2023 was barely recognizable to his old D.C. friends. And that's just the way he liked it.

■

To hear Carlson tell it, he wound up on TV by accident one day in 1995. He was writing for *The Weekly Standard* at the time, and a producer called up the magazine, desperate for a guest to talk about the O. J. Simpson trial. One hit led to another, and his pursuit of a paying TV job became deliberate. "I had financial demands," he said, namely a growing family. By 2000, when CNN tried him out on *Crossfire,* he had three young kids at home. His fourth was born in 2002.

Crossfire, the long-running left-versus-right head-butting show, had a rotation of hosts, some of whom were in their sixties. Carlson was only thirty-one. "Producers liked him: He was young, he was fresh, he was conservative but not extreme," liberal cohost Bill Press told me. Press liked him too: They became close friends and worked the paid speaking circuit together, for a time making more money from public appearances than from CNN. Part of the point, Press said, was to demonstrate that "we could disagree but still remain friends."

Carlson was not a party-line Republican, which sometimes affected the topic selection at *Crossfire.* Several CNN staffers said the show steered away from conversations about abortion when Carlson was hosting because he was pro-choice, just like the show's liberals. Carlson was also more supportive of gay rights than the average right-wing commentator.

As the 2000 election careened toward a recount, Press and Carlson were given a late-night show called *The Spin Room.* Rewatching the episodes twenty-plus years later, I noted that Carlson was able to hide his alcohol dependency (he told a biographer that, at his lowest point, he was downing four vodkas at breakfast, before sobering up in 2002), but mostly I was just struck by how fun it all felt, with Republicans and Democrats existing in the same reality and assuming most of the same facts.

It didn't last. *The Spin Room* was canceled and *Crossfire* was cut in half, from sixty minutes to thirty. Maybe the political stakes felt higher after 9/11 led America into two all-consuming wars. Viewers soured on *Crossfire,* and Carlson began to plot a way out, but then Jon Stewart—at the height of his powers as the host of *The Daily Show*—paid a visit in October 2004.

As soon as he appeared on set, Stewart disrupted Carlson, who seemed to be expecting a Borscht Belt comic firing harmless one-liners, and then-cohost Paul Begala. Stewart assumed the role of psychologist. "Why do we have to fight?" he asked right off the top. The hosts exchanged puzzled glances. Stewart kept going: "Why do you argue?" For fourteen excruciating (for Carlson) and spellbinding (for viewers) minutes, Stewart shredded the show he was on, telling the "partisan hacks" at the table that *Crossfire* was "hurting America."

"You're doing theater," not debate, Stewart said, pointing to Carlson's signature bow tie as proof.

"You have a responsibility to the public discourse," he said, "and you fail miserably."

He even called Carlson a "dick." Carlson did not appreciate the lecture one bit. "You need to get a job at a journalism school," he said.

"You need to go to one," Stewart shot back.

No one at CNN should have been surprised by this. Stewart had been reluctant to appear on *Crossfire* and had told two of its booking producers about his low opinion of the show. But they kept lobbying, and he had a book to promote, so he showed up. The live studio audience rallied to his side. By the end of the segment, Stewart implored the hosts to "please stop."

And stop they did. Barely two months later, CNN's newly installed president, Jonathan Klein, announced he was canceling *Crossfire* and cutting ties with Carlson. Klein said his plan had been to move away from the frothy debate genre all along, regardless of what Stewart had said, but he told *New York Times* reporter Bill Carter that "I agree wholeheartedly with Jon Stewart's overall premise." That basically drove a stake through Carlson's CNN career. "We just determined there was not a role here in the way Tucker wanted his career to go," Klein said. "He wanted to host a prime time show."

Carlson tried the familiar "you can't fire me, I quit" trick, telling Carter that he was joining MSNBC to helm the 9 p.m. hour. The deal wasn't actually done yet, however. I want to linger on this fact for a moment because Carlson lied about it for years afterward, seemingly to protect his self-worth after the double battering by Stewart and Klein. He told an interviewer in 2018 that "I was long gone from CNN and employed at another network by the time *Crossfire* got canceled." This is quite easy to disprove because the cancellation (effective in June) was publicized on January 5, and Carlson's final broadcast was on January 6. His leap to MSNBC was announced in February.

To be fair, Rick Kaplan, who had run CNN when Carlson joined *Crossfire,* and now ran MSNBC, saw something in Carlson's TV chops, and hoped that *The Situation with Tucker Carlson* would jump-start his third-place schedule. Carlson was ecstatic about the do-over. He decided to stop wearing his trademark bow tie, because, as he colorfully said to me, "it took me twenty years to realize that wearing a bow tie is like wearing a middle finger around your neck." Carlson moved his family into a $3.3 million mansion in Madison, New Jersey (he decided that living in Manhattan would be too expensive), and started to put down roots, foolishly, since the beginning of *The Situation* was bleak, with only 200,000 viewers a night, fewer than half as many as *Crossfire.*

After only six weeks, Kaplan moved Carlson to 11 p.m., telling me that it was always designed to be a "late-night show." Then it was moved again, to 4 and 6 p.m., and renamed *Tucker,* like he was a budding Oprah. Around this time, as he sought both promotion and pocket cash, he agreed to do ABC's *Dancing with the Stars.* If you're in need of a laugh, search YouTube to see him cha-cha-cha to "Dancing in the Street." He was the very first contestant voted off the show. Carlson remarked to a friend (who later shared the anecdote with me), "Do you know how desperate you have to be to do *Dancing with the Stars?*" Carlson did know. He was never literally poor—he just always wanted more. One year after *Dancing* he taped a pilot episode of a game show titled *Do You Trust Me?* CBS decided no, and scrapped the project.

These Hollywood dalliances did not help Carlson's day job. *Tucker* was canceled in early 2008, and it's only remembered now for catapulting Rachel Maddow to MSNBC superstardom. Maddow, an Air America radio host at the time, was Carlson's go-to liberal panelist. She took over the 9 p.m. time slot in September, just as the economy crashed, and scored ten times as many viewers as Tucker had. Meanwhile, he wondered how he was going to pay his mortgage. He went hat in hand to Roger Ailes.

∎

I first got to know Carlson during his lost years at MSNBC, when I was a college student in Maryland running a blog about cable news and he became a reliable reader and patron. When I solicited donations, he tipped $100—the single greatest sum I received from anyone. We went to dinner and he booked me on *The Situation;* on both occasions, he heaped praise on my blog, which I understood to be a campaign of flattery to induce positive coverage. I wasn't the only one—he kept in touch with other media beat reporters, partly to stoke his own ambitions, but also because he was an inveterate gossip.

By the time Carlson fell out of MSNBC, I had joined *The New York Times*. When I interviewed him for the paper, he described MSNBC as a "slow-motion departure," and probably an inevitable one, as "it's just a different network than it was when I joined." MSNBC, in the twilight of the George W. Bush years, was finding its liberal voice, and "there wasn't a place for me anymore," Carlson said.

CNN certainly wasn't taking him back. So that left Fox. Luckily for Carlson, the founding CEO of Fox News took pity on him. For thirteen years Roger Ailes had been building Fox into a conservative alternative to the rest of the American media. After 9/11, it took off. Conceived as a counter to the "mainstream" media, which conservatives always believed stuck a thumb on the scale to make it tip leftward, Fox had morphed into a dedicated propaganda organ willing to throw an entire bloated carcass on the scale to load it up on the right. "Ailes built the defining misinformation medium of its time," news industry analyst Ken Doctor said.

Fox was light on reporting, heavy on opining about what others were reporting, and was almost a make-work program for conservative commentators. Carlson would fit right in. But Ailes put him in his place first. "You're a loser, and you screwed up your whole life," Ailes told Carlson. "But you have talent."

Ailes ruled through fear and control. He really liked washouts like Carlson because he wielded power over them. "I'm doing him a favor," Ailes remarked to an associate at the time, "and he's going to owe me."

Plus, Ailes added, "if I can make him a success here, we make those two assholes"—CNN and MSNBC—"look bad."

It was exactly the mindset that made Ailes a GOP kingmaker for thirty-plus years.

Ailes's I-own-you speech was still on Carlson's mind when I spoke with him about his new role at Fox. I'm doing "whatever they want me to do," he said. His first appearance was on *Fox & Friends* at 7 a.m. on his fortieth birthday. "This is the very first thing I'm doing in my forties other than shaving," he told me, all hopped up on the possibility of a host position in the future. But Ailes had nothing like that to offer at the moment; he signed Carlson as a contributor, meaning he would just be a guest on others' shows.

Fox definitely didn't amount to a full-time job, so Carlson—who moved his family back to D.C.—hatched a plan with his college roommate Neil Patel to launch *The Daily Caller,* a right-wing politics site inspired by the left-wing *Huffington Post. The Daily Caller* squeezed out a profit, but the big money was in TV. Carlson, according to two sources, openly campaigned for a seat on the weekend edition of *Fox & Friends,* and in the winter of 2013 Ailes gave it to him. The job helped with private school tuition, but Carlson absolutely hated it. This was a guy who still fancied himself a writer, who devoured *The Atlantic* and *The New Yorker* and *The Weekly Standard* and *Vanity Fair,* and now he helmed cooking segments and rode go-karts on the Fox plaza in Midtown Manhattan. One time, he dozed off on the morning show couch during a broadcast; some viewers thought he was play-acting, but he was actually sleeping. Another time, he climbed into a dunk tank wearing a full suit; he said he trudged back to his hotel shoeless and soaking wet. The hotel room was a symbol of his misery: "He hated the weekend hours," a source said, and "he hated being away from his family." The show was in New York, his family was in Washington, so he was up and down constantly, with nothing but Amtrak Guest Rewards points to show for it. He went for early-morning jogs in Midtown to clear his head. Sometimes he even tried fly-fishing in Central Park.

His ticket to weekdays, and normal waking hours, and more quality time with his kids, only came in 2016, through a domino effect that began when Gretchen Carlson accused Ailes of sexual harassment. Ailes urged Fox's female stars to defend him, and that's exactly what 7 p.m. host Greta Van Susteren did; after the number of accusers multiplied, and Ailes was forced out, a chagrined Van Susteren invoked the "key man" clause in her contract that said she could walk if the "key man," in this case Ailes, left. She was obviously trying to renegotiate her contract to land a big payday, but Rupert responded by ending her show and enlisting Carlson to take over. *Tucker Carlson Tonight* launched on November 14, six days after Trump clinched the presidency, and the timing was perfect. Carlson's show, more than any other, was going to epitomize the Trump years: The MAGA movement's rage, glee, cruelty, and contradictions, perfectly distilled into a TV show that rarely mentioned Trump at all.

■

Unlike most cable news hosts, Carlson did not begin his hour by previewing all the segments that the producers had planned. Instead, he barreled right into his first guest. In the show's early months, that person was often an unprepared college professor or unlucky reporter, someone who had agreed to come to dinner without realizing that they were the feast. The on-screen banners said "TUCKER TAKES ON DEMOCRATIC CONGRESSMAN," "TUCKER TAKES ON BUZZFEED EDITOR," "TUCKER TAKES ON SATANIST." In other words, he did to random media bystanders what Jon Stewart had done to him.

As the one-sided cage match shtick became better known, the

gullible marks stopped saying yes and the pugilistic confrontations subsided. But to the Fox base, Carlson was instantly and permanently imprinted with the same identity as Trump: As a fighter. And a bully.

Carlson clearly saw some of himself in Trump—or wished he did. The host said years later, elevating Trump's bumptious Queens street swagger to some form of conscious political savvy, that "effective populists are the ones who critique from the inside," naming Trump, Ross Perot, and Teddy Roosevelt (of all people) as examples. Carlson wrote of Trump, "he's a whistleblower, a traitor to his class," and that's definitely what Carlson imagined he himself was. The prep school kid who got his start at the Heritage Foundation, who sometimes ate at The Palm twice in one day, who emailed his neighbor Hunter Biden for help getting his son into Georgetown—that's who now condemned the D.C. "elites" every night.

Carlson was more interested in Trump's ideas—restricting immigration, fortifying the border, and ending foreign wars—than Trump himself. Carlson was all too aware of the president's flaws and thus preferred not to talk much about him at all. But Trump's addiction to Fox made it hard to sidestep the shitshow. On a Saturday in February 2017, just a few weeks after the inauguration, Trump made a bizarre comment about something terrible that happened "last night in Sweden." Trump said it at a rally while railing against threats posed by terrorists. Swedish officials were flummoxed by sudden requests for comment. Nothing unusual had happened the night before; certainly no acts of terror. It took a while to figure out that Trump was making a hash of a Carlson segment from the previous evening. Carlson had interviewed an obscure conservative filmmaker who was pushing bogus news about a crime wave in Sweden tied to lax immigration policies.

All Trump knew was what he watched—to his detriment, and to the country's. But Carlson didn't fret about this, at least not in 2017, when he was suddenly Fox's shiniest new toy. The network was in flux and *Tucker Carlson Tonight* was the beneficiary. When Megyn Kelly decamped for NBC, leaving a sudden hole at 9 p.m., Carlson was the plug. Three months later, amid a sexual harassment scandal, the king of cable news, Bill O'Reilly, was fired from the 8 p.m. hour that had defined Fox for a generation. Carlson was once again the solution to a scheduling problem. Viewers followed him to every new time slot. By the end of the year, the new cable world order was complete: Martha MacCallum's conservative newscast at 7, Carlson at 8, Sean Hannity at 9, and Laura Ingraham at 10. Hannity, the longest-tenured host, was also the highest-rated (since TV is all about habit and familiarity and repetition) and the closest personally to Trump. But Carlson, the ideas guy, seemed the most in tune with Trump's permanently aggrieved base. Trump and Carlson employed the same techniques: the "I'm a very honest guy" claim to truth-teller status; the "people are infiltrating our country" demagoguery; the "we are in danger" allusions to strong-man rule; the "I've been treated very unfairly" plays for sympathy. In the same way that Trump claimed he loved his businessman life and didn't have to run for president, Carlson told puff-piece-writers that he didn't own a TV and would rather be out fishing, but was compelled to speak truth to power. "Everyone else is too afraid to say obvious things," he contended.

Republican Voters Against Trump founder Sarah Longwell, who held focus groups with voters across the country, told me that Carlson and Trump "both convinced voters that they are the only ones who are telling the truth."

And "that creates a bond with the audience," she added. "It's very cult-like."

Like many Republican voters, Carlson covered for Trump's mess-making and firehose of lies by being anti-anti-Trump. Carlson's December 2015 comment to an old bud, the poisonous, ultraright conspiracist and radio host Alex Jones, was prophetic: "There are things about Trump that I don't agree with. . . . But none of that really compares in emotional impact to the feeling I get watching the press whine about him and declare him dangerous. Every time I hear that I feel like sending him money."

Carlson never made any such donation, but his on-air cover for Trump was of value beyond measure. He rationalized; he normalized; he deflected; and he memory-holed. When candidate Trump—in a bald-faced burst of religious prejudice—proposed a "total and complete" ban on Muslims entering the United States "until our country's representatives can figure out what the hell is going on," Carlson told Jones it was a "totally reasonable and rational conclusion to reach." Five years later, when interviewer Aidan McLaughlin brought up that campaign promise on a podcast, Carlson reacted with laughter and disbelief. "Where did he say that?" Carlson said he didn't remember one of the chief controversies of the Trump presidency, one that had been replayed and rebuked endlessly, one that had caused years of court battles. To McLaughlin, this apparent forgetfulness showed "how much whitewashing people like Tucker have to do to pretend Trump is a palatable political figure."

"You are not crazy"

During the Trump years, while Carlson's show skyrocketed, civility plummeted. Americans more and more defined themselves by who or what they opposed, detested, denigrated. Instances of political violence spiked. So did threats to media outlets. In mid-October 2018, a Fox-addicted, Trump-dedicated Florida man named Cesar Sayoc sent mail bombs to CNN and prominent Democrats. The government called it a domestic terrorist attack.

A few weeks later, Carlson felt attacked when a band of about twenty left-wing protesters showed up on the street outside his $3.8 million home in Northwest Washington. They called Carlson a "racist scumbag" and chanted: "Tucker Carlson, we will fight! We know where you sleep at night!" He was across town at work, preparing for his show, but his wife was in the kitchen, and she called 911, believing the protesters were trying to break in. Carlson valued law and order above all else; he feared volatility and unrest. Now disorder was knocking at his front door (which he claimed was cracked even though the police observed no damage). The police, in his view, failed to punish the vandals. The protesters were not chastened by the bad press for their tactics. They said Carlson must be held accountable for promoting a white nationalist agenda. Fox's top executives defended him and denounced the protest, but that was not enough. The incident led Carlson to escalate rhetorically—and retreat physically. He withdrew further from public life.

Carlson already longed to escape back to his childhood vacation idyll of a pond in Maine, where he could fish every day; after the disturbance, he put his D.C. residence on the market. He already described urban life in nightmarish terms; after the disturbance, he got even louder and more explicit about it. He fiercely stoked white fright, blasted the "diversity agenda," and reserved many of his foulest insults for minority politicians. He began to cite the so-called great replacement, a racist and anti-Semitic conspiracy theory about a cabal replacing whites with people of color. He warned that "we're being invaded." He called Mexico a "hostile foreign power." He said illegal immigration was changing America "completely and forever."

He repeated this stuff on a loop. One night he suggested that migration "makes our own country poorer and dirtier and more divided," and the result was blanket outrage and an advertiser boycott. Yet Fox let him go back on TV to defend his "dirtier" claim by showing images of trash at the southern border. "We're good," Carlson reassured colleagues after the episode, implying he had taken advantage of his direct line to Lachlan Murdoch, and that Lachlan had his back.

See, Carlson, looking for a protective rabbi, had struck up a personal relationship with Lachlan, the new CEO of Fox Corp. Most Fox hosts didn't know Lachlan personally, but Carlson did, and he made sure everyone else knew he did. "You couldn't ask for a better relationship," he bragged of the Murdochs in 2019. "They are completely supportive. They are nice. They are fun to eat with. They've never asked me to go easy on this person or tough on that person." Media reports about the stream of controversies Carlson invited on himself and the company often emphasized this family connection, as if to say, *"Doesn't matter; he's safe."*

Internally too, Carlson and his senior executive producer Justin Wells routinely dropped Lachlan's name to get their way: *"I'll talk to Lachlan." "Lachlan told Tucker he could do this."* The portrayal they encouraged—of Carlson and Lachlan as regular dinner mates, just two middle-aged dads working together to right all that was wrong with the world—was powerful. But it was discredited when both men were deposed by Dominion's lawyers. When asked about Carlson, Lachlan said they only spoke "rarely." When asked the same question about Lachlan, Carlson chose the same word, "rarely," volunteering that "it's not on a weekly basis or even a monthly basis." A text message from Carlson to Lachlan in September 2020, obtained by Dominion, also suggested some serious distance between them: "Lachlan, it's Tucker. Hope you're great. Thanks for staying strong through all this insanity. We're all grateful for it." With its whiff of obsequiousness, that sounds like the way you address the guy who owns your company, not a close friend.

The "poorer and dirtier" controversy in 2018 appeared to be another case of Carlson projecting invincibility, or at least of Lachlan having it both ways. When Dominion questioned Lachlan under oath, he said he couldn't recall if he spoke to Carlson directly about the upsetting episode, but he said, "I'm very pro-immigrant. My family are immigrants as well." He added, "I think the insinuation" made by Carlson "is absolutely wrong."

Yet Carlson kept making it, month after month, year after year, and it played. It was exactly what the base wanted to hear. The right-wing media was also white-wing media. Michael Anton, author of a pro-Trump essay in 2016 titled "The Flight 93 Election," wrote in 2019 that Carlson was the New Right's leader, "more in tune than anyone else with the mix of populism, economic centrism, immigration restrictionism, and war fatigue that motivates today's disaffected Right."

Carlson's critics explained the appeal more plainly: racism. Derek Black, the son of a Ku Klux Klan grand wizard who turned against his racist family, said Carlson mainstreamed white nationalism more than anyone else in public life. "My family watches Tucker Carlson's show once and then watches it on the replay," he told CNN, "because they feel that he is making the white nationalist talking points better than they have and they're trying to get some tips on how to advance it."

The white male backlash was real even if Carlson and his fan club didn't want to recognize they were a part of it. When surveyed, a mind-boggling 73 percent of Republicans said discrimination against whites was as big a problem as discrimination against minorities, and 60 percent of Republicans agreed that society punishes men just for acting like men. Fox stoked those fears—Carlson most of all.

■

On August 3, 2019, a twenty-one-year-old white male drove 650 miles across Texas to a Walmart near the Mexican border in El Paso. Before entering the store, he logged online and uploaded a 2,300-word screed purporting to explain what he was about to do. "This attack is a response to the Hispanic invasion of Texas," he wrote. "They are the instigators, not me. I am simply defending my country from cultural and ethnic replacement brought on by the invasion." Then he entered the big-box store with a semiautomatic rifle. He murdered twenty-three people and injured another twenty-two.

Although Carlson's name and Fox's brand were never invoked in the killer's manifesto, Carlson's commentaries and the man's rants were frighteningly similar. Carlson, on his back foot, went on Fox two nights later and said the problem wasn't his "invasion" alarmism, or white nationalism, or gun worship. No, the real problem was that young men were adrift, angry and alone, afflicted by a "suffocating culture" in a "stagnant dystopia," an environment that was sure to spawn a few mass shooters. That they happened to be white, nativist, racist, and packing military-grade weapons was irrelevant. Carlson's America was the land of the repressed, home of the weak. As the scrutiny of his "replacement" rhetoric intensified, Carlson went back on air and claimed that white supremacy was "actually not a real problem in America." He said it was a "hoax" and a conspiracy theory "used to divide the country and keep a hold on power." When a young Fox producer posted a tweet distancing herself from his BS, Carlson called her from a blocked number and

NETWORK OF LIES |

said "shut your mouth." He later denied doing so, but was told never to call the producer again.

Carlson was on a well-worn path of radicalization at the same time he was surging into first place in the intramural Fox ratings race, leaving Hannity and Ingraham and everyone else in his foamy white wake. He kept saying "they" were all out to get him, and by extension "us," to crib the words he used on air so often. The premise of his show was that he had access to secret knowledge that the elites were afraid to share. It was the same pose that animated QAnon and countless other conspiracy theories. His straight-to-camera essays were usually about some perceived enemy—globalism, progressivism, transgenderism, ism-ism—and why elites were allowing it to ruin the country. Carlson "treated his audience with contempt," political scientist Jennifer Mercieca said, "regularly attacking their minds by convincing them that politics is war and the enemy cheats, and the whole world is out to get them."

Carlson presented himself as their protector. He kept tapping— and tasering—his audience's deep vein of concern about cultural displacement, but he began to do it from his remote studios in Maine and Florida, where he didn't have to interact with any of the people he was denigrating. One former Carlson friend posited to me that he felt safer delivering his monologues while far removed from any D.C. protesters. The host loved to claim that he did not hear his detractors at all. "I never Google myself, I'm never on my Wikipedia," he said in a podcast interview with Adam Carolla. It was one of the rare occasions when he opened up about the mother who abandoned him. Carlson said his "difficult" childhood "definitely inoculated me against caring what people who don't like me think." Critics of his work? They are like "dogs barking," he said. Their criticism is a "foreign language."

This was just a pose, obviously, and I was living the evidence, because whenever I reported unfavorably about Carlson at CNN, he shot back on his show, calling me a "creepy kid" or a "marionette" or his favorite insult, "eunuch." When I produced a documentary about disinformation for HBO, Carlson said "I want to live in a world where impressive people rise to the top, and unimpressive people park my car. Brian Stelter should be parking my car, but he has an HBO show."

When I wasn't the target, it was Alexandria Ocasio-Cortez or Bill Kristol or Nancy Pelosi or Don Lemon. Carlson saw a battle under way between "destroyers" and "creators," in which he claimed to be on the side of the creators but spent so much time and creative energy trying to destroy. It was what his viewers wanted, for sure. But he gave every indication that this was what he enjoyed: doing damage, laying waste. He was inside a vicious cycle of his own making: More viewers and more attention brought more craziness and more criticism, which spurred more viewers, and more ad boycott campaigns, and more attention, and so on. He was like an avant-garde filmmaker (in his case mischief-maker) who felt under pressure to keep getting more and more outré in what he put on camera so he couldn't be accused of "going Hollywood."

"He just felt a constant need to top himself," one insider told me.

He wasn't the only one. I cannot overstate Fox's fixation on ratings, on winning, on keeping viewers hooked around the clock. Every day Scott and her lieutenants received an email titled "Fox News Executive Scorecard" with segment-by-segment breakdowns of which stories and which guests had rated well. Spreadsheets and line graphs showed the audience's hunger for Republican red meat and its distaste for anything remotely positive or respectful about Democrats. The preeminent question was rarely "was it true?"—it was instead "did it rate?"

On one occasion when Carlson topped 4 million viewers and out-rated every other prime-time show across all of U.S. TV, he touted his ratings on air and said "you are not alone" even though "you may feel like you are." He got pretty blunt: "Millions and millions of Americans agree with you. You are not crazy. Your views are not evil."

The message affirmed that Carlson was so much more than a talk show host. He was something much closer to a modern-day Father Charles E. Coughlin, the demagogic radio priest who, in a 1930s version of far-right talk radio, preached against "Jews owning banks" and openly supported other fascist tropes pushed by Hitler and Mussolini. The conservative columnist Bret Stephens made the comparison overtly, though he suggested Carlson's fascism was born of theater, not conviction: "At least Coughlin was an honest-to-God fascist, a sincere bigot, whereas Carlson only plays one on TV for the sake of ratings."

Other observers thought Carlson was turning into a true believer. Either way, the audience trusted Carlson. A significant sliver believed so strongly that they became keyboard warriors for him. They signed on as carriers of his network of lies.

"That cunt"

Depending on his mood, Carlson could come across as a committed Fox loyalist—"I'll die here," he once said—or a guy just cashing a paycheck worth $20 million a year. When Fox accurately reported that Biden won the 2020 election, and the MAGA audience that Fox coparented with Trump took sides, mostly against the network, Carlson mused to 6 p.m. anchor Bret Baier, "I've got four more years here" so "I'm stuck with Fox. Got to do whatever I can to keep our numbers up and our viewers happy."

Carlson's contract ran through the end of 2024, and he was known to seek out early contract extensions, wanting as much job security as possible. In early 2023 his people (TV hosts always have "people") claimed that he was talking to Fox about a contract that would take him all the way till 2029. The TV business writ large was edging toward collapse, with cable subscriptions dwindling and streaming ventures bleeding money, but Carlson thought he deserved a new nine-figure deal.

Maybe that's why he still managed to put on a smile—and his trademark cackle—most nights. But six years in prime time had reshaped him, darkened his heart, driven him to the edge. He berated Fox News executives in New York. He belittled people (like me, his former pal) who scrutinized him. He oozed hatred from his every pore, and from the depths of his psyche. Of Trump, he said "I hate him passionately." (That was one of the many, many candid texts that Dominion obtained through its defamation suit.) He detested the anti-Trump Republican establishment even more. "I hate them so, so much," he texted. Carlson inspired the same emotions in others. He knew Democrats "hate-watched" his show. He was once confronted by a man at a fly-fishing store in Montana who told him, "You are the worst human being known to mankind." Carlson noticed someone filming the altercation and started to laugh—his big, hysterical, hyena-like laugh. But nobody around him really thought it was funny.

Carlson had said so much, offended so many people, that some of his producers genuinely worried he would be assassinated, like Huey Long, the Louisiana political boss, or George Tiller, the Kansas abortion doctor. Carlson coached his staff to "act like every day is our last show." He remarked to one, "It's not going to last forever," with "it" meaning his 8 p.m. show on Fox, but also probably this land, this liberty, this way of life. It was the apotheosis of his apocalyptic messaging: The woke mobs and warmongers and UFOs were coming for us all.

Unbeknownst to Carlson or anyone else, his final week of Fox episodes began on Monday, April 17, when he had a sit-down with Elon Musk. The rest of the week was predictable fear porn. Carlson cited crime in Chicago as evidence of "civilization unraveling" and said liberals "want race hate and violence." He hyped antivaccination rhetoric and claimed the rest of the media shilled for Big Pharma's "sketchy products." He suggested that gender fluidity hastened the mass suicide of the Heaven's Gate cult in 1997. He reiterated his long-held conspiracy theory that Democrats were importing migrants to "flood the suburbs" and force "demographic change." And he promoted his latest streaming documentary about a globalist plan "to make you eat bugs."

Two presidential candidates appeared on his show on consecutive nights. On Wednesday he welcomed Robert F. Kennedy Jr., hours after RFK vowed to challenge President Biden in the Democratic primary. On Thursday he invited Larry Elder, who used the platform to announce his even more long-shot bid for the Republican Party's nomination. Elder was visibly grateful for the chance to plug himself. So many people in GOP politics—and some outside it, like RFK—coveted Carlson's stage and jockeyed for a place on it. Aides to Ron DeSantis were feverishly working on a plan to have the Florida governor launch his presidential campaign on Carlson's show. But in the "Tucker primary," Trump held an early lead, notwithstanding Carlson's private comments in 2020 about the Trump years being a "disaster"; about Trump being a "demonic force"; about how "he's only good at destroying."

When Dominion made those comments public in February 2023, Trump got Carlson on the phone, and Carlson flattered his way back into Trump's good graces. Within weeks they were chummier than ever, and the Fox host was at Mar-a-Lago in April for the first sit-down since Trump was arrested and charged with hoarding classified documents and refusing to give them back to the government. The interview was a wet kiss. Carlson called Trump "moderate, sensible, and wise." One reviewer said "Carlson would have been better off lending Trump his studio and taking the night off."

On Friday, April 21, Carlson did the next best thing and pretaped his 8 p.m. show. As he signed off, he said "we'll be back on Monday," proving that he had no idea what was about to happen.

Carlson rallied the faithful at the Heritage Foundation's fiftieth anniversary gala on Friday night, then flew back home to Gasparilla Island, a barrier island in southwest Florida where he owned adjoining houses. For all of his theatrical shock about society's decay, his sorrow, his rending of garments, he was personally at peace. He wanted to be surrounded by wood and wool and trees and animals, so he was. No drywall, no DEI seminars, definitely no droning executives. Get him spun up about HR departments and he would get vulgar in a hurry. But he was far removed from all that. He lived six months a year in the tarpon-fishing capital of the world. Minutes before airtime, he drove a golf cart less than a mile to the Gasparilla Inn & Club resort, where his Florida studio was headquartered. He sometimes let locals watch the broadcast from the back of the room. His life was arranged exactly as he wanted it to be. Thus he was 1,000 percent caught off guard when, at about 11:15 a.m. on Monday, April 24, Fox News Media CEO Suzanne Scott called to tell him he himself had been yanked from the sea.

"We're taking you off the air," she said.

To Carlson, it was like somebody canceling Taylor Swift in mid-tour, or removing *The Crown* from Netflix before anyone could stream the ending. It was, in effect, a public execution, because Carlson was being stripped of his powers, his mic, his gilded soapbox, and he was unable to do anything about it. He was not offered a final month or a final week or a final day. He wasn't given a path to sign off and pretend like it was on his terms. There would be no final soliloquy. There would just be a statement, a pithy but pitiless string of words, sent by Fox News PR to the media reporters Carlson once derided as "self-righteous muppets."

I was one of those muppets. Having been fired from CNN just eight months earlier, after a nearly decade-long run hosting the network's *Reliable Sources* program, I thought I knew what he might be feeling. A new management regime decided to cancel my show, thereby subjecting me to "pay or play," a form of purgatory that I learned about when I signed my first TV contract. With "pay or play," networks don't have to play you—put your mug on TV—as long as they pay you.

At CNN, I'd had an inkling that *Reliable* was on the chopping block, and even crafted a memo trying to defend the show, citing its high ratings and low production costs. By the time I got called in to the CEO's office, I knew what the meeting was about. I wasn't told why the show was finished, but I was offered a chance to announce the cancellation on my own terms and anchor a final broadcast. Why? Because there was mutual respect. I had known the exec who fired me, and his boss, and their spouses, and their PR people, for more than a decade. I trusted they wouldn't trash me on the way out and they trusted I wouldn't light a match on their air.

Carlson, by contrast, was a pyromaniac. There was no trust at all between Carlson and Scott, in either direction, for reasons that will soon become clear. But during that brief Monday morning phone call, Scott did offer Carlson one thing—not a final show, or control over the timing of the newsbreak, but the chance to include his own comment in the press release. For a moment, Carlson thought about saying yes; maybe he did want the breakup to sound truly mutual and mutually beneficial. But he quickly snapped out of that. He'd been dumped and he wanted everyone else to know it too. He wrote a farewell email to his staff at 11:27 a.m. The news erupted at 11:28. "Fox News Media and Tucker Carlson have agreed to part ways," the announcement said, glaringly lacking any quote from him. "We thank him for his service to the network as a host and prior to that as a contributor."

Carlson's production team was not given a heads-up, so they found out the same way as everyone else, through smartphone news alerts or texts from friends. Within minutes, they learned that their boss, Wells, had also been ash-canned, but the rest of the staff was supposed to stay at their keyboards and whip up a replacement show that very night.

While the other cable newsers began wall-to-wall coverage of Carlson's ouster and what it meant for the Republican Party, Harris Faulkner, the anchor of Fox's 11 a.m. hour, gingerly told viewers that Carlson and the network "mutually" decided to split up. "Mutually" was just another Fox lie. Not a single soul believed it. (I later heard that the wrong script was loaded into the teleprompter for Faulkner to read.)

Whatever had happened, it happened fast, or so it seemed. The press release said that different hosts would fill in at eight o'clock on the amorphously named *Fox News Tonight*. The fact that Fox had no firm plan for the time slot—no splashy outside hire, no new graphics, no innovative new format—betrayed how suddenly and sloppily

Carlson had been terminated and added to the shock value. Donald Trump Jr. said it was "actually mind-blowing." His dad felt the same way. "I'm surprised," the former president said. "He's a very good person, a very good man and very talented, and he had very high ratings."

■

While the outside world was gobsmacked by Carlson's cancellation, some of his own staffers were not nearly as surprised. "It was always going to end badly," one of my sources at the show said. "We knew we were burning too bright."

The royal "we" was something Carlson always used. He portrayed his production team—and *only* his team—as a force for good in the battle against the evils he presumed nightly. His entire show was about "us" versus "them," and this approach extended to the rest of Fox, where *Tucker Carlson Tonight* resembled a rogue unit. According to Grossberg's lawsuit alleging harassment and a toxic workplace, the bro-fest environment was antagonistic toward other Fox shows, including Maria Bartiromo's, where she had worked before. Grossberg said she was hauled into the executive producer's office in her first week on the job and asked, "Is Maria Bartiromo fucking Kevin McCarthy?" (No, she said.)

Grossberg soon discovered that Carlson's producers and writers were more loyal to him than to Fox as a network. Sometimes known as the "Tuckertroop," which was the show's in-house email alias, they were a saboteur squad of true believers, regarding the mothership as almost enemy territory, since as a Fortune 500 company, Fox Corp had policies in place promoting diversity and supporting transgender employees—the very types of things Carlson railed against on air.

Carlson always specified that he worked for the Murdochs, which was a way to elevate his standing and diminish what the org chart said: that his opinion show, like all the others, reported up through executive vice president Meade Cooper to Scott, who was a rare female CEO in the male-dominated TV business. According to sources on the staff, Carlson shit-talked both women as well as his #1 enemy within Fox News, the entrenched public relations boss Irena Briganti, whom he called a "cunt."

Carlson's internal critics, of whom there were many, viewed his treatment of the female executives as part and parcel with the misogyny displayed on his show. More than a dozen current and former Fox staffers brought this problem up to me, unprompted. "Tucker is very titillated by misogyny," a host said. Some of the staffers theorized that his mother's mistreatment of him engendered a negativity toward women. (Mom disappeared from his life when he was six, which certainly fits some clinical descriptions of "abandonment." He did not speak of her often, but when he did, it was in the worst of ways. "Cruel." "Abusive." "A full-blown nut case.")

The counterpoint I heard from a Fox lifer was that "Tucker didn't respect anyone of any gender." Yes, in private messages obtained by Dominion's attorneys, he was seen calling numerous women "cunts," including other female leaders at Fox. (His text message referring to Trump ally Sidney Powell as "that cunt" was important to the case.) But Carlson hit men with the same slur too, so, according to Fox News boys-will-be-boys etiquette, he was apparently an equal-opportunity basher. Remember, this was supposed to be a defense of him.

Carlson told a friend that " 'fuck' is so overused it's lost all its power and meaning," and "cunt" was more effective: "It's super naughty, but it's to the point." His brand, weird as it was, revolved around the idea that he could call anyone a "cunt," or anything else, at any time; he could say anything, do anything, and never be held accountable, so long as he commanded the attention and affection of millions.

Directives from network executives like Scott, critiques from detractors, concerns from advertisers—from the outside, none of it seemed to matter. And on the inside, that was partially true. Scott, for example, was personally disgusted by some of Carlson's on-air comments and off-air conduct, but felt hemmed in by Rupert and Lachlan. She was in charge—except when she wasn't. "The executives could not stop him," Boughton allegedly told Jason Donner.

But in truth, Carlson had alienated so many people, instigated so many internal and external scandals, fanned so many flames of ugliness, that his firing was inevitable. After all, he'd been fired from CNN and MSNBC already. That's why, at Fox, he puffed out his chest and pretended to be immune to attack. To be tight with Lachlan. To be too popular to cancel. His long relationship with career vulnerability caused him to foster an image of untouchability.

It was bullshit. But outside Fox, where perception mattered more than reality, he had seeded a compelling story—that he controlled one of the most powerful TV brands in America. That he fearlessly defended free speech from the censors and the liars. That he decided what was "news" for millions of people. Carlson was no ordinary TV host, he was "a movement," Wells proclaimed. Like most of Carlson's stories, it was wildly hyperbolic, but hypnotically powerful to the people primed to believe it. Fans told him all the time that he should run for president in 2024. That he was the only one who could make America great again, again. There was even a "Draft Tucker" super PAC.

And so that's why, on that Monday morning in April, as Carlson processed the why and how of his own defenestration, he didn't think long about finding contentment from cancellation and retiring from public life. His carpenter in Maine texted him "more time for fishing?" when the news broke, but the answer was no. He needed this time to exact revenge on Fox and build back better.

His brain ballooned with theories about his dismissal. He suspected it was the father's doing, not the son's. He wondered if it might be related to Rupert's recent romantic entanglement. The idea sounded crazy; but, then again, the cornerstone of the Fox News schedule wouldn't be fired without the patriarch's knowledge. And Rupert, King Rupert of Tabloidia, had been acting erratically for months.

"Messenger from God"

The best way to understand Rupert Murdoch is through his divorces.

His first divorce, circa 1967, from Patricia Booker, a former flight attendant and fellow native of Melbourne, Australia, was years in the making. In the end it was bitterly contested but not publicly painful. Rupert was a man in a hurry, trying to rebuild and expand his family's newspaper empire, and smitten with a journalist at one of his papers, Anna Torv, thirteen years his junior. By one account, Rupert and Torv were already shacked up while his marriage to Booker disintegrated; the new pair tied the knot later that same year. Him: "I thought she was a very pretty girl." Her: "He was like a whirlwind coming into the room. It was very seductive."

Rupert's only child from his first marriage, Prudence, or Prue for short, soon had half-siblings from the second marriage to Torv: Elisabeth, born in Australia in 1968; Lachlan, born in London in 1971; James, also in London in 1972. The growing family, Prue included, moved to Manhattan's Upper East Side as Rupert gobbled up American brands like the *New York Post* and built the News Corp empire. In the 1980s he launched satellite networks in Europe and established Fox as the fourth broadcast network in the U.S.; in the 1990s he expanded into Asia with Star TV and founded Fox News in the U.S.; he was a workaholic, always eyeing the next deal, which strained his marriage after three decades. "I remember Rupert telling me that they weren't happy and they were having counseling," his late mother, Dame Elisabeth Murdoch, recalled, "and I said, 'Rupert, you're going to be terribly lonely, and what will happen is the first designing woman will come along and will snap you up.' He said, 'Don't be ridiculous, Mum, I'm too old for that.' But that's exactly what happened."

Rupert partially admitted as much. "I was traveling a lot," he said, "and was very obsessed with business and perhaps more than normally inconsiderate, at a time when our children were grown up and home was suddenly an empty nest." Torv explained the divorce more explicitly: She said he cheated. "I think that Rupert's affair with Wendi Deng—it's not an original plot—was the end of the marriage."

Wendi Deng grew up in the polluted Chinese city of Xuzhou with no electricity, no phone, and no hot water. "You didn't know you were poor. It's just the way it was," she said. "So to get anyone's attention you had to be smart." At age nineteen, Deng befriended a California couple who were in China working on a factory project. The couple sponsored her for a U.S. student visa and set her up in their home, but the husband was love-struck, and left his wife to marry Deng in 1990. They only lived together for "four to five months, at the most," he said, but the marriage lasted the two years necessary for Deng to receive a green card. Deng worked her way into a scholarship at Yale; graduated in 1996; and returned east, becoming a very junior executive at Star

TV in Hong Kong. That's where Rupert met her, in much the same way he met Torv, a dazzling twentysomething catching the boss's eye. Rupert insisted that he didn't ask her out until separating from Torv in 1998. But the rumors about Deng made the divorce talks even testier—and more expensive for the mogul.

Rupert was now in the grandfather stage of life, as Prue raised three young kids in London, and Torv's friends had said she wanted Rupert to slow down, take a step back from his empire-building, act more like an ordinary Pop Pop. To Rupert the thought was terrifying. He told an interviewer that if he retired, he'd "die pretty quickly."

Deng brought him new life and enthusiasm about his businesses. Many observers wondered if his obsession with cracking China's satellite TV market was part of what made Deng so alluring: "If he marries Deng, he will be marrying the market," a British paper commented. The inevitable wedding was held on Rupert's yacht, *Morning Glory*, in June 1999, the same month his divorce from Torv was finalized. He was sixty-eight and she was thirty, the same age as his youngest daughter, Elisabeth.

Rupert's wife swap devastated Elisabeth, Lachlan, and James, all three of whom now worked for the family firm. They watched as he forced Torv off the News Corp board of directors. (Lachlan pointedly followed her out of the boardroom after her tearful final meeting.) All of the children sided with their mom but, in a pattern that would repeat itself for decades, they gradually warmed back up to Dad. James, who oversaw Star TV, worked closely with Deng as she became an informal News Corp diplomat in China, forging relationships and guiding investments there.

With Deng, Rupert was rejuvenated. He moved downtown with her to a hip SoHo loft. He started to wear more casual clothes. He dismissed as "laughable" the notion that "what was driving me was fear of death." But a bout with prostate cancer in 2000 was a reality check. Deng canceled her Beijing trips while Rupert received treatment in Los Angeles. Once his doctors said the cancer was in remission, he quipped, "I'm now convinced of my own immortality!"

■

Rupert said "fuck off" a lot less than the *Succession* character he inspired, Logan Roy, but Rupert's lieutenants marveled at all the other similarities. He lorded over a $30 billion media empire, exploited the political power of his outlets, and pitted his children against each other. For years Lachlan was said to be the heir apparent; then James was said to be "the one"; then Lachlan again. Magazine cover stories and gossip columns endlessly chronicled the ups and downs. Then Deng gave birth to two daughters, Grace and Chloe, which made the dynastic shape all the more complicated. Rupert's divorce agreement with Torv was said to protect the four adult children's inheritance, known as the Murdoch Trust. The trust divvies up both billions of dollars and control of the media empire, including Fox News. Under oath with Dominion's lawyers in 2023, Rupert confirmed the precise structure: "There's eight votes," he said. "The four older children each have one, and I have four, which go away when I die."

In the mid-2000s Deng wanted the trust expanded to include Grace and Chloe. This desire precipitated a bitter family feud. Rupert essentially compromised by giving the girls financial stakes in the trust but not voting rights. He revealed the plan during a TV interview with Charlie Rose, enraging Deng, who hadn't been told yet. The couple nearly broke up afterward. But they stayed together, in a wounded way, until 2013, Rupert's big breakup year. First he split his company in half, with Fox News and his other TV assets placed under the Fox umbrella, and his newspapers under News Corp. Then he dumped Deng just as suddenly as Fox would jettison Carlson a decade later. Reason number one: Rupert had become convinced that Deng—who mastered the elite social scenes he thrust her into—was having an affair with former British prime minister Tony Blair. (Her side denied that.) But as with any other bad breakup, there were so many other reasons. The couple spent far more time apart than together. When they *were* together, they fought so loudly that Rupert's allies accused Deng of "verbal abuse." Rupert wondered about Deng's relationships with other men. It seemed as if he tolerated Deng and looked the other way for years—until one day he cut her off.

Rupert behaved the same way in his business dealings. He would scapegoat an executive or shut down an unprofitable division and never speak of the failure again. "Rupert is loyal, loyal, loyal, loyal, loyal—until the minute you're dead," one of his former deputies remarked to me. That had been his approach for decades both at work and at home.

Rupert's next infatuation was with Jerry Hall, previously the longtime partner of Mick Jagger. Gossip columns quipped that his new girlfriend was "almost age-appropriate" since they were only twenty-seven years apart. On the wedding day in 2016, Rupert walked into the historic St. Bride's Church on Fleet Street with Lachlan on his right and James on his left. All three men were uneasily sharing custody of the media empire at this point, with the knowledge that, as Lachlan put it, "Rupert's never retiring." Fox was structured in such a way that all the assets, from Fox News to the movie studio to the Sky satellite networks, reported up to both brothers. It was never going to work long-term, but Rupert was trying to keep the peace; he viewed Lachlan as his successor but didn't want James to quit the family business.

A $52 billion deal with Bob Iger sort of solved the problem. Rupert agreed to sell the bulk of 21st Century Fox to Disney at the end of 2017. He envisioned James taking an executive role at Disney and Lachlan running the rest of Fox's remaining assets with him. Lachlan was incensed at first. "Why the fuck would I want to run this company," he asked, if it was just a shell of its former self? Disney would be getting Sky and the studio and most of the cable channels. For that very reason, James championed the deal talks; he saw that Disney needed scale to compete with the likes of Netflix and Apple, and he could also see a place for himself high atop the corporate hierarchy, perhaps even putting him in line to succeed Iger someday. James and Lachlan both tried to undercut each other as the talks progressed. But Rupert got the deal done, and the price eventually rose to $71 billion after Comcast instigated a bidding war for the assets. Rupert's four adult children received $2 billion each—for Lachlan, money to soften the blow since he was running a slimmed-down company, and for James, money to invest in new ventures since a Disney dream job never materialized.

After the deal dust settled, James thought of the new Fox as just "an American political project." Lachlan ostracized James as a deluded liberal. The two brothers stopped speaking. It became increasingly clear that James could not abide the reactionary, radical direction Fox News was heading in. He was disgusted by Fox's prime-time hosts. "They're spewing poison," he told confidants. His wife, Kathryn, agreed. Kathryn was active in the fight against climate change, which meant, as one interviewer wrote, she was trying to "remove partisan obstacles to climate progress that her family's empire helped build." Both James and Kathryn felt Fox News was a growing threat to pluralistic democracy. And they blamed Lachlan, who, in James's view, was both more conservative than Dad and more checked-out.

James walked away. In mid-2020 he quit the News Corp board, stating that "my resignation is due to disagreements over certain editorial content published by the company's news outlets and certain other strategic decisions." James was finally totally free of any corporate responsibilities tied to his famous/infamous last name. No board meetings. No phony grip-and-grins. He was intent on building his own media holding company while funding progressive causes that made his brother retch.

But he still had a vote. Because of the way the Murdoch Trust was set up, Lachlan and James were on a collision course as their father cruised through his nineties. When *Hoax* came out in 2020, I floated a question: One or two or ten years into the future, could James and his sisters effect regime change, fire Lachlan, and put a muzzle on Fox News? The question hung in the air two months later when James agreed to an interview with *New York Times* columnist Maureen Dowd, who reported that James was "aligned" with Elisabeth and Prue. Kathryn, an unmistakable liberal influence on her husband who called herself a "radical centrist," said James was "free of that tension" at News Corp. But "when a family is very involved in the business, it's a big decision to leave that. I don't know if it's ever ending. It's always, you know, ongoing."

Ongoing. James was busy making investments in film festivals and streaming companies—not to mention serving on the board of Tesla—and he didn't want people to think that these were merely pit stops on the way back to Fox Corp; but, well, that's what many thought anyway. There was a macabre aspect to these conversations since it was all predicated on the *when*.

There had already been a number of close calls, like the time Rupert fell on Lachlan's yacht and broke his back, and the time when he was hospitalized with pneumonia. When Rupert semi-retired in late 2023, he said he was in "robust health." But the bottom line was that, whether death knocked next month or next decade, the Murdoch Trust could be reshaped in any number of ways. Networks could be spun off. Divisions could be sold. Different kids could take control of different parts. A takeover by James was far from a fait accompli. He was deferential to his sisters, and careful not to assume anything. And that was a wise strategy, because Rupert's "chairman emeritus" shift was the ultimate signal that he wanted Lachlan to stay in charge. To dethrone him, "James would have to get two siblings who know their late father's wishes to completely ignore those wishes," an insider pointed out to me.

However, power brokers in conservative media circles assumed that, should James indeed come to power, Fox would be defanged. As one said to me, "Rupert's death will change politics more than Trump's descent down the escalator." Trump talked about it too: He reportedly groused to Rupert in 2017 that Fox News was "going to become too liberal when James takes over." Trump's intel, as usual, was incorrect; Lachlan shortly thereafter emerged as the chosen son. But nothing in media lasted forever, including Rupert's marriages.

■

"Jerry, sadly I've decided to call an end to our marriage," Rupert wrote in an email to Hall in June 2022. "We have certainly had some good times, but I have much to do."

I have much to do. Rupert, at ninety-one, was starting anew for a fifth time. The thought of dying alone—or not having enough time to peruse Billionaire Tinder—evidently didn't faze him.

Hall's absence was noticed when Rupert hosted his annual summer party in London. British prime minister Boris Johnson and dozens of other pols showed up to bow and scrape and pay homage. Days later Rupert was in the Cotswolds for the wedding of one of his granddaughters. His life was rich in all the senses of the word—but he still went ahead and blew it up by sending Hall a shock email that said, in effect, "lose my number." He wanted to communicate solely through lawyers now.

Hall's friends said Jerry didn't see it coming. But his side said the isolation and intensity of the pandemic created conflict. After the divorce news hit, papers owned by Rupert's rivals filled with stories about family friction; Rupert's adult children "thought that Jerry was keeping them from him," a source told the *Daily Mail*, while she merely thought she was encouraging wise Covid-era protocols around testing and masking.

Hall and Murdoch had married in the U.K. but Hall filed for divorce in California, as they had spent the winter there at Rupert's Bordeaux-style vineyard estate in Bel Air, in the Santa Monica Mountains. Rupert and his lawyers immediately knew what the California maneuver meant. Divorces in the state default to a 50/50 split of cash and assets accrued during the marriage, so Rupert was incentivized to reach a tidy settlement, lest his income and tax affairs dribble into public view. The divorce was finalized within six weeks, out of court, and Hall moved out of Bel Air. She promised she would supply no plot lines to *Succession*, and she came away with Holmwood House (their $15 million Covid quarantine locale) but not the Montana cattle ranch that they purchased from Koch Industries in 2021. The cows all belonged to Rupert.

The sudden split from Hall caused whispers about Rupert's mental acuity, which grew louder when, come autumn, he perplexed many outsiders by proposing a re-merger of Fox Corp and News Corp. Rupert had split the two companies apart a decade ago, for good reason, to "unlock shareholder value." Bankers and analysts had a hard time seeing why they should be plugged back together. T. Rowe Price, the largest News Corp shareholder after the Murdoch family, loudly objected, and other dissenters joined in, including, significantly, James. He sent letters to the boards of both companies pooh-poohing the proposal. In January Rupert backtracked and withdrew the idea altogether. "There was a time when Rupert would say jump and people would say how high. But not anymore," a longtime lieutenant said.

With a corporate reunion off the table, but Rupert forever revved up by mergers and acquisitions, was Carlson removed because Rupert and Lachlan were readying Fox Corp for a sale to some Big Tech player or sovereign wealth fund? Carlson certainly entertained that theory, along with a more imaginative, more speculative one. On St. Patrick's Day, barely six months after divorcing Hall, Rupert, at age ninety-two, proposed to yet another woman—Ann Lesley Smith, age sixty-six. "We're both looking forward to spending the second half of our lives together," Smith said, overcome by the optimism of love (or the proximity of billions). Rupert doled out the news to Cindy Adams, the gossip columnist at his beloved *New York Post*, and said the wedding was set for late summer.

Carlson met Smith on his late-March trip to California and learned a happy coincidence: She was an ardent fan of his. The meeting was out of the pages of a romance novel: a meal with the newly engaged couple at Rupert's estate in Bel Air. Carlson told his staff afterward that Rupert seemed genuinely smitten. But there was also something awkward about the scene, something that may explain why, in a matter of days, Rupert called off the engagement. Apparently the mogul had gone queasy when Smith read to Carlson from the Book of Exodus.

On April 4, when *Vanity Fair*'s Gabriel Sherman broke the news of the abruptly broken engagement, he wrote that "one source close to Murdoch said he had become increasingly uncomfortable with Smith's outspoken evangelical views." One week later Sherman relayed this outstanding quote from the same close-to-Rupert source: "She said Tucker Carlson is a messenger from God, and he said nope."

This was, by any measure, a humiliating turn for the nonagenarian. Was it also a tale of betrayal? The Carlson-vineyard-prayer-meeting was not revealed until after Carlson was fired, but this image of Carlson-as-angelic-envoy, Carlson-as-something-approaching-Jesus, along with this idea that Rupert was repulsed by it—*that* much was in print by mid-April. Rupert knew that only a small number of people were privy to the intimate dinner. He surely didn't leak it to *Vanity Fair*. Did Carlson? Did Rupert perhaps retaliate by firing him? Rupert's history of divorces showed a retaliatory instinct.

Carlson's friends believed Rupert was freaked out by his fiancée's comments about Tucker, plus sketchy details about her past marriages, and thus called off the wedding and, perhaps to rub it in, canceled her favorite show. This hewed closely to a witticism Elon Musk had shared with Carlson in their L.A. interview: "The most entertaining outcome is the most likely."

But there was a slightly more convoluted way to read the situation, starting with Rupert pegging Carlson as a leaker, ending with the firing of Fox's biggest star—and biggest headache. Either version suggested combustible and worrisome volatility within the C-suite. Rupert's broken heart may have been the straw that broke Carlson's back channel with Lachlan.

My reporting pointed to a different chain of events altogether. Lachlan, not Rupert, made a cold-blooded business decision to break ties with Carlson; notified Scott on Friday; and waited until Saturday to notify Rupert, according to two C-suite sources. The execs made a conscious choice not to state a reason for the breakup. Thus Fox PR took a vow of silence about Carlson (knowing he'd accuse them of shivving him no matter what) and a dozen different possibilities filled the information vacuum.

One theory held that Lachlan was showing his skeptical siblings James and Elisabeth that he was a suitable long-term leader of the firm. "He's trying to position himself so that they can all get along and he can keep his power but they have some input too," a source told *Insider*.

Another theory focused on the Fox Corp board of directors and its belated awareness of damaging text messages from Carlson— texts that Dominion intended to display for the first time at trial. The most incendiary as-yet-unpublished message was from the day after January 6. Carlson reflected on watching a video of three or more "Trump guys" surrounding an "Antifa creep" and "pounding the living shit out of him."

"Jumping a guy like that is dishonorable obviously," Carlson wrote. "It's not how white men fight. Yet suddenly I found myself rooting for the mob against the man, hoping they'd hit him harder, kill him. I really wanted them to hurt the kid. I could taste it. Then somewhere deep in my brain, an alarm went off: this isn't good for me. I'm becoming something I don't want to be."

The moral of his story was about the dangers of dehumanizing political opponents, but the words "it's not how white men fight" are what startled some Fox board members. It similarly disturbed Dominion executives who read it during the discovery process. The text indicated a view of racial superiority that contradicted Carlson's frequent (and much doubted) claims of color blindness—and set up an excruciating cross-examination scenario in court.

This much is known for sure: The Fox board retained Wachtell, Lipton, Rosen & Katz, a notoriously powerful white-shoe law firm, to investigate Carlson and any other malign messages that might exist. "There were major concerns about liability," a Fox executive told me. The legal probe was a conceivable reason why he was ousted—but it was hard to square the purported distress over the text with the disturbing performances that Carlson put on night after night.

So what else could it be? Carlson's position on Russia's invasion of Ukraine—for which he was accused of pro-Putin sycophancy—was thought, by some of his supporters, to be another reason for Lachlan's action.

Carlson's allies kept coming up with new theories, new ways he had transgressed, which only reinforced his opponents' view that he was long overdue for a comeuppance. *It could have been this! It could have been that!* It could have been a dozen different factors.

Adding to the mystery, Fox resolved to keep Carlson in "pay or play" for months. To fix that, Carlson retained a L.A.-based litigator, Bryan Freedman, whose presence in a media biz dispute often portended conflict. If Fox really planned to pay Carlson to hunt and fish until his contract expired at the end of 2024, well, Freedman thought that was a flagrant and unjustifiable attempt to keep Carlson on the sidelines—during a presidential election, no less—and kill Carlson's value to future employers.

"They're not going to shut him up through the election," a Carlson-friendly source promised me. "There's nothing Tucker hates more than being shut up."

"Pain sponge"

Rupert and Lachlan wanted all of the profits from Fox, all the prestige, all the power, but none of the blame. They achieved this by appointing leaders of their various divisions who absorbed all the headaches and heat. In the immortal words of billionaire mogul Lukas Matsson on *Succession*, they hired a "pain sponge."

Suzanne Scott was the Fox News pain sponge. Rupert and Lachlan left all the messy stuff for her to clean up. For example, when GOP Speaker of the House turned Fox board member Paul Ryan urged a certain bent to the prime-time programming, Rupert brought up Scott right away, as if to say, "She's the boss." This had been a Murdoch family signature for decades. They delegated; they had plausible deniability about any ugly specifics at their businesses; and they enjoyed their yachts and retreats and vineyards.

Only up to a point, however; they also proved willing to take out any deputy if the going got too tough. Layers of executives were an expensive and powerful form of insulation. For the most part, the layers worked: "Suzanne keeps all their secrets," an associate remarked.

Dominion obtained emails showing that Rupert and Lachlan communicated to Fox News through Scott, rather than directly with hosts and executives. For better and for worse—often for the worse—they did not meddle. (And on the occasions when they did, "they left no fingerprints," because the messages were transmitted through Scott, a former Fox exec told me.)

Scott's account, under oath during her Dominion deposition, was that when she received emails from Rupert or Lachlan, they were just a "suggestion." She said "I make my own decisions" and "if I pass something along, I expect those leaders to make their own decisions."

Lachlan—described in 2020 as "a laid-back executive who doesn't spend his days watching Fox and is sometimes surprised to learn of a controversy it has generated"—gave the same account under oath. As if to prove the point, he said he didn't know whether certain Fox News SVPs and VPs were still employed by the network. "I'm not the CEO of Fox News," he remarked. "I'm not responsible for the editorial on Fox News. I don't make editorial decisions on Fox News. For me to criticize or to endorse or even talk about a newspaper article or a Fox News opinion piece, I think it becomes very challenging."

In other words, the CEO of Fox Corp relieved himself of responsibility for what aired on his news network.

"I do provide Suzanne Scott with feedback," he added. "Because she is the responsible executive." Under his description, it was not his management style to make demands. Like his dad, he just made suggestions, he claimed. "I don't tell journalists what to do," Lachlan swore.

And how could he? The landlords were usually several time zones away from their properties. They were dependent on the property managers to keep tabs on things.

This absentee landlord approach distressed Preston Padden, a former Fox Broadcasting exec who worked closely with Rupert in the 1990s. Padden emailed with Rupert at the height of Covid and knew his old boss was taking it deadly seriously. "He told me that he did not leave his house without a mask and I should not either," Padden told me. "He told me that he was going to be among the first to get vaccinated and that I should do the same. Then I turn on the channel and see hosts disparaging masks and fueling vaccine hesitancy."

Back when Padden worked at Fox, he said, "what Rupert said is what happened, period. Maybe Rupert is so desperate for Lachlan to succeed that Rupert is willing to step back and cede control."

■

Scott learned from the Murdochs' hands-off approach. She ran Fox News the same way—pushing responsibility downward—which is why so many rank-and-file staffers complained about a lack of leadership during her tenure. Reporters and commentators felt like no one was firmly in charge. "She let the hosts go rogue," one producer complained. Another especially critical staffer likened Scott to a "dodo," that long-extinct bird that could never fly. Perhaps they misunderstood her approach to the portfolio. "I have leadership in all areas of the business," she testified, "and it is their job to handle the editorial of the shows, the guest bookings, all of that. I'm running a business. I'm not granular. I'm looking at it . . . from a 50,000-foot view. I'm not granular in the weeds. I really entrust the leadership team I have in place across the businesses."

Scott was, at one time, an unlikely choice for the top Fox News job, since she started at the network as an executive assistant. But she trained under Ailes's deputy Bill Shine and committed to improving the network's culture (read: make it more bearable for women) in the wake of Ailes's ouster. In 2018 she won the CEO title. Scott wanted to be viewed as a red-America pioneer, leading Fox News into categories like lifestyle, history, books, and weather. *"Come to Fox for everything."* That's the way she articulated her strategy.

One of the very few times she gave an interview, Scott—whose mother was a real estate agent—depicted the prime-time shows as just "one little piece of real estate." That piece gets lots of attention, she said, but "I have 230-plus contributors, reporters, hosts and personalities on some platform at any given moment."

From Scott's vantage point, prime time was a thing to be managed, or sponged up, while the growth potential was elsewhere—in streaming subscriptions and Christmas movies and conferences and so forth. Objectively she wasn't wrong. More importantly, Lachlan believed she was right.

Lachlan had a broadcast network, Fox, in steep secular decline; a set of local TV stations with the same challenges; a live-event franchise, Fox Sports, with constantly ballooning costs; a nascent streaming and ad-targeting platform; and a handful of digital businesses and production companies. This amalgamation of assets might have made sense a decade ago, but in the 2020s, no way. I remember visiting the company's local station in Philadelphia, Fox 29, where my wife used to report the traffic, and noticing that it had no real connection to Big Fox. By the same token, Fox gained vanishingly few synergies by having news operations in various metros. Philly's live shots and taped reports almost never appeared on Fox News. (And when they did, it was usually to denigrate the city.) Fox News wasn't striving to be the best-in-class compilation of news from across the country. It was better off being called Fox Opinion, a right-wing talk channel that had more in common with Carlson's old site *The Daily Caller* than with KDFW in Dallas or KTVU in Oakland.

Fox News was far and away the most profitable part of the enterprise, supplying the cash for Fox's expansions onto new turf. Most of the quarter-to-quarter revenue came from the monthly bills paid by every cable-subscribing household in the U-S-of-A. In 2020, Fox News earned more than $2 per month per household. Come contract renewal season, Lachlan wanted his negotiators to break past the $3 mark.

The immovable nature of long-term contracts meant the cable fee monies were basically fixed in place. The big revenue line that Lachlan could control, could manipulate, was advertising sales. In theory, higher ratings should translate to higher ad revenue—but not with *Tucker Carlson Tonight.*

As Carlson gained adherents, he *lost* advertisers, creating quite the conundrum for Fox Corp. Carlson spun up so many scandals that Fox couldn't realize his full value because his racist rhetoric was so toxic to most advertisers. "Bye-bye, Tucker Carlson!" tweeted Mike Sievert, the CEO of T-Mobile, when his firm stopped pitching wireless discounts during Carlson's show. His rebuke stung the ad sales execs at Fox who lost blue-chip sponsors (and their commissions) left and right. There was so little advertiser interest in Carlson's show that the commercial load shrank and shrank, to the point that the producers had to come up with filler content in place of the usual ad breaks. MyPillow CEO Mike Lindell propped up Carlson—he ordered tons more spots and became far and away the show's top sponsor. But Lindell also got in a public pissing match with Fox over the 2020 election results. This was so awkward, and he was so important, that Scott arranged to send a personal note and gift to Lindell.

Fox needed Lindell; Lindell needed Fox. But if a MAGA pillow and blanket and slipper brand was the best ally Fox had, well, that was a sign of serious trouble.

Yet Lachlan, and by extension Rupert, kept reaffirming their support for Carlson's show even as the 8 p.m. time slot became an ad sinkhole. Were the Murdochs really 100 percent sold on Carlson's high-costs-of-free-speech belief system? Or were they making a severe miscalculation about the value of an individual host—any individual host, in a place that had lost many big ones before, like Glenn Beck and Megyn Kelly—versus the value of the Fox brand?

■

Some of the same questions had arisen before, when Fox was sued for defamation by ex-Playmate Karen McDougal in 2019. McDougal was one of two women (the other being adult-film actress Stormy Daniels) who had accused Trump of infidelity in a very public way. Carlson, in turn, had accused McDougal and Daniels of seeking a "ransom," saying, "Two women approach Donald Trump and threaten to ruin his career and humiliate his family if he doesn't give them money. Now that sounds like a classic case of extortion." He also said, "Remember the facts of this story. The facts are undisputed."

What facts? McDougal never approached Trump for money. Instead, as the 2016 election approached, she considered telling her story to ABC News, until *National Enquirer* publisher and Trump pal David Pecker arranged to buy McDougal's story and bury it— because Trump had that little presidential thing happening. Thus did most of the country learn the publishing term "catch and kill." Trump lawyer and fixer Michael Cohen went to jail for his role in the hush money scheme. The week Cohen was sentenced, Carlson made his false "ransom" claim, prompting McDougal to sue Fox for defaming her.

The case found its way into the arms of Judge Mary Kay Vyskocil, who, lo and behold, was a brand-new Trump appointee. The case, accompanied by words and music about "First Amendment rights" and "actual malice," a theme that would recur with haunting effect a few years later, drove Fox to an inventive, though inadvertently brutally honest, defense that boiled down to: "Nobody should take a word this guy says seriously."

Lawyers for Fox argued persuasively, according to Judge Vyskocil, that "given Mr. Carlson's reputation, any reasonable viewer arrives with an appropriate amount of skepticism about the statement he makes." McDougal's case was dismissed because, the judge concluded, "whether the Court frames Mr. Carlson's statements as 'exaggeration,' 'non-literal commentary,' or simply bloviating for his audience, the conclusion remains the same—the statements are not actionable."

That didn't make them "not mockable," and Carlson was subsequently treated to a hectoring chorus of "even his own network says he's a joke" every time he unleashed a new stream of bile about honest white American folk facing the invasion of the replacement people. But the outcome may have lulled Fox's executives and high-powered lawyers into complacency about future defamation claims. The First Amendment and the *"hey, who would take any of this seriously?"* defense was always there to protect them, so why worry about a little voting company bashing?

■

The Dominion case ultimately had profound consequences for Fox. Observers wondered if Scott would take the fall. Instead, she soaked up more of the pain; she managed the Carlson cancellation and coped with the resulting ratings collapse and navigated the aftermath.

The year 2023 was always going to be unpleasant for Scott, Tucker or no Tucker, settlement or no settlement, because the fat and happy years of cable were over. Companies like Fox were able to offset cord-cutting for a while by making the corded pay more . . .

but that trick was played out. Lachlan told Scott she had to seriously trim head count. In the spring she canceled several shows, laid off veteran reporters, basically dissolved the investigative reporting unit, and froze spending in certain areas. Some staffers said they were told that Scott had to cut costs by 15 percent due to the Dominion debacle, and quickly, but this haircut was already in progress before the deal was done in Wilmington. Fox executives pointed out that other networks were forced to make far sharper cuts.

On top of the TV industry challenges, Scott was juggling more egos than anyone safely could. Every day Scott was "tiptoeing through a minefield," one ally said, managing a business that also happened to be a Republican political machine. And the party's leader roared against her network and her bosses, the Murdochs, whenever he wasn't being interviewed by Hannity or Bartiromo. To put it simply, Trump was impossible to placate.

All throughout 2023 Trump's political hand seemed to strengthen and Fox's resistance to him weakened. Rupert telegraphed why in one of his post-insurrection emails that Dominion shared with the world. Reporters jumped on his remark about making Trump a "non person" but mostly overlooked the crucial caveat he included: "We want to make Trump a non person. Fairly easy *unless they charge him and he remains in the news.*"

By the beginning of April, Trump was charged in the hush money case and he was the news. And by the end of the month Carlson was fired. Long-simmering feuds boiled over, and sources on both sides were newly willing to spill. Carlson's side said the execs who were supposed to be in charge—women, they misogynistically went out of their way to note—were invisible to them. The other side said Carlson's people were obnoxious and obstreperous. For example, Carlson's widely criticized trip to Hungary, where he cozied up to

Eastern European strongman Viktor Orbán, was never approved by the network, according to an executive who was involved.

For weeks after Carlson's cancellation, right-wing websites were filled with allegations of a secretly "liberal" Fox agenda. The most preposterous one was about Fox encouraging its employees to read about glory holes in celebration of pride month. It didn't take a forensic scientist to find Carlson's fingerprints on the bad press.

The post-Carlson ratings free fall reminded many people of the post-election period in 2020, when Fox's audience staged a revolt and hosts like Carlson panicked. Now another rebellion was under way—and Carlson was leading the charge. How did it come to this? I'll show you. Let's go back in time.

PART TWO

"They will cheat big"

Halloween is usually a carefree night of cheap thrills, fake scares, sugar highs, and bar crawls. It is one of the best nights of the year to be in Manhattan: Costumed revelers fill the avenues, laughs and shouts echo down the side streets, and the city exudes a sense not of danger, but of celebration—and possibility.

But in 2020 the vibe was different. There was something distinctly, genuinely scary about All Hallows' Eve in the teeth of a global pandemic. The masks were just pieces of cloth, but they were frightening. Everyone was afraid—of the virus, of political unrest, of riots, of each other.

Covid case counts were at an all-time high in the U.S., and vaccines were not yet available. Experts were issuing dire warnings about the winter months ahead. ("We're in for a whole lot of hurt," Dr. Anthony Fauci warned in a Halloween interview.) With parades canceled and parties called off, New York's normally bustling streets were ghostly, save for the contractors who were hammering plywood to shuttered storefronts. With memories of the previous spring's mass looting and lawlessness still fresh, store owners were taking no chances. They were boarding up because the presidential election was three days away.

Some Fox staffers noticed the sea of plywood as they walked through Rockefeller Center on the way to Fox News HQ on Sixth Avenue between 47th and 48th Streets. But most didn't see it firsthand because they were told to stay home and work virtually to reduce the chances of Fox stars and producers being sickened and sidelined on election night.

A control room being crippled by Covid was a real concern, but that was far from the scariest scenario. The election season had been unbearably toxic. The televised debates between Trump and Biden had made viewers wince. Disinformation had fallen like acid rain. And the fear was palpable. In North Carolina on Halloween afternoon, police deployed pepper spray when African American civil rights protesters held a march toward a polling place. In Texas, Trump diehards surrounded a Biden campaign bus on an interstate and tried to run it off the road. So liberals warned about voter suppression, for good reason, while conservatives stoked fears about mail-in ballot fraud, with far less justification. For the record, Rupert Murdoch voted by mail.

During the final days of the campaign, Fox News fueled fears of a Democratic takeover as only Fox could. Shows hyped the "LEFT'S WAR ON AMERICA." Sean Hannity claimed America would be "unrecognizable" if Biden won. In private, though, Fox producers whined that an elderly white male presidential candidate—one with a recently deceased military vet son—simply wasn't as appealing a villain as Barack Obama or Hillary Clinton. That's why the shows talked so much about the African American, Asian American woman Biden had picked for VP, Kamala Harris, and demonized her as an un-electable radical, not from the "real" America. Fox constantly assailed liberals like Harris as anti-American and un-American. But what, *Los Angeles Times* columnist Jean Guerrero asked, "could be more anti-American than a company that cons millions of people into denigrating their democratic institutions?"

■

Former president Barack Obama—who had called the Fox-era information war "the single biggest threat to our democracy"—was out on the socially distanced campaign trail on Halloween, promising that with Joe Biden as president, "you're not gonna have to think about [Trump] every day." Politics, he said, "won't be so exhausting." Indeed, voters told pollsters they wanted a break. Biden's lead was substantial in pre-election polls. But the average Biden supporter was scared to believe it (dreading a repeat of 2016) and the average Trump supporter had stopped believing the polls long ago. It was well known among insiders that Trump voters were notably reluctant to respond to pollsters, and sometimes downright eager to lie to them, which made Trump's true strength difficult to measure accurately. Fox host Maria Bartiromo epitomized that MAGA mindset: In spite of all the polls, even Fox's own poll, showing Trump trailing Biden badly in the national popular vote, she predicted a "landslide" for Trump on Tuesday.

Bartiromo placed that bet in a text message thread with Fox Business senior vice president Gary Schreier on Saturday. "Hope you're right," Schreier responded. "I think he can win but I'm just not as confident as you are. I worry about Arizona. States like that. And cheating.

"There will be a lot of cheating," he added, signing on, as many at Fox did, to the concocted GOP talking point that American elections are unsecure—though countless investigations had proved just the opposite.

"They will cheat big," Bartiromo agreed. "But they'll get caught."

"I just hope it matters when they do," Schreier replied.

There *was* a lot of cheating, by Trump and his allies, many of whom were actively plotting numerous schemes to undermine, and, if needed, overturn a Biden victory. But in Bartiromo's imagined scenario, the Democrats would be the cheaters, because she lived in a MAGA madhouse of her own twisted making.

Bartiromo was still dining out on her 1990s reputation as a

sharp-elbowed business broadcaster, and thus still landed interviews with Fortune 500 CEOs with some regularity, but by 2020 she was so Trumpified that she was primarily seen as a political operator. Longtime friends said they didn't recognize Bartiromo anymore. She found solace in her airtime: fifteen hours a week on Fox Business, hosting the network's before-the-opening-bell morning show, plus a Friday night recap of the week, and an hour-long Sunday morning talkfest on the flagship Fox News. Rupert was said to be very fond of Bartiromo, even though he had noticed that her Fox Business show had "zero audience . . . Well, very little. It is the smallest of the day." Her Sunday morning broadcast was far more successful and more overtly political, reflecting who Bartiromo had become: much less "Money Honey" (her old nickname from CNBC) than "Trumper pumper"—apologist for Trump, a friend of the family, a propagandist posing as a journalist.

In her Halloween chat with Schreier, Bartiromo fantasized about what a newly emboldened second-term Donald Trump would do. "By Nov 6th," she wrote, Trump will fire CIA director Gina Haspel and FBI director Christopher Wray, two frequent subjects of deep state conspiracy theories Bartiromo had signed on to. She added a "100" emoji to underscore her confidence. When Schreier sounded skeptical about Haspel, she said "Yes both will be fired." (They were not.)

Bartiromo based her bogus "landslide" forecast on nothing rational, nothing statistical, just her plain contempt for Biden. "I just do not see how anyone outside of massive lefties could seriously believe Biden is fit for office," she wrote. "It's just so obvious. From his mental state to his years of corruption. It's just not feasible." Schreier had the savvier take. "I don't think this election is about Biden at all. It's about Trump," he wrote. "People are voting for him or against him."

"We love competition"

The Big Lie was premeditated.

Trump spent the last few days before the election laying the groundwork for his "heads I win; tails Joe loses" plan. He told aides that he would address the nation and declare victory if he was ahead on Tuesday night, all the later ballots be damned.

Trump was *expected* to have an early edge given the "red mirage" that political analysts were forewarning the public about. The mirage occurred when in-person ballots cast on Election Day, a method favored by Republicans, were counted first, while mail-in ballots, more often preferred by Democrats, were counted later. Trump spent months deriding vote-by-mail options and, abetted by Fox and other conservative megaphones, sowed distrust in the process. He said Sunday night that "I think it's a terrible thing when states are allowed to tabulate ballots for a long period of time after the election is over." He exploited the intricacies and idiosyncrasies of America's decentralized elections system and simplified them for his own advantage.

Fox's head honchos knew this was coming. They knew Trump would claim victory regardless of reality and would cry "fraud" if he fell behind. "It was commonly understood among those of us working in Washington that, yes, this was going on and that it was intentional," digital politics editor Chris Stirewalt said.

Fox skeptics—including top Biden campaign aides—wondered how the network would navigate this inevitability. Stirewalt said he personally believed that "when the most powerful person in the United States is trying to subvert the democratic process and break the republic, you've got to stand taller. You have to stand stronger." But would they? How would the Fox News decision desk, led by polling expert Arnon Mishkin, react to Trump's pressure? What about pressure from Fox's owners? As *Slate* put it in a foreboding—and eerily prescient—headline two months before the election, "The Fox News Decision Desk Controls the Fate of American Democracy."

I asked Fox News PR chief Irena Briganti about that *Slate* piece, and some of our texts were swept up in the Dominion discovery process. Our conversation began about Mishkin because I had gone around the PR department and messaged him directly. It always irritated the famously prickly Briganti when I did that, but, hey, a guy's gotta try. Like a loyal soldier, Mishkin forwarded my outreach right to Briganti and referred me to her. Briganti was protective of Mishkin; "he's been with us for 20 years," she pointed out, vouching for his utmost integrity.

Mishkin, a registered Democrat (a fact that Team Trump would predictably use against him), led a team of eight statistical and political pros, a purposeful mix of Republicans and Democrats. They were guided by the numbers, not personal preferences, and they knew their reputations were on the line with every race call. No one who knew Mishkin thought that his team would bend their projections just to please (or enrage) Trump. But there were legitimate questions about how the projections would be reported on the air.

"What about when Sean Hannity contradicts your decision desk?" I asked. "Do you have thoughts about what happens then?"

"I have a statement if you're doing a story," Briganti replied, because "I'm expecting everyone to ask the same question between now and Election Day."

Everyone did. Fox never really answered.

■

Biden began his Election Day with Catholic Mass at his home parish in Wilmington, Delaware, then visited the grave of his late son, Beau. Trump began Election Day by worshipping *Fox & Friends*.

The president groggily called into the show that started it all, the show that put him on the road to the White House.

"This has been a very special show for me," Trump said, blabbing about how he was honored to be back on. This was telling because he'd lately been bashing Fox with regularity, claiming the network had tilted left, implying Rupert or Lachlan or Paul Ryan was to blame.

"Fox has changed a lot," he shouted agitatedly during the phoner. "And somebody said, 'What's the biggest difference between this and four years ago?' and I say 'Fox. It's much different now.'" He said the *Friends* were still great, and so were Tucker and Sean and Laura, but "Fox is a much different place." No matter how much praise Fox lavished on Trump, if it was not impassioned enough, or it was couched in some questioning or even some genuine honesty about his record, it was never, ever enough. But he was still addicted to the slavish attention anyway: He mentioned that he watched Monday night's *Tucker Carlson Tonight* and praised Carlson's segment about his "massive crowds." Biden, of course, consciously held socially distanced events to adhere to Covid guidelines. But Fox viewers didn't want to hear that, and the hosts had no interest in saying it. Trump also bragged about the stock market's performance, even though the gains in Obama's first four years outpaced Trump's first four years; again, Fox viewers didn't want that fact-check and the hosts didn't provide it.

Trump mostly used the *Friends* chat to sow disinformation about the vote count process. He encouraged his fans to distrust the results in states like Pennsylvania, predicting that "Philadelphia will be a disaster," foreshadowing his blame-big-diverse-cities plan. He practically demanded to know the winner of the election by midnight, which in any close election would be an impossibility. He wanted the Fox audience to assume that the election would be rigged against him—and them.

■

While the rest of America voted, Lachlan Murdoch pronounced Fox to be the ultimate winner of the election. "This very moment, as we speak," Lachlan told investors on an 8:30 a.m. quarterly earnings conference call, "our viewers are starting their Election Day turning on their TV sets to where they left them last night, the Fox News Channel, or opening their web browsers to FoxNews.com, or checking the Fox News app for the latest report."

Lachlan did his best impression of his dad on these calls, sparing no adjective to describe Fox's supremacy. "Fox News has been the most-watched network in all of television, from Memorial Day through Election Day," even bigger than the Fox broadcast network, Lachlan said. Total day ratings were up 31 percent in the demo. Prime-time ratings were up 54 percent. "Last Tuesday," he bragged, "*Tucker Carlson Tonight* on the Fox News Channel had more total viewers than the season premiere of NBC's *This Is Us*."

Lest anyone say Fox had brainwashed only conservatives, Lachlan highlighted Fox's performance in swing states and its appeal among independents. He claimed that this was a testament to "the quality of our journalism and the balance of our reporting." But saying people watched Fox for the journalism or the balance had the ring of the old line about reading *Playboy* magazine for the articles. That wasn't what most people were looking for.

Left unmentioned was the fact that Fox News had just laid off sixty to seventy people, largely from the reporting ranks, including the so-called Brain Room of researchers who tried to keep the network's coverage somewhat straight. The Brain Room department was "always a reliable and unbiased source for us," a disappointed staffer told me. "Seeing the company cut down on their staff only further reinforces the idea that the likes of Sean Hannity and Tucker Carlson are running the asylum."

For the entirety of the Trump years, the story was the same: Opinion won, news lost.

Toward the end of the conference call, Michael Morris of Guggenheim Securities lobbed a question about a buzzy idea at the time: that Trump might start his own network if he lost. Lachlan very much enjoyed the chance to swat away the notion of MAGA TV. "We love competition," he said. "We have always thrived with competition, and we have strong competition now." He meant CNN and MSNBC, not the further-right and harder-to-find channels Newsmax and One America News, which, as far as Lachlan was concerned, were mere flies on the back of his elephant.

One America, or OAN for short, was the most cravenly pro-Trump and conspiratorial of the bunch, and it was so puny that it wasn't even rated by Nielsen. Newsmax was more respectable but still resembled Liberty University's college TV station. According to Nielsen, Newsmax averaged 50,000 to 100,000 viewers in the evening hours when Fox averaged 3 to 5 million; its highest-rated hour, *Greg Kelly Reports*, at 7 p.m., was one-fortieth the size of *The Story* on Fox at the same time. Trump tried to help out Newsmax by appearing on Kelly's show in late October, but barely made a ratings dent, managing a measly 112,000 viewers. So Lachlan's confidence in Fox's dominance was backed up by data.

Election Day was the last day that would be true.

"Call Rupert"

At 1:36 in the afternoon on Election Day, the man known as Trump's "shadow chief of staff" messaged the real one, looking for reassurance.

"Hey," Sean Hannity wrote to Mark Meadows, "NC gonna be ok?"

Meadows replied two hours later, knowing that Hannity was currently in the middle of hosting his nationally syndicated radio show, his straight shot into the ears of the GOP base.

"Stress every vote matters," Meadows wrote. "Get out and vote."

"Yes sir," Hannity replied, offering a verbal salute to the marching orders. "On it. Any place in particular we need a push?" The conversation continued:

> *Meadows:* "Pennsylvania. NC AZ."
> *Hannity:* "Yup."
> *Meadows:* "Nevada."
> *Hannity:* "Got it. Everywhere."
> *Hannity:* "Is turnout low?"
> *Meadows:* "No. Seems good. But some of our people said it was going to be a landslide. Don't want that out there."
> *Hannity:* "Agree."

This was Hannity in his element—not a journalist, not even really on the Fox team, but a soldier in the cause of conservatism, a spokesman, an operative, really, for the Republican Party, ready to do their bidding when called to serve.

While Meadows and his adjutant, Hannity, were coordinating talking points, Lachlan was texting with Suzanne Scott, who passed along a secondhand prediction that Trump was going to suffer a "historic popular vote loss" but was "going to win the Electoral College."

"If that happens, god willing, we will have to defend the Electoral College aggressively," Lachlan wrote back, enlisting the deity in the endorsement of Trump—as well as the defense of an election system that would elevate someone suffering "a historic loss."

This is how media executives' nervous energy on Election Day gets expended—through endless what-are-you-hearing texts with associates. "Caught up with Hemmer," Scott wrote at 5:04, referring to Bill Hemmer, who manned the network's touch screen on election nights and showed real-time vote totals. "He thinks Trump is going to have a very good night. Big lead in FL."

Lachlan wrote back, citing the *Wall Street Journal*'s editorial page editor Paul Gigot, "that's what Gigot has heard as well."

At 5:20, Lachlan flagged a story on the *Daily Mail* website about a Biden campaign trail gaffe. The story was headlined "Joe confuses his two granddaughters and then introduces one of them as his dead son—and he could be US President in HOURS."

"If this is real," Lachlan wrote, "can we get up on website?" Scott said she would check. Then:

Scott: "It's real and we are getting it up."
Lachlan: "Should be lead story for now."
Lachlan: "Thx."
Scott: "Copy."

Lachlan and Scott and Gigot and the *Daily Mail*—the right's band of influencers were talking among themselves like BFFs on Snapchat.

Fox's special report, led by Bret Baier and Martha MacCallum, began at 6 p.m. Eastern. It was like an unwelcome early ice bath for Fox's viewers, a numbing shock to the system, since the network had strongly suggested that the race was a toss-up. Before 6 p.m., on-screen banners celebrated "MASSIVE ENTHUSIASM FOR TRUMP" and promised that he was "CLOSING THE GAP IN KEY BATTLEGROUND STATES." In reality, Biden had consistently maintained almost every advantage in national polls heading into election night. But Fox downplayed the polls—even its own polls—that said so. The network had for months stuffed its viewers, blindly, wrongly, with promises of a second Trump term. It was all smoke and bubbles. And bubbles were about to burst.

At 6 p.m., Fox suddenly became all about numbers, not narratives. While Laura Ingraham and weekend host Jeanine Pirro mingled at Trump's election night party in the East Room of the White House, Baier and MacCallum helmed the anchor desk inside the sprawling Studio F in New York. Mishkin's decision desk made the projections; Fox's D.C. managing editor Bill Sammon verified the calls; and Chris Stirewalt went on the air to discuss the calls.

Fox wanted to show off its A-team. After the 2016 election, at great expense, the network broke away from the other broadcasters and their National Election Pool, which conducts exit polls to help with projections and tabulates all the local-level votes. Fox partnered with the Associated Press and established a new system. The AP called it VoteCast, and Fox called it the Fox News Voter Analysis, a mouthful of a name that described a massive survey of Americans in all fifty states. (One of my favorite aspects was that it included nonvoters to more fully capture the national mood.) The AP and Fox believed that their system was superior to the in-person exit polls that had occasionally led the networks astray in past election cycles.

It had worked well during the 2018 midterms: Fox projected that the Democrats would regain control of the House almost an hour before the other networks. This was its first presidential test.

Mishkin's team modeled all the swing states, studied the survey data, and compared the actual raw vote counts to what they expected would happen. Executives at Fox's rivals said Mishkin's decision desk was aggressive—meaning they tended to make key race calls more quickly than rivals—but impressive. The callers were really, truly walled off from political and financial influence. "We called it the nerdquarium," Stirewalt recalled in a Dominion deposition, "a fish tank for nerds." He said it was run in a "wonderfully hygienic way." No one else was allowed in the tank—not even the Murdochs.

This might sound too good, too ethical to be true. But Scott's interactions with Lachlan on election night backed it up. At 8:26, when the information had to be sketchy at best, Scott wrote, "I'm hearing POTUS will win FL GA Ohio Iowa NC and AZ. He will win but close. Problem is MI WI PA."

"Hmmm," Lachlan replied. "How far behind is he in PA?"

"Only 5% in."

At 9:07, Scott sent a web traffic update: "Over 2.1 million" concurrent visitors. "By a mile," she said, it was Fox News Digital's "best day ever."

Lachlan was attuned to the Trump of it all. At 9:22, he asked, "Why are we not calling Florida at this stage?"

Scott, his link to the inside, replied, "I asked it's not callable yet. Close but not yet."

"Momentum in Pennsylvania looks good," Lachlan wrote at 9:43 before taking a dig at presumed-lib Stirewalt, who was on air at the time, and not saying anything like that: "Stirewalt is dripping sweat." Scott said, "I told Jay our viewers don't like him and we should use sparingly." Yes, Lachlan affirmed, "and Chris has to be careful tonight if the momentum moves to Trump. He needs to look truly neutral."

Lachlan was anything but neutral. At 10:03 he exclaimed: "Trump now ahead in Wisconsin!" At 10:47: "Trump ahead in popular vote so far! Amazing." He also consumed international coverage of the U.S. race, and at 11:06, he texted Scott, "Australian media is reporting that Biden has to win Arizona to have a chance of winning. Is that right?" Even when forewarned about the timing of the "red wave," Lachlan couldn't see it behind his red-colored glasses.

"Yes," Scott wrote back at 11:09, "I also think Trump needs it."

"And hearing it's tight," she added.

Tight she could live with. But the network's investment in a new, improved decision desk was about to pay off in the most aggressive early call in years. The nerdquarium was ready to make the call that would come to redefine Fox in the minds of many Trump voters. And not in a good way.

Remember, three hours earlier, Scott told Lachlan she was "hearing" that Trump would take Arizona. But Mishkin's team was now confident that Biden would win the state—a confidence that challenged the expectations of their employer as well as an audience conditioned to believe everything Fox said. The decision team was actively debating "is it time yet?" to make the call public. "AZ is leaning Biden," Scott texted Lachlan at 11:10, laying the groundwork for what was coming. Her next text, ten minutes later, was just two words: "Biden Arizona."

The simple, declarative words had the impact of "Oh the humanity." The call was shared on air at the same moment, ineptly. Hemmer was at the touch screen running through various "what if . . ."

scenarios that showed how Biden and Trump could both reach the 270 electoral vote mark when he stopped himself and pointed his index finger at Arizona, suddenly awash in blue on the oversized TV monitor. "What is this happening here?" he asked.

"Why is Arizona blue?"

"Did we just call it?"

Fox had botched the critical moment. It was just a fluke of timing—Sammon had just checked the box in the computer system, turning Arizona blue on Hemmer's map, and Hemmer noticed before Sammon told the control room to have Baier announce the projection. This was exactly what TV networks tried mightily to avoid on election nights: uncertainty, confusion, chaos.

The director called for a split screen, with the anchors on the left and Hemmer on the right. Baier was still wearing his glasses, not expecting to be on camera. "If you lose Arizona, where do you win now?" Hemmer said ominously, clearly referring to the Trump team's hopes.

"Okay, time-out," Baier said, "this is a big development. The Fox News decision desk is calling Arizona for Joe Biden."

In his own war room at the White House, Trump was watching, of course. Not believing he could possibly be seeing what he was seeing, he erupted. "Call Rupert," the president shouted to Jared Kushner. "CALL RUPERT."

■

At that moment, Rupert was confident that Trump was a goner. In the six months leading up to Election Day 2020, the elder Murdoch had grown more and more pessimistic about Trump's shot at reelection. He told pals to expect a President Biden. By the time Election Day dawned, he believed that Trump was going down, possibly in a landslide, and thus his corporate marriage of convenience (and contention) was almost over.

Rupert and Trump spoke often during the early innings of Trump's presidency. They talked about policy moves, Fox personalities, ratings, women, all sorts of things. Several of Trump's biggest bootlickers, like Lou Dobbs, were on the low-rated Fox Business Network, and more than once, Trump said he wanted his interviews with Dobbs to air on the highly rated original Fox News. Rupert bragged to his friends that he "refused" Trump's requests.

Rupert's telephone relationship with POTUS fizzled out in 2020: Trump called him only twice, once in February, and once in September. The February call was largely about the looming Covid-19 pandemic, which Trump was soft-pedaling, even likening to a Democratic "hoax." Rupert warned him to take it seriously. "You better be careful," he said. "It is a big deal."

"Well," Trump responded, "some people say that."

To ride out the pandemic, Rupert flew from his vineyard in California to his mansion in Henley-on-Thames, forty miles from London. He was cooped up there at Holmwood House, "bored in the country," he said, with his Trump-hating, Fox-hating wife Jerry Hall, and what he read and saw of Trump's pandemic mismanagement made him apoplectic. Trump wasn't following any of his advice; instead, Trump was taking cues from the reckless commentary on his networks. Dr. Anthony Fauci told me he believed that some of Fox's prime-time talk about the pandemic was downright "outlandish." So for all of Rupert's feelings about the president's own failings in dealing with Covid, he should have looked inward.

Before the pandemic Rupert usually gave directions in person or on the phone. But in 2020, stuck at home with "nothing to do but write stupid emails," he began to write his directives more often—

creating a discoverable record for Dominion's attorneys. In one emblematic message before the 2020 election, Rupert encouraged Fox to cover "some of the close Senate races and give a little exposure to Republicans fighting to" hold or win key races. Scott's #2 Jay Wallace said he would get it done. Rupert was explicit in his aim to help the GOP, particularly his personal friends like Mitch McConnell, the Senate majority leader, and Dr. Mehmet Oz, who was running for Senate in Pennsylvania. Had the head of CNN or ABC or CBS or NBC come out and said their network should give exposure to candidates from one party to help them hold the Senate, the reaction would have been nuclear. But with Fox, it was expected—another sign that the network was a propaganda organ more than a news operation.

Trump called Rupert one more time in 2020, on September 15, six weeks before Election Day. Afterward, he emailed Lachlan and Scott and summed up the conversation:

> *Talked a little about a few things but he insisted on talking about our people! Loved twice over Lou Dobbs, loves Hannity, loves Maria B (known her for thirty years), but we have a bad person (do you know him? Sammons). "Hates Trump!"*
> *I didn't tell him he might be right!*
> *That's all.*

"Sammons" was a reference to Bill Sammon, the longtime head of Fox's D.C. bureau. Sammon was a fifteen-year veteran of Fox with a long history in conservative politics and journalism. He was about to be offered a new three-year contract. Perhaps Rupert innocently misspelled the man's name, but the email suggested that Rupert was so far removed from Fox's day-to-day operations that he didn't know

Sammon at all. Or maybe Rupert was at an age where he simply didn't remember.

■

Fox's Arizona call was the pivot point of the night, dramatically narrowing Trump's paths to 270. Arizona was the first state to flip from red to blue versus the 2016 election results. So it was a clanging signal that Biden was on the way to winning the White House—and a breaking point for MAGA heads who turned off Fox in disgust and rage.

To this day, election forecasters still debate whether Fox's projection was premature. But it definitely did turn out to be right. Besides, the polls were already closed, so howling about one network's "projection" would have no effect whatsoever on the ultimate outcome. But Trump had always, first in business and then in politics, built his reputation around perception, not reality. Fox, which Trump had reason to think of as "my Fox," was on the air creating the perception that he was going to lose. For both strategic and psychological reasons, Trump had an overpowering need to change that perception. Strategic, because losing Arizona would conflict with his plan to declare victory early and insist only fraud could alter that result. Psychological, because being perceived as a loser could tear him apart.

But at the moment it came down, Mishkin's team did not think it was a decisive moment in the presidential race—or American history. They viewed Trump v. Biden as an Electoral College dogfight and thought Trump was still very much in it. The Trump campaign's furious reaction, however, signaled that Arizona was the knockout round, sudden death, Waterloo, pivotal to their math and their path to victory.

On the third floor of the White House residence, Trump demanded that someone do . . . something. "They've got to change it," one source recalled him saying. He was crying out for a shazam moment, a magic trick to make reality disappear. Trump dispatched Kushner and Meadows to call the Murdochs and Baier and Hemmer and Sammon—maybe even the floor manager or the guy who ran the coffee cart—anyone they could think of.

It's "way too soon to be calling Arizona, way too soon," Trump senior adviser Jason Miller texted Sammon. Miller then tweeted a public version of the objection while Meadows called Sammon and asked how Fox justified the call. Sammon's answer: "Math." He was in the nerdquarium with Mishkin and was not at all surprised by the Trump White House's bluster. As he explained it, "One guy wins, the other guy always pushes back."

But this time "the other guy" had friends in very high places at Fox. Hope Hicks epitomized this: After helping to get Trump elected, Hicks had jumped to a much higher-paying job at Fox Corp in 2018 to run communications, and in 2019 she brought Raj Shah, previously one of Trump's top spokesmen, over to the company in a senior VP role. In early 2020 Hicks returned to the White House, so come election night, she was part of the bully-Fox-into-backing-down campaign: She messaged Shah and, according to a source, pushed for the Arizona call to be reversed.

Rupert said he never considered changing the call ("I trust these people. I do not interfere in that sort of thing") but his son wasn't quite so placid about it. At 11:52, Lachlan texted Scott, "Team is doing a great job. With the possible exception of the decision room."

"Yup," Scott replied. "Getting complaints about the AZ call but the decision team stands by it."

Scott still gave Lachlan some hope that Trump would win reelection, texting, "My gut [says] Trump wins PA and MI." (Her gut needed fine-tuning: Trump wound up losing in both states.) But her broader point was that neither candidate would be getting to 270 anytime soon.

On Fox's live broadcast, guest after guest heaped doubt on the Arizona call, even though they didn't have access to Mishkin's models or data sets. Finally, at 12:33 a.m., more than an hour after the call had been made, and with no other network having joined Fox on its lonely limb, Baier brought Mishkin on air, and assumed a detective role. "Arnon, we're getting a lot of incoming," he said, "and we need you to answer some questions. Arizona: Are you 100 percent sure of that call?"

Mishkin said yes and explained the math. He even said "I'm sorry," to no one in particular, as he reaffirmed his ruling: "The president is not going to be able to take over and win enough votes to eliminate that seven-point lead that the former vice president has."

Trump, undeterred, decided to address the nation, or at least whatever small sliver of the nation was still awake. He stepped before a bank of live TV cameras at 2:21 a.m. and delivered his pre-planned declaration of victory in the face of defeat. "We have won Georgia," he lied. He went on to lose Georgia. "We're winning Pennsylvania," he lied. He went on to lose Pennsylvania. "We are winning Michigan," he lied. He went on to lose Michigan. "Frankly, we did win this election," he lied. He lost that election.

The speech turned the toxic soup up to boiling, with Fox squarely in the pot. The network was once again torn between Trump and the truth. Initially the truth won: Chris Wallace said on the air right afterward, "This is an extremely flammable situation" and "the president just threw a match into it. He hasn't won these states." But Trump believed that his noise machine could outmatch news coverage. And having watched him do it for four years, I could see why he thought so. He had suggested bleach as a Covid treatment; fired an FBI chief for investigating him; and redrawn a National Weather Service hurricane map with a Sharpie so it fit a lie he'd made up . . . and still suffered no discernible loss of support from his voters or attention from the media. The network of lies—dozens of Fox opinion shows and a hyperpartisan universe of Fox-wannabe podcasts and websites and social networks—insulated him.

When the sun came up Wednesday, Mishkin was booked on *Fox & Friends* to explain why states like Pennsylvania weren't called yet. A few minutes later, another guest on the show, Trump adviser David Bossie, mocked "your so-called expert" from the decision desk.

Scott, feeling the pressure from Bossie types, proposed at an 8:30 a.m. meeting that Fox stop making any further projections until the state-by-state results were certified. This concession to Trumpism would have busted decades of political journalism norms. Network calls in presidential elections were the Super Bowl of the business: Getting them first (and right) made you the winner. What was the point of the game if you didn't keep score? Scott did not implement her idea, but tensions were clearly coming to a head.

■

On election night, during the prime-time 8 to 11 p.m. hours, when it looked like Trump very well could win a second term, Fox News averaged 13.6 million viewers, which was even higher than its 2016 election average of 12.1 million. CNN came in second place with 9.1 million. Near midnight, however, minutes after Fox called Arizona for Biden, Fox's audience started to shrink and Newsmax's audience started to grow.

The shift was minor, all things considered, since Newsmax had a measly 500,000 viewers. But the Newsmax base held steady until two in the morning, while half of the Fox base went to bed. When I revisited the Nielsen numbers months afterward, I realized that this was the very first sign of an eyeball exodus. A sliver—but a noticeable one—of the Fox audience was so invested in Trump, and so infuriated by Fox's Arizona call, that they went off in search of a safer space. They were like sports fans who didn't want to see the action live if it meant their guy was in a dogfight and might lose. They just wanted to see the parts where he was winning.

And so they landed on Newsmax, where there was no decision desk, where Arizona wasn't blue, where Trump was still a "contendah." On Wednesday the Fox-turned-Newsmax audience was audible outside an election office in Maricopa County, Arizona, where pro-Trump protesters alternated between two slogans, "Count the votes" and, more alarmingly, "Fox News sucks." How had Fox replaced CNN in that familiar chant?

Raj Shah sent an email to his two deputies, Elliott Schwartz and Alex Griswold, both former reporters from the *Washington Free Beacon*, a conservative political site. This team—which they dubbed the Brand Protection Unit in emails—tracked Fox's status in the social media universe and counteracted advocacy groups like Sleeping Giants that wanted to starve Fox of ad revenue. In the Twitter analytics for election night, Shah found a "sharp spike in conservative criticism of Fox." The most common specific complaints were about the decision desk. There were the usual gripes from liberals, but "85% of all negative engagement was from tweets sent by conservatives," Shah wrote. The network was sinking in MAGA quicksand.

By Wednesday afternoon Fox and the AP showed Biden on the cusp of winning the presidency, with 264 electoral votes, thanks in part to the Arizona projection. At this point, Fox had put more points on the scoreboard for Biden than any other network, fueling the outrage that the home team's announcers had not only been unfair to the home team fans, they had out and out betrayed them. Mishkin had to defend his Arizona call both externally and *internally.* "We are not pulling back that call," Mishkin told MacCallum on the air. Trump was closing the gap with Biden in Maricopa County, but it wasn't going to be enough to flip the state to red. So Trump and his brainwashers needed to make an emotional rather than mathematical argument. That's what Wednesday night was all about. Hannity asked leading questions: "Is the fix already in?" "Do you believe these election results are accurate?" Laura Ingraham blamed "the propagandistic media." Mishkin's truth was buried by brokenhearted whining and innuendo. "Holy cow, our audience is mad at the network," Tucker's executive producer Justin Wells wrote in a late-night email. "They're FURIOUS," anchor Shannon Bream replied. And it was about to get so much worse.

"Those fuckers"

Operating on little sleep, and even less tea and sympathy from the audience, some of Fox's stars petitioned the decision desk for a do-over. The Arizona call is "hurting us," Bret Baier wrote in a 7:41 a.m. Thursday email to Sammon, Stirewalt, and Jay Wallace. As Election Day turned into election week, and everyone was strung out and stressed out, Baier wanted to be on the record about what was going on.

"I know you guys are feeling the pressure," he wrote. "But this situation is getting uncomfortable. Really uncomfortable. I keep on having to defend this on air. And ask questions about it. And it seems we are holding on for pride."

Baier was remarkably sympathetic to the Trump camp's arguments that Trump might close the gap and win Arizona's eleven electoral votes. So he urged Sammon to revoke the call. "The sooner we pull it—even if it gives us major egg. And we put it back in his column. The better we are. In my opinion."

But Arizona was never going to be in Trump's column. What Baier proposed would have artificially swung the election toward Trump for no reason other than TV anchor discomfort (and viewer bitterness). It would have been the worst media blunder during an election since the calling of Florida back and forth between Al Gore and George W. Bush in 2000.

Sammon said he appreciated Baier's honesty, but "it's not pride that's got us sticking to the call—it's math. I'm confident we will be proven right and all will be well. We just have to tune out the outside noise as much as possible. We're gonna get there!"

Baier told his friends that it was a "shitty call." But he felt like his concerns fell on foolish ears. He wasn't the only one. Chief White House correspondent John Roberts, who wanted to move into a day-time anchor role and soon would, wrote to Sammon and Wallace at 9:31 a.m. and said the Tuesday night call "is really beginning to hurt us as a network" since the raw vote gap in the state between Biden and Trump continued to shrink. "I am hearing from people that I have never heard from before, and not just flame throwers," Roberts wrote.

The rebellion was happening on Fox's air, as well. "Arizona is going the other way," Kellyanne Conway insisted on *Fox & Friends*. Co-host Brian Kilmeade awkwardly said that "we stand by the Arizona decision, but that's done by the decision desk," quickly shifting the blame. People who defended the decision, like Stirewalt, were getting clobbered by social media trolls. "When I defended the call for Biden in the Arizona election, I became a target of murderous rage from consumers who were furious at not having their views confirmed," he recalled. *Murderous rage.*

As the day dragged on, Fox's shows noticeably shifted, and hosts began to cast doubt both on Arizona, specifically, and the legitimacy of the election, broadly. At noon, Harris Faulkner said Arizona was "too close to call," even though Fox had called it. At 5 p.m., Lou Dobbs said the Justice Department should "move in" to ferret out mass voter fraud. This rhetoric inflamed the president and an incalculable number of his fans. At 6:47, Trump walked into the White House Briefing Room and accused his opponents of the very thing he was doing: "Trying to steal an election." He smeared patriotic poll workers and derided entire states. "They want to find out how many votes they need, and then they seek to be able to find them," Trump said, in an almost literal foreshadowing of what he himself would say to try to get Georgia to swing its vote to him.

Afterward, Baier and MacCallum pretended like it was perfectly normal behavior for a sitting president. In reality, it was so abnormal, so grotesque, that most other networks cut away and refused to air Trump's remarks live. "What a sad night for the United States of America," Jake Tapper exclaimed on CNN. Trump, he said, was attacking democracy with a "feast of falsehoods."

"When he wins the state, it's legitimate," Tapper said, ridiculing the president. "When he loses it's because the vote is being stolen from him. It's not true. It's ugly. It's frankly pathetic."

Tapper was flanked by political journalists Dana Bash and Abby Phillip. "This president clearly knows that this is not going to end well for him," Phillip said, "and he's trying to take the rest of the country down with him." Bash said she texted senior Republican lawmakers "to ask when the intervention is going to happen." Tapper agreed: "It's time for some Republican lawmakers to find their spine."

But over on Fox, not a single host or guest denounced Trump's undemocratic conduct and comments. Not a single one. Baier, who was at the anchor desk when it happened, privately called the speech "heinous," but didn't dare say so on air. When I asked why no one spoke up, I heard excuses and evasions that always led to the real answer: The pressure from the audience was debilitating—and emasculating.

The Trumpian right already distrusted almost everything and everyone. Fox was one of the only *semi*-trusted brand names on the right. But because of the decision desk, Fox had forfeited a great deal of that trust. Less trust meant lower ratings, a less powerful network, a weaker business, and less lucrative contracts for the hosts, so the hosts were desperate to claw that trust back. Thus, at 8 p.m., Tucker Carlson implored the news media to "slow down" and stop making "hasty calls."

"If people air concerns, resolve the concerns," he said. "Don't call them names, don't sweep those concerns under the rug, don't shut them down artificially with unelected news anchors. Let our system work."

It was a pointed message to Carlson's unelected news side colleagues. During the commercial break, when producer Alex Pfeiffer complimented the monologue, Carlson texted back, "That had a very specific audience."

"We worked really hard to build what we have," Carlson wrote. "Those fuckers are destroying our credibility. It enrages me."

Carlson also held a brief conference call with Hannity and Ingraham during the four-minute ad break. "They're highly upset," he told Pfeiffer.

Carlson's whole hour hyped Trump's lies under the guise of get-

ting to the truth. If you watched with the sound off, this is what you
saw on screen:

CLAIMS OF VOTER FRAUD FROM ACROSS AMERICA
CHAOS ERUPTS IN PENNSYLVANIA OVER BALLOTS
TRUMP: THERE IS EVIDENCE OF A RIGGED ELECTION
AMERICANS ARE LOSING TRUST IN THE ELECTION PROCESS

Carlson interviewed a pro-Trump poll watcher in Philadelphia
who howled about vote count "corruption." The guy "was super
nuts," Carlson admitted to Pfeiffer afterward. But the segment "will
help" restore the audience's faith, Pfeiffer said. Being "nuts" on air
clearly was not disqualifying.

Hannity tried to do the same thing as Carlson—and he went so far
that he triggered some alarms inside Fox. He declared at 9 p.m. that
"any call of Arizona was premature." He claimed "it will be impossible to ever know the true, fair, accurate election results." (He might as
well have declared "democracy as we know it is over.") He insisted that
"Americans will never be able to believe in the integrity and legitimacy
of these results." He was doing his best to make certain of that.

"Hannity is a little out there," Raj Shah remarked to a friend as
they both watched Hannity's rant.

After the broadcast, Irena Briganti emailed Viet Dinh, Fox
Corp's top lawyer, and flagged "some press heat" around Hannity's
fist-waving commentary. "Thanks," Dinh replied. "Let's continue
to buckle up for the ride for [the] next 24 hours. Hannity is getting
awfully close to the line with his commentary and guests tonight."
Which raised the question: Where was the line if that was only *close*
to it? Just a little outside "Anarchy-ville"?

These execs could see what was really going on. When Hannity brought on Senator Ted Cruz, Shah admitted that Cruz was "saying really wild shit on air." But people like Shah, whose reputations were forever tied to Trump, wanted (or maybe even needed) to believe something was amiss. As he watched another Philly-bashing segment on Fox, he asked, "Why are they defying a court order letting election observers within 6 feet?"

"I don't know," his friend replied, "but I do know that these sorts of disputes are routine and generally inconsequential. I haven't heard the other side, I just hear relentless focus on this one incident in order to undermine confidence."

That was exactly right. Obsessive coverage of one kerfuffle was meant to sully an entire election. Fox was willing to swallow outrageous claims whole, and then feed them back to an audience they had conditioned not to be able to digest the truth. If they could find one legit case of one dead person voting, or one precinct where voting machines failed, even temporarily, that could be enough to build the scaffolding that election deniers could climb to attack the foundation of a system that was standing in their way.

■

Baier was like a human Gumby toy, being stretched in multiple directions, liable to snap at any moment. He was pushing to withdraw the Arizona call to appease the base. But he was also disturbed by some of his fellow appeasers. When he saw that Maria Bartiromo was posting unhinged tweets about fraud, referring to an imaginary "4am dump" of pro-Biden votes and a "vote fairy" that supposedly stacked the deck for Democrats, Baier was furious. He wanted it stopped. Baier alerted Sammon and said "we have to prevent this stuff. While [we] cover the real issues."

"Holy crap," Sammon responded.

"We need to fact check," Baier said.

Late at night, Baier texted with some of his golfing buddies, and the real Bret came out—the father of two who joined Fox in its infancy and worked his way up to chief political anchor with a $6.5 million limestone mansion in Northwest D.C. to show for it. He wanted to be back there—in the Covid era he often anchored his 6 p.m. show from a spare room—but he was stuck in New York as Election Day turned into election week. "I am tired. And pissed. And running out of suits," Baier wrote to his friends. There are "no fucking bars open," he wrote, "and I may just tear some Trump campaign spokesperson's head off tomorrow." When one of his friends commented that "it ain't over," Baier replied, "There is NO evidence of fraud. None."

But the Fox audience needed to hear otherwise.

"Sore loser"

On Friday, November 6, Biden was inexorably closing in on the presidency, and all eyes were fixed on the vote count in Pennsylvania. Rupert was tuned in to *Fox & Friends* while writing Scott a good-morning email. "Nice to see plenty of breaks!" he wrote. Ever the businessman, he observed that CNN was forgoing commercial breaks due to all the breaking news, while Fox was still running loads of ads.

As deeply partisan as Rupert had been during his entire career, he was ultimately a pragmatist: "With several states now disappointingly favoring Biden," he wrote to *New York Post* editor Col Allan, it's "hard to claim foul everywhere." He wrote to Scott that "everything seems to be moving to Biden, and if Trump becomes a sore loser we should watch [to make sure] Sean especially and others don't sound the same. Not there yet, but a danger." Rupert wanted to warn against Trump dragging Hannity—and the rest of Fox—down into the sewer of fabricated evidence with him.

Scott forwarded Rupert's message to prime-time supervisor Meade Cooper and marked it confidential. Cooper and her deputy Ron Mitchell took the temperature of the hosts, sometimes through their executive producers, and Mitchell then remarked in a text to Cooper, "I feel really good about Tucker and Laura. I think Sean will see the wisdom of this track eventually, but even this morning he was still looking for examples of fraud."

Still trying to find fraud. *Still* trying to prop up Trump. It was sad, in a way, like a teen reader of *Tiger Beat* seeing her idol rejected by America. Several people tried to nudge Hannity back to reality. In an ongoing text chain with Hannity and several producers, Hannity's longtime producing partner Porter Berry said they have "gotta be super careful on any allegations" of fraud since people can say "you're pushing that [the] American democratic system can't be trusted. Just have to be 1000 percent sure and very careful." Hannity didn't respond. Later in the day, he sent the group an outlandish tweet from Georgia GOP Senate candidate Herschel Walker dreaming about making seven contested states "vote again." If laws were broken, Hannity wrote, "what other remedy is there?"

Back in the real world, Biden pulled ahead in Pennsylvania, as all the decision desks expected he would, and the major networks prepared for the inevitable moment when Biden would cross the 270 electoral vote threshold.

CNN's prime-time team had signed off at midnight and resumed anchoring at 7 a.m. Friday—a crystal-clear sign of an imminent projection. But Fox handled it very differently. *Fox & Friends* kept acting like Trump's lies were the real story. In at least two divisions of Fox, staffers were told to keep up this act even after Biden reached 270: My CNN colleague Oliver Darcy obtained a memo telling some staffers not to call Biden "president-elect" once Biden was the projected winner, and I obtained a different note sent to a different set of staffers with the same gist. The memos cited Trump's bogus legal challenges. "Former Vice President Biden does not become 'President-elect' until the votes are certified," one of the memos stated. "Please stick to something along that phrasing." Keep Trump's hopes alive—that's what some Fox execs were telling the rank and file. But when Darcy and I reported on the existence of the memos, there was a freakout inside Fox, and management forswore the guidance.

Shortly before noon, Baier interviewed Republican National Committee chair Ronna McDaniel and pressed for tangible evidence of the fraud she was still imagining (and selling), then pointed out that she didn't have any: "There's all kinds of stuff flying on the internet. But when we look into it, it doesn't pan out." That's what Fox viewers needed to hear, over and over again: "We lost, guys; we're sorry." But Baier's fact-check was an aberration. Rather than help Trump fans process their shattered hearts, hosts like Hannity stoked their rage in explicit collaboration with Trump and his party. McDaniel was on with Hannity on Friday night, and it was scripted like World Wrestling Entertainment, but with American democracy cast as the Heel. NPR's David Folkenflik obtained an internal RNC memo that, he said, "set out in great specificity the intended flow of the show's lengthy opening segment—including its guests, articles and subjects—and the primary points Hannity would make."

Hannity was coordinating with the Trump White House too. Rupert knew it because he asked Scott, at 5:22 p.m., "Has Sean spoken to POTUS yet? And his opinion?" (Rupert later explained the email by saying Hannity "had a closer relationship with Trump than anybody else.")

Scott replied six minutes later and noted that Hannity was still on his radio show, "so no update from him, but he seems to understand where this is heading," meaning a Biden triumph. "However," she said, he will continue to "focus on the litigation for now," giving Trump and his fans vaporous hope about a legal avenue to victory. Scott added: "I told him he should pivot to the wins for the Republicans and Senate fight in Georgia." Rupert replied: "Good."

"A Trump explosion"

Instead of being first with the biggest projection of the year, Fox was last.

On Friday night, Mishkin and Sammon were ready to call Nevada, and thus the White House, for Biden, but Jay Wallace said no. He wrote in a text message, "I'm not there yet since it's for all the marbles—just a heavier burden than an individual state call." Decision desks were inherently competitive. Every team wanted to be first. But in this extraordinary case, Wallace believed the audience backlash wasn't worth the journalistic benefit.

Therefore, at 11:24 a.m. on Saturday, November 7, CNN became the first network to project that Biden would win Pennsylvania and surpass 270 electoral votes, evicting Trump from the White House. NBC followed forty-five seconds later, then CBS thirty seconds after that, and ABC and the AP, all within a frenetic two-and-a-half-minute window. Street parties broke out in New York, Philadelphia,

Washington, Atlanta, Los Angeles, and smaller blue precincts across the country. Anyone who flipped over to Fox News wanting confirmation or contradictory coverage or conservative tears saw . . . ads for MyPillow instead.

Neil Cavuto, who usually anchored a two-hour block on Saturdays, stuck to his pre-planned rundown for a full fifteen minutes. At times he alluded to the projections of other networks but noted, "We at Fox have not yet made that call."

Where was the Fox decision desk? Jon Favreau of *Pod Save America* fame joked on Twitter that Mishkin was "still tied up in a Fox News basement somewhere." But the delay was not his fault—sources blamed the holdup on the special events producers who, like undertakers loath to start the funeral until the family emerged from denial, failed to have Baier and MacCallum ready for the climactic moment. On CNN Wolf Blitzer and company were on marathon, stay-on-your-toes duty for this very reason, but Fox stuck with regular programming instead. That's why Saturday was such a mess. Baier did not break in with the official projection until 11:40. "Keep in mind," MacCallum said, adding an asterisk to the coverage, "the Trump campaign is in the midst of waging legal challenges in several states, but the path is clear for the new president-elect."

Rupert had a heads-up about the impending news. At 11:33 he told *New York Post* editor Col Allan that Fox was about to make the call and wrote, "I hate our Decision Desk people! And pollsters! Some of the same people I think. Just for the hell of it still praying for AZ to prove them wrong!" (With Pennsylvania, though, Biden didn't even need Arizona. And Arizona proved them right.)

Rupert was evidently unaware that Wallace had stopped Fox from being first on Friday night. "We should have and could have gone first," Rupert wrote to Lachlan, "but at least being second saves us a Trump explosion!" (They were actually no better than sixth.) "I think good to be careful," Lachlan replied. "Especially as we are still somewhat exposed on Arizona."

Politicians in the U.S. have to win an election every two or four or six years. But political TV hosts are campaigning to stay in office every single day. The Nielsen ratings are like a nightly election, and when the ratings sag low enough for long enough, a host is liable to be . . . unseated. On Saturday, hundreds of thousands of Fox fans, with gnashing of teeth, went running to Newsmax.

For the first time since launch day in 1996, Fox was facing true competition from the right. It was visible on TV, at Newsmax and OAN, and on the web, at streaming sites like Right Side Broadcasting. The most devoted members of the Trump cult refused to believe, accept, or countenance that Biden was president-elect. They swore off Fox and lumped it in with—gasp—CNN and NBC. Charles Herring, the owner of OAN, felt the eruption in the form of viewer feedback emails and messages. "A massive wave of former Fox News viewers have abandoned Fox and have found a home at OAN," he told me. He scrolled through the emails from new viewers and said that disillusioned former Fox watchers "believe new pro-left voices have infiltrated the network."

Newsmax CEO Chris Ruddy sensed the same opening as Herring. "Newsmax has not called the election for Joe Biden," he proudly proclaimed during a live interview with me on CNN. This was Ruddy's new pitch to viewers: We haven't accepted reality like Fox has. We won't offend you with the truth. In our world, numbers are just squiggly lines that don't add up to anything.

Ruddy and Trump had gabbed on the phone earlier in the week. "He's very disappointed in Fox News," Ruddy told me. Chris Wallace's moderation of the first Biden-Trump debate, when he was forced to wrangle a totally unruly Trump, "was terrible," Ruddy said. "It really hurt, I think, the president. And then, you know, they call the election." As in: They reported the news. Ruddy brought up Arizona and suggested a nefarious scheme was at work: "What was going on at Fox News that they didn't want to give the president the sense that he was winning or had the potential shot of winning?"

There was no such conspiracy at Fox. Lachlan's messages showed that he was openly rooting for Trump's reelection. Rupert's emails showed more disillusionment with Trump but a keen desire not to offend the Trump-watching base. But this anti-Fox plotting took root in the conspiracy-drenched soil of the far right anyway. It was a symptom of the fallout from years of Fox stoking the rage and paranoia of a group of citizens disaffected with their place in America. As time went on, they were more and more willing to believe anything that made them feel better about themselves, and about the country they wanted "back," the country as they fantasized it to be—in their memories.

Ruddy, in particular, knew how to press these buttons. And he was in touch with one of Fox's stars who wanted to help. Jeanine Pirro, the host of *Justice with Judge Jeanine* on Saturday nights, was one of Trump's steadiest allies at Fox—which, in this context, meant she proselytized for him and shrieked absurd things about Biden. In August she had predicted the Democratic nominee was "not even going to be on the ticket" by November. Weeks later, she "interviewed" Trump, and he charged Biden—wildly, nonsensically—

with using performance-enhancing drugs. "I think there's probably, possibly drugs involved. That's what I hear," he said, and she sat quietly, never batting a fake eyelash. Pirro, shamelessly, titled her next book *Don't Lie to Me* and dedicated it "to one person": President Trump. (Who says there isn't comedy on the right?)

During post-election week Pirro was determined to deny Biden's victory—but Scott's deputy Meade Cooper denied her the airtime. Cooper and weekend programming chief David Clark talked on Friday about preempting *Justice* on Saturday, sensing that Biden's win would merit extra hours of (what Fox considered) straight news coverage, but also recognizing that Pirro would murder the truth. "Her guests are all going to say the election is being stolen," Clark wrote, "and if she pushes back at all it will just be token." His suggestion: "Perhaps we need a PT news block," using shorthand for prime time.

So Pirro got sidelined. But why? Speculation filled the explanation vacuum. "They took her off cuz she was being crazy," Justin Wells wrote to a friend. "Optics are bad. But she is crazy."

Pirro made sure that Ruddy heard about her unplanned bye week. Newsmax threw up a breaking news banner: "JEANINE PIRRO SUSPENDED FROM FOX NEWS." No, she was not; it's "BS," Cooper told Irena Briganti in an email. "As you know we totally revamped programming today." Briganti said she was pushing back. Meantime, Briganti's #2, Caley Cronin, fielded a PR inquiry of a very personal sort—her own mother-in-law was watching Newsmax when the "suspended" story aired. "She wanted to make sure we knew," Cronin wrote. Cronin said it was "scary she was watching them—and a bit telling given she's [a Fox] die-hard."

"Yep—our viewers left this week after AZ," Briganti remarked.

It was a weird case of Fox staring at its own image in an even more twisted mirror.

Newsmax's bogus Judge Jeanine story spread to several far-right blogs that were gullible enough to believe it. "She is planting this stuff," Clark wrote to a colleague. "Angling for a job somewhere else. 100%. Cuz it ain't coming from us. And guess what??? Bye bye!!!" Clark said Pirro was "the biggest headache of my 40 plus year career."

Pirro's phone blew up with sycophants who wanted to see her. "Can't believe your show isn't on!" one friend wrote. "The media keeps saying Trump needs to show fraud and when someone tries to expose it, they get shut down!"

"I know," Pirro replied. "This is nuts. We're still fighting."

Pirro personified the Fox-Trump base far more than Cooper or Clark or any of the executives on the org chart. The base wanted to break out the torches and pitchforks and fight. They ignored Biden's call on Saturday night to "put away the harsh rhetoric, lower the temperature, see each other again, listen to each other again." What they wanted to see were, in the immortal words of Kellyanne Conway in 2017, "alternative facts." Conway birthed that phrase on the weekend of Trump's inauguration, when only a modest crowd showed up at the National Mall, in dismal contrast to Obama's swearing-ins. Her twisting of the truth about a gathering on the Capitol steps was an eerie foreshadowing of the rioters who, fed by "alternative facts," would storm those very same steps in 2021.

"The network is being rejected"

Networks can broadcast for twenty-five years but be defined by just five of the days. That's what happened at Fox between November 8 and 12. By the end of the 12th, a morose Sean Hannity was texting his colleagues that "in one week . . . they destroyed a brand that took 25 years to build and the damage is incalculable." His "they" were Fox colleagues, but they were on the "news" side, the facts side.

On the 8th, the morning after Biden clinched his win, the *New York Post* featured an editorial titled "President Trump, your legacy is secure—stop the 'stolen election' rhetoric." The piece represented Rupert's personal views: Within an hour of the president-elect projection, Rupert had mused to Col Allan in an email, "Should we say something Donald might see?" An hour later, a draft of the editorial was in Rupert's inbox. His son Lachlan said it looked great. Rupert agreed but, ever the newspaperman, flagged a few typos.

The editorial gave Trump point-by-point directions, starting with his personal attorney: "Get Rudy Giuliani off TV. Ask for the recounts you are entitled to, wish Biden well, and look to the future." As soon as it was posted online, Scott told Lachlan she would circulate it inside Fox, and then she wrote to Briganti, "I'm sending this around to our staff."

The *Post* editorial eliminated any doubt about the POV of Fox's patriarch. Behave with "dignity," the editorial said. Stop with the "baseless conspiracies." The hosts of *Fox & Friends Weekend* were told to stay away from election fraud claims, and the Pirro preemption also spoke volumes. Despite all that, Maria Bartiromo was waiting in the wings, all gassed up on rage and righteousness, about to heap shame onto the network and cost the company hundreds of millions of dollars.

■

During her weekly show on Fox News, *Sunday Morning Futures*, Bartiromo became the first Fox host to utter the name "Dominion."

She did it intentionally and repeatedly in front of millions of viewers. What she started, on November 8, was the mainstreaming of a truly diabolical conspiracy theory which, by the 12th, was being repeated in all caps by the president.

Of her two big guests on the 8th, Bartiromo thought Rudy Giuliani would be the trickier one because he had been publicly accusing Fox of tipping the scales to favor Biden. (Giuliani, once the internationally admired mayor of New York City, was reduced to shilling for Trump, and would eventually face severe legal consequences.) Before the show, Bartiromo told producer Abby Grossberg that she would call up Giuliani and ask him not to bash Fox on Fox's own air. "It's also a pretape," Grossberg noted, "so if it goes completely off the rails, we could always try to cut" his insults out.

That turned out to be the least of their worries. The much bigger problem was their other guest, a Texas-based lawyer named Sidney Powell, who transformed from a federal prosecutor in the 1980s to a critic of prosecutorial overreach in the 2000s. Powell achieved MAGA celebrity status for her savage criticism of Special Counsel Robert Mueller's probe of Russian interference in the 2016 election and her representation of Lt. Gen. Michael Flynn (ret.), the MAGA hero whom Trump pardoned for lying to the FBI about Russia. She was a regular on Lou Dobbs's show. (Maggie Haberman reported in *Confidence Man* that Trump started speaking with Powell "after being impressed by her appearances" with Dobbs.) Now Powell was on the president's legal team, or at least that's what Bartiromo said when she welcomed Powell onto the show. Powell alleged, in her very first answer, "a massive and coordinated effort to steal this election from We the People of the United States of America, to delegitimize and destroy votes for Donald Trump, to manufacture votes for Joe Biden."

The ball of noxious fabrications rolled downhill from there, thanks in large part to Bartiromo's prodding. The moment it ended, Briganti's deputy Caley Cronin texted her and warned that the Powell interview was "problematic"—like a plague of locusts is problematic. Yes, Briganti replied, "tons of crazy—I am screaming at Stelter via text so I missed some of it."

Yes, it's true, Briganti and I exchanged some very pointed texts during the 10 a.m. hour on Sunday. I was about to go live on CNN and castigate Fox for "enabling Trump's delusions about the election." It wasn't just Bartiromo doing so: Long-ago House Speaker Newt Gingrich went on Fox at 9 a.m. and said "thieves" in big cities stole the election—a merry dog whistle for the racists in the viewing audience. Trump immediately tweeted out Gingrich's words.

It's Journalism 101 to ask a subject for comment ahead of time, so I frequently checked in with Fox PR before anchoring *Reliable Sources* segments. On this day Briganti argued that Fox hosts were reporting on newsworthy allegations—POTUS was still claiming he won—and were pushing back on controversial claims. We were busy texting so I didn't see just how little Bartiromo "pushed back" on Powell until later.

"Sidney," Bartiromo said, "I want to ask you about these algorithms and the Dominion software. I understand Nancy Pelosi has an interest in this company." Then she tossed to break. "Stay with us," she said, delivering the tease perfectly. (The Pelosi link was made up, by the way.) After the ads for hearing aids and telehealth doctors, Bartiromo came back on camera and said "Sidney, we talked about the Dominion software. I know that there were voting irregularities. Tell me about that." Powell alleged fraud: "They were flipping votes in the computer system or adding votes that did not exist."

Bartiromo should have said "who's they?" and asked "what proof do you have?" but she barely challenged Powell at all. Bartiromo sounded more amazed than doubtful and told Powell to "please come back soon." Cronin told Briganti that the show was so "crazy" she decided not to send the transcript to the reporters who usually received highlights from Fox's Sunday morning shows—an indication that at least someone at Fox already knew the show was becoming increasingly deranged. Briganti said Bartiromo is "one of our biggest issues now."

What they didn't know was that Powell's Dominion smear was rooted in a ludicrous email from one, random, especially unglued Trump fan. Stay tuned for more about that.

As for the Giuliani interview earlier in the hour, well, it was ultimately deemed just a footnote. "Maria did a good job with Rudy," Fox Business exec Gary Schreier wrote to his boss Lauren Petterson afterward. "She did well," Petterson agreed. "It's just going to be hard to get her back to business news for a while."

"I know," Schreier wrote. "It has to play out. The question is after it does and if it lands where we think it will land will she move on. I really don't know." He could have extended his inquiry to the entire right-wing media machine: If Trump's lawsuits fail and Biden is inaugurated, will they "move on"? If only.

Schreier commented to Petterson that Bartiromo "has GOP conspiracy theorists in her ear and they use her for their message sometimes. I wish she had that awareness." These execs were technically responsible for Bartiromo, yet they were passively bemoaning how bad actors "use" her, and they were not intervening. It was an early sign that Fox was not going to stop, never mind correct, the torrent of irresponsible sludge Bartiromo was pouring out on their air.

■

One of the Murdochs' messages to Suzanne Scott on Sunday was about being "careful" with guest bookings. But they weren't worried about the likes of Sidney Powell; they were fretting about having too many Democrats on the air.

We're "getting creamed by CNN," Rupert wrote in an email to Scott. "Guess our viewers don't want to watch it. Hard enough for me! They'll return (not for Chris Wallace!)."

Scott forwarded the email to Jay Wallace after having what she dubbed a "long talk" with both Rupert and Lachlan. She told them the "first 72 hours will be the worst of it." She said "they are expecting" the following:

- "Major overhaul of polling."
- "Audiences don't want to see too much of the Mayor Petes [Buttigieg] and [Sen. Chris] Coons etc in the news hours. Need to be careful about bookings next 2 months—especially in news hours."
- "Breaking news reporting and investigative units need to get back in the game."

This was the beginning of a battle plan aimed at winning back the Trump-loving audience. Rupert's view, as he expressed later, was that "we'd been through this with Obama winning. We would go down in the ratings, and [in] a few weeks they'd come back." Internally, according to a source, execs thought the rebuilding process would take a whole lot longer after Arizona—maybe six to twelve months. But that's not the type of timeline that the heads of a publicly traded company, trained to impress shareholders three months at a time, like to hear.

■

Meanwhile, back in the world of rooms with stars on the doors, Tucker Carlson was leading a text message chain where Hannity and Ingraham bitched and moaned about all their "enemies" and "liberals" within Fox. The trio had a complicated history and very competitive staffs; the cable grind encourages petty rivalries and backbiting. But they also had something very specific in common that no one else understood. They were the faces of Fox, plastered on huge banners outside Fox headquarters on Sixth Avenue, for better and for worse, and after the Arizona call, it was for worse, much worse. Late that Sunday, in the prime-time text chain, Ingraham and Hannity mournfully shared links to anti-Fox stories on Breitbart.com, where angry comments from former fans piled up.

"We are screwed," Ingraham wrote.

Hannity: "News or opinion?"

Ingraham: "All."

The trio detested the "news" side. "We are tainted too—not as much" as news, she said, "but their turn toward Biden was so pronounced and obvious that it bleeds across network." Hannity concurred: "The network is being rejected."

Carlson looked at his phone fifteen minutes later and added to the pity party. "I've heard from angry viewers every hour of the day all weekend," he wrote, "including at dinner tonight."

"Same same same," Hannity said. "Never before has this ever happened."

Ingraham said she'd been on the receiving end too—"including at Mass!!" Was she cold-shouldered during the sign of peace?

Carlson was furious at Fox's mis-management team. He asked VP of morning programming Gavin Hadden, "Do the executives understand how much credibility and trust we've lost with our audience? We're playing with fire, for real."

"I hope so," Hadden replied. "I'm worried."

Fox was being confronted with a new paradigm: They don't trust us anymore because this time we didn't lie.

The conversation continued:

Carlson: "Some of this will pass but once you lose people's trust
 it's tough."
Hadden: "We certainly have gone against 'the customer is always
 right.' But hopefully our product is strong enough to with-
 stand."
Carlson: "I sure hope so. I sincerely believe it's important to have a
 strong Fox News."
Hadden: "There is no question."
Hadden: "And Newsmax with all our castoffs is not the answer."
Carlson: "With Trump behind it, an alternative like Newsmax
 could be devastating to us."

On Monday the 9th, the start of a new workweek, fear of Newsmax was like a burning rash spreading over Fox's thin skin. Fox was
being depicted as insufficiently loyal to Trump and the GOP. The
MAGAsphere felt betrayed. "We're bleeding eyeballs," a producer
said to me. So there had to be changes. And there had to be scape-
goats.

Sammon and Stirewalt were being fitted for horns. They
came under withering criticism from top execs as well as talent. In a midday email to Jay Wallace and Briganti, Scott said
"Sammon not understanding the impact to the brand and the
arrogance in calling AZ and how that played out by him is astonishing." She distinguished between Mishkin, whom she called a
"scientist," just following the data wherever it led, and Sammon,
who "is supposed to be a top executive whose job it also is to protect the brand."

Moments later, Scott spoke by phone with Lachlan, who wanted Raj Shah's Brand Protection Unit to get more involved. Shah had been sending out weekly reports for a year, largely about liberal groups' attempts to turn advertisers against Fox, but now his reports were about the ugly conservative backlash. Scott asked Briganti to call Shah and "walk him through everything we are doing." Shah, in an email an hour later, assumed a crisis posture: "We are under pretty heavy fire with a fast moving situation on our hands." Shah described Monday as "Day 3," meaning Saturday, the day Biden was declared president-elect, was Day 1. It was like a post-disaster diary.

Briganti and Shah strategized about how to land pro-Fox commentaries from conservative thought leaders. "The biggest folks aren't going to rush to our defense," Shah wrote, "but the Tier 2 folks might write." They divvied up who would pitch whom.

Shah had a curious side gig as a liaison between Tucker Carlson's show and Briganti's PR staff, which was born out of Carlson's antipathy for Briganti. Carlson felt he didn't have anyone advocating for his show and his brand. So he went directly to Dinh and asked for the unusual arrangement. On Monday, Shah told Briganti that "Tucker's team [is] telling me his monologue should be base/viewer pleasing."

Please the base sounded faintly pornographic, but Carlson knew he needed to perform. Carlson was angry both at management and at colleagues like Bartiromo who were, in his view, hurting the cause with crazed claims about voter fraud. He texted his team and said "the software shit" Powell hyped on Bartiromo's show "is absurd." He worriedly speculated that "half our viewers have seen the Maria clip" and he wanted to push back on it.

■

The biggest news story that day was an early-morning announcement by Pfizer and BioNTech that their Covid-19 vaccine was more than 90 percent effective in preventing the virus. The headline: Lifesaving vaccines were on the way. "I think we can see light at the end of the tunnel," Pfizer boss Dr. Albert Bourla said on CNBC. Rupert emailed Scott: "Huge story. People will be hungry for every detail. What if it happened two weeks earlier!?" His insinuation was that the vaccine news could have shifted votes toward Trump. "Yes on it," Scott wrote back. "Lots of good stories for us today. Time to pivot." He said "right," and she elaborated: "Pivot but keep the audience who loves and trusts us . . . we need to make sure they know we aren't abandoning them and [are] still champions for them." Rupert agreed and—tacitly acknowledging that the Fox audience contained a high quotient of unhinged MAGA-ites—said "lots of sane Fox viewers still believe in Trump."

Indeed, an astonishing number of Republicans were in denial about the election result. Trump and his aides were stoking a resistance to reality. The journalistic—not to mention patriotic—thing to do was to defend the truth and debunk disinformation. Yet the incentive structure at Fox in November of 2020, fed by its addiction to those reliably juicy ratings, rewarded those who deflected the truth and delivered disinfo.

Take business anchorman Neil Cavuto, the veteran anchor of Fox's 4 p.m. hour. On Monday Cavuto tossed to a Trump campaign press conference being held by White House press secretary Kayleigh McEnany. Her two-timing was unethical and possibly illegal, because it seemed to be a violation of the Hatch Act, which limits electioneering activities by people in the executive branch. When Cavuto heard her cite "fraud" and "illegal voting," among other unproven charges, he cut in. "Whoa, whoa, whoa," he said as he interrupted. "I just think we have to be very clear: She's charging the other side as welcoming fraud and welcoming illegal voting; unless she has more details to back that up, I can't in good countenance continue showing you this.

"I want to make sure that maybe they do have something to back that up," Cavuto continued. "But that's an explosive charge to make, that the other side is effectively rigging and cheating. If she does bring proof of that, of course, we'll take you back." He summed up his view this way: "Not so fast."

And good for him. Cavuto was brave. But his bravery won him no medals. Instead it earned him the charge of being, in the words of Shah's team, a "brand threat." In other words: We're Fox. Unproven, completely scurrilous charges? That's our brand.

"We're taking incoming," Shah wrote. His team initially thought the "threat level" was low but senior execs disagreed. Scott later made her view crystal clear in an email: "Neil doesn't think the American audience is smart [enough] to make a decision for themselves in watching a press conference? Terrible."

Fox's C-suite was united in its belief that Cavuto had undermined its recovery efforts. He cut away from McEnany "just as we were trying to shift the narrative on the right, which led to further backlash and an even more difficult environment to pitch in," Briganti wrote to her bosses.

Lachlan was alarmed. In a text exchange on Monday night, Scott, as though talking about the death of a loved one, told him that the audience was "going through the 5 stages of grief. It's a question of trust—the AZ [call] was damaging but we will highlight our stars and plant flags letting the viewers know we hear them and respect them."

Yes, Lachlan replied, but it "needs constant rebuilding without any missteps. Cavuto was bad today I hear." Cavuto had spoken up for the facts, the truth, and that, for Fox, was the dead-wrong decision, a bad mark to be checked against his name.

Lachlan added that Jay Wallace "has to be very strong"—to tamp down the rest of the rebellious truth-telling integrity-preserving newsroom. Yes, Scott affirmed, "today is day one and it's a process." She said "Bush to Obama took a few months." She was desperately trying to calm her owner's nerves. She referred to the "Neil incident" and assured Lachlan that Wallace handled it "head on."

Separately on Monday, a liberal activist and internet oddball named Timothy Burke posted video from an internal Fox feed. His caption: "Sandra Smith, off-air, reacts to her colleague Trace Gallagher indulging a nutjob who denies the outcome of the election even after Fox News had called it for Joe Biden." This video, from Saturday, was known as a "hot mic" moment because Smith, a daytime anchor, was off-screen but could still be heard and seen by the control room and others within the network. She was heard viscerally reacting to a guest who dismissed Fox's presidential projection: "What? What is happening? Like, Trace, we've called it."

Fox officials had no idea how Burke obtained the video. But they thought it was yet another alarming setback. They were on edge all day and night. It was almost midnight on the East Coast when Lachlan was watching the late-night conservative newscast anchored by Shannon Bream. He texted Scott and asked, "Is Shannon's show run by news Dept? I ask because Chad Pergram [was] really terrible." The CEO was belittling Fox's whip-smart Congress expert, who was on the show with a segment about the "unlikely friendship" between Biden and the Republican Senate leader Mitch McConnell. When Scott woke up Tuesday morning, she asked Jay Wallace to look at Pergram's hit (TV-speak for a correspondent's report) and see if anything was objectionable. There wasn't. Scott also texted Wallace about another immediate concern of Lachlan's: the continuing visibility of moderate Democrats on Fox's shows. Figures like Pete Buttigieg were supposed to be, if not invisible, hard to spot. Yet correspondent Peter Doocy "was still using Buttigieg sound in his reporter hit" last night, Scott pointed out. "On it," Wallace responded.

Yes, the panic inside Fox was so profound that the head of the network was worrying about random sound bites—or fleeting glimpses of the enemy—that might upset viewers (or her boss).

What Scott called "rebuilding" involved quieting the truth about Biden and shouting alternatives that might salve the audience's grieving hearts. As the *Washington Post*'s Philip Bump wrote, "Fox News earns the trust of its audience not by conveying the truth but by bolstering the right's agreed-upon falsehoods." The right was quickly coalescing around the agreed-upon Big Lie, so Fox stars felt pressure to show solidarity. Even Baier, the man who'd announced Biden was president-elect, went there: He told viewers on Monday that "we are not going to stop digging and following up on leads" about voter fraud. The language of journalism was being exploited to cover farfetched theories in a cloak of legitimacy.

Carlson started his Monday night show by spinning a crowd-pleasing fairy tale, claiming that there were several "massive" sources of "election interference" that had tipped the scales against Trump. Imperfect polls, he said, in an especially fantastical touch designed to project serious charges against Republicans back onto Democrats, were tantamount to "voter suppression." Covid-era changes to voting procedures, he said, were intended to "move votes." Move was the ideal word, because it didn't require proving anything nefarious had actually happened to the votes, it only had to *sound* like something cheaters did. Carlson privately thought Powell's claims about Dominion were absurd, but he publicly played along: "We don't know how many votes were stolen," he said. "We don't know anything about the software that many say was rigged. We don't know. We ought to find out." It was a variation on Carlson's just-asking-questions shtick. Would it be enough to please the base?

On Tuesday the 10th, the Monday ratings report hit like a right-cross smack in the face of the champ. Newsmax, previously a Rocky-like tomato can, was surging. Greg Kelly's 7 p.m. show on Newsmax topped 800,000 viewers, a spectacular 1,000 percent increase from his pre-election average. Kelly's 6 p.m. lead-in, cohosted by Sean Spicer, also grew by 1,000 percent. In sixteen years covering television, I had never seen a show score a ten-times increase in one week.

It was obvious where these viewers were coming from. Fox's afternoon and evening hours were down dramatically, despite the epic news cycle. This was so much more precipitous than an ordinary post-election slump. "Our audience hates this," one exec told me. "They're pissed," said a second source. "Seething," said a third. Fox's ratings were still far higher overall, but Newsmax's sudden gains were "a bit troubling," Scott admitted, pretty understatedly, in a text to Wallace. His reply more accurately reflected the high-alert agitation boiling inside Fox: "Trying to get everyone to comprehend we are on war footing."

On Newsmax, Biden was not president-elect and Trump was not a loser. "IT ISN'T OVER YET," Newsmax's on-air banners proclaimed. Fox was still only flirting with election denialism at this point, while Newsmax was already cuddling up in bed with it. Newsmax "truly is an alternative universe when you watch," Scott texted, "but it can't be ignored." Her lieutenants began to monitor Newsmax's bookings to assess which guests were appearing on both channels. The intent was to pressure guests to stop saying yes to Newsmax—and to "pause" booking those who didn't abide.

Every other segment on Newsmax seemed to be a tirade against Fox. "They are just whacking us," VP Porter Berry wrote as he watched. "They definitely have a strategy across all shows to try to target and steal our viewers," Petterson replied. I was struck by her use of the word "steal." Pro-Trump activists were organizing, in Orwellian fashion, around the undeniably catchy and alliterative phrase "Stop the Steal," which succinctly stated the bogus argument that the election was "stolen" from them. Trump and Fox were now operating on parallel tracks, racing further and further away from facts, and signing on to the same mission: "Stop the Steal."

"Respect the audience"

"Omg I'm so depressed," Maria Bartiromo wrote to Steve Bannon. She was texting during a commercial break in the middle of her show on Tuesday.

"I can't take this," meaning Trump's loss, Bartiromo exclaimed.

"I am watching the world move forward. & it's so upsetting Steve," she wrote. "I want to see massive fraud exposed." She claimed to be contradicting Fox's decision desk: "I told my team we are not allowed to say" Biden is president-elect "in scripts or in banners on air. Until this moves through the courts."

Bannon was in a destructive posture; he outlined a plan to "destroy" Biden's presidency "before it starts, IF it even starts." But Bartiromo said "I'm scared and sad."

"You are our fighter," Bannon replied. "Enough with the sad! We need u."

Hannity was down in the dumps too, according to a text exchange he had with his liege, Mark Meadows, later in the day. It read like two teammates commiserating:

Hannity: "How u holding up?"

Meadows: "I am doing well. Working around the clock. We are going to fight and win."

Hannity: "You really think it's possible. I'm beginning to feel down. To [*sic*] much disorganization. We need [Trump-defending congressman] Jim [Jordan] to front the messaging. Someone that's credible."

Meadows: "Arizona now down just 12813. Still ballots to count. Very disorganized but I have been busting heads yesterday and today. Let NOT your heart be troubled my friend."

The White House said it wasn't over, but most of the folks at Fox knew it was. Carlson didn't repeat his "rigged" rhetoric on Tuesday. He pivoted to anti-Biden, anti-Dem storylines. But this attempt to move on, to accept the laws of political physics, riled up his viewers. It led to this remarkably candid text exchange with producer Alex Pfeiffer *during* the show:

Pfeiffer: "You told me to tell you if we are getting attacked on Twitter so I will. Many viewers were upset tonight that we didn't cover election fraud."

Carlson: "Yeah. Probably should have."

Pfeiffer: "Yeah I didn't get why we didnt. Assumed it was some sort of decision not to. But it's all our viewers care about now."

Carlson: "Mistake."

Carlson: "I just hate that shit."

Pfeiffer: "Yeah its honestly awful."

As Carlson signed off, Pfeiffer sent a tweet quoting a *Washington Post* story—a specific quote that eventually became infamous in political circles. The *Post* quoted a "senior Republican official" who said it was okay to let Trump blow off steam about losing the election by lying to the base. The official said, "What is the downside for humoring him for this little bit of time? No one seriously thinks the results will change. He went golfing this weekend. It's not like he's plotting how to prevent Joe Biden from taking power on Jan. 20. He's tweeting about filing some lawsuits, those lawsuits will fail, then he'll tweet some more about how the election was stolen, and then he'll leave."

Pfeiffer correctly argued that the official was wrong: "It's like birtherism 2.0. A grassroots movement the GOP leadership thinks they can control and will go away but this won't."

"This is a wise tweet," Carlson responded.

Monday's conspiratorial commentary clearly wasn't enough. Carlson hated the fraud "shit" and sometimes claimed he hated Trump but felt he had to go there again. His audience wanted the scoreboard to show a different result, with more points for their team, some way for them to believe their hero would still be POTUS. So Carlson and Pfeiffer conjured up a new way to signal to viewers *we're with you.*

■

"Do we have enough dead people for tonight?"

That's what Carlson asked Pfeiffer at lunchtime the next day.

It was Wednesday the 11th, and the Trump campaign was supposed to be sending over some names of "dead people" who voted in the election. The implication was that live people exploited outdated voter rolls. It was perfect for Carlson, who told Pfeiffer that

Trump's lies were "disgusting"—"I'm trying to look away"—but needed for competitive reasons to be lie-curious, open to the possibility.

The problem at lunchtime was that the campaign wasn't coughing up the names as quickly as Carlson wanted. The host said he would call the campaign directly if need be: "Obviously they need to do whatever they can to help us." *Obviously.*

Because more and more it was a *joint* effort.

By 8 p.m., Carlson was satisfied, and he started his show by saying that the Trump voters who "believe this election was fundamentally unfair" were right. Democrats stoked fraud by encouraging mail-in ballots, he claimed. Then he started naming some dead people who voted by mail.

You can probably guess what happened next. It turned out that several of the allegedly deceased voters were still very much alive. Actual reporters—not from Fox, it goes without saying—went to their actual homes, knocked on some actual doors, and found out the truth. Trump's campaign and Carlson's team had totally bungled the story. Fox buried a correction but it didn't matter: For Carlson, "dead people voted" was a success. Fox viewers heard what they wanted to hear: We didn't lose. The other guys cheated. It was conservative virtue signaling.

Carlson also adjusted his guest bookings to show "respect" to the frenzied audience. Dana Perino, the George W. Bush press secretary turned Fox anchor, was one of those reality-based Republicans who mostly kept her credibility intact during the Trump years, but was often derided as a RINO (Republican in Name Only) by the base. Post-Arizona, Perino's regular appearances on Carlson's show were put on hold. "It's only temporary," Carlson assured her. But Perino was irritated about being dumped. She told a friend, "This day of reckoning was going to come at some point—where the embrace of Trump became an albatross we can't shake right away if ever."

■

Instead of shaking it, many of Fox's stars embraced it. As the week went on, key programs all seemed to see the destination—Trump and his voters were the victims of a "rigged" election—and they tried out various ways to get there. Carlson was more subtle about it than Bartiromo and Dobbs, who went all-in on very specific, *X-Files*-style conspiracy theories about hackers and algorithms. Dobbs booked Giuliani on Thursday the 12th and brought up Dominion, triggering the first of many smears about rival company Smartmatic on the network. "All of its software is Smartmatic software," Rudy lied, "so the votes actually go to Barcelona, Spain." Dobbs threw around terms like "overthrow," "cover up," and "election nightmare."

If Dobbs was at one end, and reality was at the other, Hannity was somewhere in between. Hannity pretended the outcome of the election was still in doubt, citing "outstanding votes that have yet to be counted" and "more reports of dead people voting from beyond the grave." Most importantly, he found a new villain to stand in the lineup before the fretful Fox viewers. He talked at length about Dominion, dropping innuendo like breadcrumbs for the flock to follow, all about "security concerns" and "fraudulent software." The president watched and cheered. He began his Thursday by rage-tweeting against Fox, but after Hannity's show that night, he wrote, "Must see @seanhannity takedown of the horrible, inaccurate and anything but secure Dominion Voting System which is used in States where tens of thousands of votes were stolen from us and given to Biden. Likewise, the Great @LouDobbs has a confirming and powerful piece!"

A Fox News PR aide forwarded Trump's tweet around, saying, "Again, telling his followers to watch."

A Fox correspondent named Jacqui Heinrich reacted very differently. She tweeted that "top election infrastructure officials"—including some in Trump's government—had issued a statement that same day saying "there is no evidence that any voting system deleted or lost votes, changed votes, or was in any way compromised."

Out of nowhere: an accurate report! But in the prime-time text chain, Carlson flagged the tweet for Hannity at 11:09 and said, "Please get her fired. Seriously." Why? Because a Fox employee fact-checking Trump was bad for business. This was like Cavuto all over again. "I've fought this fight for years," Hannity replied, a fight to keep facts at bay. "They never listened."

"It needs to stop immediately, like tonight," Carlson wrote. "It's measurably hurting the company. The stock price is down. Not a joke." (For the record, the stock did droop about 2.6 percent on Thursday, but it bounced right back.)

Hannity said he had already sent the tweet to Suzanne Scott. Carlson kept riling him up: "Why would we allow some 27 year old fake reporter to wreck our network?" Hannity said he was making a drink and going to bed. But not before he sent Heinrich's tweet to his top producers along with a question (more accurately, an ugly threat): "Do they not realize I like to fight and the damage I can do here?"

Executive producer Robert Samuel responded that it's "amazing" how many Fox staffers seem to "hate" the audience. "You don't have to love Trump," he wrote, "but you have to respect the audience." They continued:

Hannity: "Oh I just dropped a bomb."

Samuel: "Grenade or nuke?"

Hannity: "Nuke."

Executive producer Tiffany Fazio weighed in with a "WTF" and said "they better get the 'news division' under control." So many Fox "News" officials delighted in disparaging their "news" division.

By now it was well after midnight. Porter Berry replied-all: "She's a huge lib and I've been raising this issue for weeks. It's insane. She's like a Jim Acosta type character. Bad news bears. She needs to be pulled off political coverage." Berry was bringing out the foulest insults someone at Fox could muster: CNN's Jim Acosta was #1 on the hit parade of Trump media enemies because of his Trump-era coverage. Heinrich was nothing like him. But the bosses were convinced she was a "lib," and therefore a menace. Scott dubbed Heinrich's fact-check "unhelpful" and emailed it to Wallace and Briganti. "Very poor form," Briganti replied. "She continues to audition on twitter for a job elsewhere—this has been going on for months." Briganti said she had flagged it for Heinrich's boss. Half an hour later Briganti followed up and said "Sean texted me" and "doesn't understand how this is allowed to happen from anyone in news.

"She has serious nerve doing this and if this gets picked up, viewers are going to be further disgusted," Briganti added. "Her job is to report—not to taunt the President of the United States and our biggest talent to further her career." She *was* doing her job—reporting, accurately—but for an organization that had thoroughly devalued that skill, reclassifying it, in fact, as a liability. After midnight Briganti flagged the situation for her PR team, writing, "Jacqui attacked Sean by tweeting this—please keep an eye out for pick up, tweets, reporter retweets. etc—she just gave us a News/Opinion divide story."

In the prime-time text chain, the divide was absolute. The popular kids had had enough of the Mensa crowd. The news division "breaks no news ever," Hannity quipped. "They hate hate hate all 3 of us."

> *Ingraham:* "Good."
> *Hannity:* "They are embarrassed by us."
> *Ingraham:* "I don't want to be liked by them."
> *Carlson:* "They're pathetic. [That is] why they're so angry."
> *Ingraham:* "THEY ARENT SMART."
> *Ingraham:* "They like the sound of being a television journalist, and the trappings."
> *Carlson:* "Exactly."

This is when Hannity said "they," seemingly referring to Heinrich and her fact-cabal on the news side, "destroyed a brand that took 25 years to build." Carlson called it "vandalism." Hannity joked about a "prime time walk out"—or maybe it wasn't a joke. Ingraham jumped on the idea on Friday the 13th and said the reason for a walk-out could be "fraud in the inducement"—a form of contract fraud. "When we signed," she said, "they sold the network as a conservative alternative. It is now the opposite and is actually hurting ALL of our established individual brands." Fox was now the *opposite* of a conservative network? They were the equivalent of MSNBC? One honest report had reductio-ed the three Fox prime-time stars to absurdum.

Ironically, management's plan for solving its "brand crisis," as Shah described it, was to lean hard on the Terrible Trio: Ingraham,

Hannity, and Carlson. Jay Wallace previewed it in a text to Baier earlier in the week: We "need to do some promoting of prime," Wallace said. "All American cookout of hot dogs and hamburgers to get us through." On Friday the 13th Fox rolled out a new marketing campaign, titled "Standing Up for What's Right," to highlight the prime-time players. "FOX NEWS," the announcer boomed, "THE VOICES AMERICA TRUSTS."

Of all the things that happened during this pivotal week, the most important was the arrival on Thursday, November 12, of an email titled "Setting the Record Straight." The email was compiled by Hamilton Place Strategies, a D.C. comms firm that Dominion had to hire a few days earlier. Tony Fratto, a White House deputy press secretary under George W. Bush, was a partner at Hamilton Place, and he thought Dominion would be a short-term engagement, since post-election fires usually burn themselves out in a month or two. But this time, they were fighting a block-wide inferno with water pistols. There were at least half a dozen different flash-falsehoods, from cries about secret CIA programs to claims about sneaky last-minute software updates. And then there was the long-dead dictator who was somehow pulling rigged voting strings from beyond the grave.

So "Setting the Record Straight" was Dominion's solution. The email was sent to hundreds of members of the media, including many at Fox. "We needed to create a fact trail," Fratto said. His team sent another corrective email on Friday . . . and another on Saturday . . . prompting Fox SVP David Clark to quip on Saturday night that he had the emails "tattooed on my body at this point."

Weekend anchor Eric Shawn, one of the few straight-as-an-arrow broadcasters still left at Fox, had forwarded the latest Dominion fact-check to Clark and said "you may need to keep this handy tomorrow." That was because Powell and Giuliani were set to be on Bartiromo's show in the morning. Fratto knew, and he had a plan. On Thursday, in concert with the fact-check emails, he began calling and messaging the folks he knew at Fox. To Baier, he wrote, "These attacks by the president and Rudy are bonkers, and untrue. I wanted you to have the facts attached below." To Cavuto, he forwarded a clip of Giuliani lying about Dominion on Dobbs's show and wrote, "You know I respect you and I have a lot of friends over there, but this is some of the most embarrassing and malicious TV I've ever been forced to watch."

Dobbs's show was even worse the following night. He mentioned the company's denial, indicating that he was aware of the "Setting the Record Straight" emails, but then gave Powell a platform to claim Dominion was "created to produce altered voting results in Venezuela for Hugo Chavez and then shipped internationally to manipulate votes for purchase in other countries, including this one." Dobbs's only pushback was to tell her to release the evidence "quick." He actually believed the election was being stolen from Trump, but he was worried Trump's flunkies were not competent enough to prove it in time.

Powell's Fox tour continued: Pirro's show was back on the schedule Saturday the 14th, and Powell was there, imagining a "huge, huge criminal conspiracy" and prompting Pirro to encourage a Justice Department probe of the matter.

All of those lies aired *before* Bartiromo hosted both Powell and Giuliani again on Sunday the 15th. Fratto had a long and friendly history with Bartiromo: He estimated that he'd been on her former CNBC show forty-plus times. "She is one of the great stars of this time," he said, "and she is a really good business news journalist." That's why he held out hope that she might be persuadable. He pinged her at 9:09 a.m. Sunday, less than an hour before showtime. "There has been a LOT of misinformation out there about Dominion," he wrote. And there was about to be a ton more. Dominion was smeared more than twenty times during Bartiromo's broadcast. Powell repeatedly made it sound like Dominion and Smartmatic were one and the same, when they were actually rival companies. Fratto emailed Bartiromo during her show: "Dominion has nothing to do with Smartmatic." And again: "What on earth are you talking about?"

Bartiromo knew how to find out who owned a company. Fratto believed she knew she was lying. Dominion was actually owned by a private equity firm named Staple Street Capital, which had acquired a 76 percent stake in Dominion for $38.3 million in 2018. The business was growing steadily, but "once the defamation happened, the world collapsed for us," Staple Street cofounder Hootan Yaghoobzadeh said.

On the air, Powell had the audacity to tell Bartiromo "I never say anything I can't prove." (Had she been Pinocchio, people could have walked on her proboscis from New York to Miami.) And Bartiromo ate it up as Powell claimed to have spoken with "several whistleblowers" over the weekend. Rewatching the broadcast several years later, I was stunned that Bartiromo was not immediately sanctioned for stirring up so much libelous nonsense. Worst of all, she actually seemed to believe it: "Wow," she told Powell, "this is explosive."

■

Fratto tried in vain to play Whack-a-Troll with the Trump puppets. On Monday, November 16, he emailed Scott and Wallace directly and said an enormous amount of "verifiable wrong information" was finding its way onto Fox's air. He asked if they would both accept a briefing from Dominion. Cognizant of the fact that he was going to the bosses, he added, "I prefer to always talk to on-air talent and pro-ducers, but I think this situation is crossing dangerous lines."

Fratto and Wallace spoke by phone later in the day. Fratto tried to appeal to Wallace's sense of newsworthiness. The bullshit is "dam-aging my client," he said, and Fox is "starting to look like News-max." Fratto asked: "Is this really what you want on Fox?" And: "Where does this end?" He warned Wallace that "you're going to be embarrassed."

Wallace was cordial but not all that concerned. He said he had urged Fox's show teams to be thorough and careful and he sug-gested he might send out another note to that effect. It's unclear if the guidance actually reached Dobbs's team, but let's be clear, hosts like Dobbs did not care one iota what some faraway, hall-monitor boss advised them to do. And this devil-may-care disregard went both ways: Execs like Wallace, who knew their audience, did not hand-wring much about the propaganda on their airwaves. (He told a colleague that "the North Koreans do a more nuanced show" than Dobbs.) Wallace later dismissed Dobbs as just "an opinion show" and excused the unrestrained slurs against Dominion and Smart-matic by saying "this wasn't being reported on as any type of news story for us."

This excuse was infuriating. Wallace and many of his colleagues clung to (more accurately hid behind) the discredited notion that everyone could tell the difference between a "news" show and an "opinion" show. To the extent that Fox viewers *could* tell, they avoided news and preferred opinion. Plus, Fox's opinion hosts pre-sented themselves as Crusading Journalists, fighting the virtuous fight by searching for the truth and striving for fairness.

Powell was back on Dobbs's show defaming Dominion and Smartmatic again at 5 p.m. on the 16th. Fratto emailed the Dobbs transcript to Wallace and said more "fucking" lies had just aired on Fox. He called Dobbs a "disgrace." Fratto wrote to Cavuto too, and called the segment "a heaping steaming pile of lies," and wrote to Baier, "there's no 'debating' this kind of crazy." Wallace forwarded Fratto's message to Petterson and Cooper. "I spoke with him earlier to calm him, but it doesn't look like it worked," Wallace wrote. "Think we need to keep an eye out here on this storyline—or at least make sure we include their response."

That was it. Just "keep an eye out." The network's hosts had ignited a conflagration of lies, throwing the reputations of two companies into the flames at every opportunity. The response was to just take note; smell the smoke; observe the damage; listen to the anguished cries of the victim. But do nothing. Just let it burn.

"Everything at stake here"

Every Tuesday around 9 a.m. I refreshed my CNN email rather obsessively. I was watching for the Sunday ratings spreadsheet to hit my inbox so I could see how *Reliable Sources* performed. On Tuesday, November 17, I noticed something right away: CNN beat Fox every hour in the key twenty-five- to fifty-four-year-old demographic except for 10 a.m., when Bartiromo won. Bartiromo and her absolutely fabulist guests, Giuliani and Powell, were one of Fox's only bright spots, ratings-wise, in the wake of Biden's win. The base tuned in just for them and tuned Fox out immediately afterward.

I wasn't the only one who noticed. Schreier texted Petterson and asked if she'd seen the ratings. "Huge," she replied. "HUGE," he repeated. "Tentpole and then some." (In TV, a tentpole is a show that pops up in the ratings between lesser performers.)

The viewers deserved better than this election denialism—but in their MAGA hearts, it was what they really wanted. And wherever there was demand to be lied to, there was plenty of supply. "One thing I can't comprehend," said Al Schmidt, the Republican city commissioner of Philadelphia, "is how hungry people are to consume lies and to consume information that is not true."

It only made sense through the prism of radicalization. Trump was the truth and the way. Fox's biggest stars not only understood that credo, they endorsed it. So it only made sense for them to enable Trump's Last Stand. Lachlan Murdoch personally set this tone; he even nitpicked an on-screen banner for being offensively "anti-Trump." When MAGA marchers gathered in D.C. in mid-November, he wrote to Scott, "News guys have to be careful how they cover this rally." Some of the remarks he'd heard on air were "slightly anti, and they shouldn't be. The narrative should be this huge celebration of the president. Etc." Later in the day, the crowd's mood changed as counter-protesters pointed out that Trump lost. Mayhem erupted in the streets. Punches were thrown. Fires were set. Police officers were injured. The violence foreshadowed January 6.

Lachlan needed a ratings rebound, and some producers explicitly said Giuliani and Powell would provide that. "Any day with Rudy and Sidney is guaranteed gold!" a producer for Dobbs's show wrote. "To keep this alive, we really need Rudy or Sidney," another producer wrote.

Then the Fox MAGA brigade turned around and tried to justify the bilge they were spewing by saying that their still mourning, and moaning, viewers felt robbed . . . a feeling that they themselves had instigated and sustained. "A lot of Americans believe this election was rigged," Carlson said on November 19. "They aren't saying that because they are crazy. They're not just saying it because they're mad. They mean it, and that is a potentially fatal problem for this country."

During this third week of November, the network of lies demonstrated conclusively that it was not capable of, to borrow Dominion's words, "setting the record straight." Early in the week Scott and Wallace held a Zoom meeting to talk about how to avoid another Arizona from ever happening. Scott called it "one of the sad realities" that "if we hadn't called Arizona, those three or four days following Election Day, our ratings would have been bigger." Maybe, she said, Fox just shouldn't call races at all? Viewers' emotions should be taken into consideration, anchor Martha MacCallum said on the call: "In a Trump environment, the game is just very, very different."

At Fox it surely was, because in their game they had played Dr. Frankenstein, created a monster, then for four years watched him stomp the village called America.

"Trump will concede eventually," Rupert predicted, ignorantly and wrongly, in an email to Scott. "We should concentrate on Georgia, helping any way we can"—a blunt suggestion to use Fox to win GOP votes in the twin Senate runoffs there. His next line was even more revealing: He said "we don't want to antagonize Trump further."

In other words, Rupert, even after the election loss, recognized who the real boss was—and it wasn't him.

Trump "had a very large following," Rupert said later, "and they were probably mostly viewers of Fox, so it would have been stupid." Stupid to provoke Trump because he would hurl abuse and they'd side with him over Fox.

Rupert made two other points in an email to Scott: He flagged a story in his *Wall Street Journal*, about Trump allies exploring a take-over of Newsmax, and said "these people should be watched, if skeptically"; and he reiterated his doubts about Giuliani, whom he had previously called "a terrible influence on Donald" and a drunkard. Everything Giuliani said should be "taken with a large grain of salt," Rupert wrote, likely sadly, because he had held Giuliani in such high esteem in the years before and immediately after the September 11 attacks. But he recognized that Rudy had be-clowned himself during the Trump years. He signed off his email to Scott with severity: "Everything at stake here."

Rupert knew that Trump was hyping the wannabe competitors to wound Fox. He was so determined to appease Trump that he talked with Lachlan about buying repeats of *The Apprentice* to air on Fox Business. Trump had an ownership stake in the show, making this a pretty flagrant way to put cash in the president's pocket to, hopefully, shut him up. But the plan didn't move forward; and Trump definitely did not shut up.

■

Carlson was fed up. All week long, he texted associates about his conviction that Powell was lying—and hurting the MAGA movement that he had helped construct. She's a "fucking bitch" and a "crazy person," he wrote in a text on November 16. "I'm starting to think she's a lunatic," he wrote on November 17. He was well aware of the claims she was making on other Fox shows—"we have so much evidence," she kept saying, "stunning evidence"—and he wasn't having it. Carlson texted her on the morning of November 17 and said "you keep telling our viewers that millions of votes were changed by the software. I hope you will prove that very soon."

"You've convinced them Trump will win," he continued. "If you don't have conclusive evidence of fraud at that scale, it's a cruel and reckless thing to keep saying."

This may be the only time I'll ever type these words: Tucker Carlson was right. He clearly knew the difference between carefully framed, suggestive BS and sloppy, unmistakable BS.

Powell *was* being reckless. She was being cruel. She was leading the viewing audience into a blind, dark alley of delusion. She's "lying," and "I caught her," Carlson wrote to Ingraham and Hannity on November 18.

"Sidney is a complete nut," Ingraham replied. "No one will work with her. Ditto with Rudy." Giuliani had appeared before a Pennsylvania judge in a long-shot bid to block the certification of the state's vote, and when Ingraham read the transcript, she felt like he had "embarrassed" Trump. The conversation turned back to Powell:

> *Carlson:* "It's unbelievably offensive to me. Our viewers are good people and they believe it."
>
> *Carlson:* "She's soliciting 'millions of dollars' in checks made out to her personally."
>
> *Ingraham:* "It's beyond bad."
>
> *Ingraham:* "Where are the hundreds of thousands of votes she said she'd show us this week?"
>
> *Carlson:* "She lied."

The next day, she lied some more. The Trump campaign orchestrated a ninety-minute press conference with Powell and Giuliani so they could, in Jason Miller's words, "present all the evidence that they had been gathering." Miller hadn't actually seen their "evidence" of game-changing voter fraud, mind you, but "they told me they had it." So his team printed up a sign that promised "MULTIPLE

PATHWAYS TO VICTORY" (weeks after Biden was declared the victor) and invited reporters to their alternative-reality festival.

When the presser began, Trump tweeted that Newsmax, OAN, and "maybe" Fox were showing it live. In a chat room with his fellow brand-protector Griswold, Shah flagged the tweet and wrote, addressing the president he used to serve, "fuck you man we're on you can see it."

"This sounds SO FUCKING CRAZY btw," Shah added.

"Rudy looks awful," Griswold said.

Yes, the presser was mainly remembered for being a literal meltdown: Giuliani's hair dye dripped down his face like a sewage leak as he melted in front of the TV camera lights. "He objectively looks like he was a dead person voting 2 weeks ago," Shah joked. Beyond the stomach-turning visuals, there was the content, including Rudy promising he could prove voting fraud "18 different ways," without actually delivering one single way. Rupert was watching, and he told Scott it was "terrible stuff damaging everybody, I fear. Probably hurting us too."

"Yes, Sean and even Pirro agrees," Scott said.

People around the globe were watching Trumpworld's antidemocratic conduct with horror. Rupert emailed with a friend who ran TV stations in Afghanistan and said Trump and Giuliani were "both increasingly mad."

"The real danger is what [Trump] might do as president" for the next two months, Rupert added. He is "apparently not sleeping and bouncing off walls!" That sounded like a good story—but Fox did not report it.

■

When Giuliani's and Powell's nutty speeches ended, the Fox anchor in the chair was Dana Perino. Because Perino knew the Trump team was full of it, and because she didn't fear saying so, the next few minutes on Fox were exhilaratingly honest. Perino tossed right to Fox correspondent Kristin Fisher, who said the presser was "colorful" but "light on facts," then dismantled the Trump legal team's manic talking points piece by piece. A second correspondent piled on, and then Perino turned to her former Bush White House colleague Karl Rove, who demanded proof for the dubious claims.

Perino had been texting with Fratto, her Bush-era buddy, during the press conference. "Where the hell did they even get this Venezuela tie to Dominion?" she asked, referring to Powell's extra-bonkers claim that the corpse of Hugo Chávez was somehow linked to the manipulation of voting machines. "I mean wtf." Fratto wrote back, "It is insane." On the air, Perino pointed out that Dominion was actually an American company, and said "I wouldn't be surprised if they decided to take some sort of action against this." She was the first television host to foreshadow Dominion's lawsuit.

Perino and Fisher took the side of the truth, muscularly, without apology. It was exactly the sort of news coverage that conservatives needed to hear. Naturally, the blowback was extreme. In the Brand Protection Unit chat room, staffers shared an array of angry tweets. This coverage "is the kinda shit that will kill us," wrote Shah, the same guy who had himself declared Rudy's rantings "fucking crazy." The unit sent out an alert within minutes: "We're seeing a number of negative reactions" because viewers feel like the coverage "was dismissive of the Trump campaign's claims." It *was* dismissive, because those claims were on par with arguing thousands of Trump ballots had been eaten by Rin Tin Tin.

Then the screaming started. Fox VP Ron Mitchell told colleagues that Scott was bellowing about Perino's post-presser coverage. ("Ron said he has never heard so much yelling and screaming," Hannity producer Tiffany Fazio wrote.) Megan Albano, the executive producer of Perino's show, told Scott that the Twitter outrage about Perino was an exaggeration, and pointed a finger at Fisher for a "highly editorialized" report. It was not; it was just a factual report. But Scott decided that Fisher was the villain.

"I'm getting major incoming," Scott wrote to Wallace, "on her editorializing and her dismissive tone and indifference to the audience. We need to manage this."

It was now 4:19 p.m., and Scott saw Fisher's face on a TV monitor, doing a live shot on Cavuto's show. "I hope she didn't double down," Scott wrote. "I can't keep defending these reporters who don't understand our viewers and how to handle stories. The audience feels like we crapped on [them] and we have damaged their trust and belief in us." She added, "We can fix this but we cannot smirk at our viewers any longer."

Smirk at our viewers? Perino and co. were trying to tell them the truth! And maybe save them from embarrassing themselves by telling their neighbors they believed Chávez was responsible for Biden being president. Privately, Perino told a friend that the presser was "insane," full of "horrible" lies. But she didn't say any of that on the air. She just sought the (nonexistent) evidence. Mitchell got it right when he told Albano, "I'm not mad at either of them," meaning Perino or Fisher. "I'm mad at those clowns at the conference who put us in a terrible place."

That's how I felt too, as a journalist who was covering this information poisoning in real time. The people at fault were the poison peddlers, not the people trying to clean up the pollution. But Scott saw it differently. When Albano defended Perino, Scott replied and said, "You can't give the crazies an inch right now . . . they are looking for and blowing up all appearances of disrespect to the audience."

Let's diagram Scott's sentence. The "crazies" were the right-wing activists who were pouncing on every "disrespectful" comment made about Trump on Fox's air. Accurate depictions of his election loss were considered disrespectful to these diehards, thus, the command was don't give "an inch" by speaking the truth. What a pusillanimous attitude from the CEO of a media powerhouse.

■

During the presser, Carlson and execs Justin Wells and Ron Mitchell traded insults about Rudy's bad hair day. Carlson said "I really want to ignore" the spectacle altogether. "It's all so desperate and deranged at the same time," Wells said. Come prime time, "I don't see how to cover this," Mitchell wrote. He said there was "just no winning on covering it from any angle." Other prime-time producers felt the same way. Hannity's producer Tiffany Fazio said that night "we just didn't talk about Sidney's claims. That's the way to handle it."

Carlson disagreed. He decided to make his case against Powell public at the top of his eight o'clock hour. He carefully wrapped it in a paean to Trump voters so as not to offend the "crazies." He sneered at the media and Big Tech and the "billionaire class" to show that he was on the same side as his viewers. He came close to attacking Perino and Fisher directly. He spent nine whole minutes allying himself with the audience, ridiculing "elites," paying "respect" to Powell, to soften the blow that came next.

"We took Sidney Powell seriously," Carlson said. "We have no intention of fighting with her. We've always respected her work. We simply wanted to see the details. How could you not want to see them?

"So we invited Sidney Powell on this show," he said. "We would've given her the whole hour; we would've given her the entire week, actually . . . But she never sent us any evidence despite a lot of requests, polite requests, not a page. When we kept pressing, she got angry and told us to stop contacting her. When we checked with others around the Trump campaign, people in positions of authority, they told us Powell has never given them any evidence either."

Rather than saying what he knew—that Powell's conspiracy theories were bananas—he sympathized with the viewers again and said he was "hopeful" she'd release the proof. He let the audience down easy.

Trump saw Carlson's segment and snapped at Powell on the phone the next day. He asked why she refused to go on the show to defend herself. "You look weak," he said.

She proceeded to repeat her rambling theories—the Venezuelans, the Iranians, the Chinese!—as Trump, along with Hope Hicks and Dan Scavino, listened through a speakerphone. Someone muted the phone so Powell couldn't hear.

"This does sound crazy, doesn't it?" Trump asked.

"Yes, yes, it does," Hicks said.

(The special counsel's January 6 indictment cited this conference call, and Trump's use of the word "crazy," as evidence that Trump knew his claims of fraud were false.)

To stick it to Carlson and Fox, Powell backed out of her Saturday booking on Pirro's show; went on Newsmax instead; and accused Carlson of throwing a "tantrum." She said her evidence of algorithmic vote-flipping was "irrefutable" and "hardcore." As Shah watched, he emailed Wells and said "it's just MIND BLOWINGLY NUTS." Carlson later commented that the Powell monologue "totally wrecked my weekend" because it caused a "shitstorm" among Fox fanatics.

"I had to try to make the WH disavow her, which they obviously should have done long before," Carlson said.

That may sound like Carlson being braggadocious, but he was serious. As Shah told his higher-ups, "our consultants and I coordinated an effort to generate Trump administration pushback against her claims." It wasn't that hard to do, since Trump and Hicks were laughing at Powell and calling her "crazy." By Saturday night, the *Washington Examiner* was hard at work on a story saying that Trump family members and aides were frustrated with Powell too. Carlson was just the first person with right-wing credibility to say it out loud.

The *Examiner* story worked. By the end of the weekend, the Trump campaign issued a statement disowning Powell, saying she was *not* working for the campaign or the president. Carlson's best friend Neil Patel forwarded it and asked "Is this because of you?" Carlson took credit. "I've got a high tolerance for crazy as you know," he wrote, "but she was too much." In a text to Shah, he was more explicit about Powell, using his favorite word: "That cunt. I hope she's punished."

"No one can tell me differently"

On November 20, Maria Bartiromo sent a text that no legitimate journalist would ever write. "This was fraud," she wrote of the free and fair election three weeks earlier. "No one can tell me differently." Had she decided the moon was made of Silly Putty, pigs could fly, and the Tooth Fairy was really a white lady from Queens named Stella, would she have been similarly unpersuadable by evidence to the contrary? Apparently, because no amount of reality could dissuade her from the fraud fantasy.

That same day, Dominion ratcheted up its pressure on Fox by sending a six-page legal letter to the network. This should have triggered emergency meetings at the top of Fox, but it did not. The attorney, Mitchell J. Langberg, was not subtle about the fact that Dominion might sue. "To list every example of false and defamatory 'facts' that Fox has broadcast about Dominion would become excessively repetitive," he wrote.

The legal threshold for a public figure to prove defamation is "actual malice," a standard set out in the 1964 Supreme Court case *New York Times Co. v. Sullivan.* "Actual malice" means "with knowledge that it was false or with reckless disregard of whether it was false or not." Langberg cited "reckless disregard for the truth" on nearly every page of his letter. He said that biased sources like Powell were on "an obvious mission to destroy Dominion's reputation," and hosts like Dobbs were "regurgitating" their lies. "The vitriol that has found voice on Fox has resulted in threats to the safety of Dominion employees and their families," Langberg wrote. "Dominion is prepared to do what is necessary to protect its reputation and the safety of its employees."

This was what's known in the business as a "retraction demand letter." Fox did not retract anything. Dominion-defaming hosts like Bartiromo didn't even wince.

■

"What happened to Maria Bartiromo?" is a question that has spawned numerous articles and countless cocktail party conversations. What's clear from her interactions with colleagues is that Bartiromo fully bought into the MAGA-against-the-world mentality that Trump fostered. "They hate him & they wanted him out" because he exposes "their corruption," she wrote on November 20. "I think he could win [t]his." Trump had lost weeks ago but she was still holding out hope. She sounded more like Alex Jones than a distinguished broadcaster.

How does this happen? How does a card-carrying member of

the Media Establishment, a regular at Davos, a CEO schmoozer, end up like this? Some observers thought her information diet was steadily poisoned once she joined Fox. Others thought she was actually quite consistent and strategic in the way she advanced her career: At CNBC, she kissed up to Wall Street, and at Fox, she did the same to MAGA. Trump was just another CEO for her to pursue.

Bartiromo was not the only Fox star who abandoned Earth for Planet Trump. Jeanine Pirro continued to give her producers regular bouts of acid reflux. She drafted an opening commentary about imagined voter fraud for her November 21 broadcast that her own executive producer, Jerry Andrews, was deeply disturbed by. "It's rife with conspiracy theories and BS and is yet another example why this woman should never be on live television," he wrote to his boss David Clark. Of all the internal comments about the wild excesses of Fox's election denial narrative this, to me, was one of the most incredible. The guy producing Pirro's live TV show thought she should never be allowed on live TV!

Andrews said the Brain Room, Fox's version of an in-house fact-checking department, was going through the script. A couple of hours later, the Brain Room sent feedback that would have dragged Pirro back toward reality, but she didn't care: "She is refusing to drastically change the open despite the fact check," Andrews reported to Clark.

At CNN, my executive producer and I were a rock-solid team. We read each other's minds and finished each other's sentences. Pirro and Andrews were the opposite. After Saturday's show, Clark sent Andrews an email about another ludicrous accusation by Powell and called it "crazy town—glad [Jeanine] didn't have her or Rudy" on the show. "Jeanine is just as nuts," Andrews responded. She was convinced the election was stolen and no one could tell her differently.

Lou Dobbs was all aboard the same crazy train. He allowed Powell to call in again on November 24, even though she had been officially excommunicated from Trumplandia; she was *not* speaking on behalf of the president. The on-screen banner said "BATTLE FOR THE WHITE HOUSE" even though the only battle still raging was between MAGA addicts and the inconvenient truth. To be fair, though, there were tens of millions of those addicts. Hannity, that same day, texted his top producers a link to a CNBC article titled "Almost no Trump voters consider Biden the legitimate 2020 election winner." And why would they? The only media outlets they trusted were operating from a conspiratorial cesspool where Trump was the rightful winner. It was a perfect case of circular reasoning: *We need to keep covering these outlandish claims of voting irregularities because millions of our viewers believe them; and they believe them because we keep covering them.*

Citing the CNBC article, Hannity said, "Respecting this audience whether we agree or not is critical. Fox has spent the month spitting at them." Right, producer Robert Samuel responded, "our best minutes from last week were on the voting irregularities." He parsed the minute-by-minute ratings and saw that the audience *wanted* to be lied to about voter fraud. We're "going to have to thread the needle as we've been doing," Samuel said, "and hold Joe accountable."

Tiffany Fazio chimed in and said Hannity was right: "Last night numbers were terrible. We are specials all week though." Because this week included Thanksgiving, the show episodes could be labeled differently, as "specials," so that Nielsen wouldn't count the low-rated episodes in the monthly and yearly averages. It was one of the tricks TV shows employed to look more popular than they really were.

Even at its lowest-rated point, Fox was still incredibly influential.

The demeaning of Smartmatic and Dominion was so scarily effective that lawyers for both companies decided to call for help. Dominion called Thomas Clare, who along with his wife, Libby Locke, ran Clare Locke, perhaps the most feared defamation law firm in the country. Clare took the call "while we were preparing Thanksgiving," he recalled, and he walked to his office by the waterfront in Alexandria, Virginia, to keep talking.

A paper trail was already established, thanks to Fratto's emails and Langberg's retraction demand, but there was so much more to do. "When we got the call, it was an easy 'yes' to get to become a part of it," Clare said.

At almost the same time, over Thanksgiving weekend, Smartmatic's general counsel David Melville left a voice mail for J. Erik Connolly, who led a defamation practice based in Chicago. Connolly, wondering if the inquiry was a prank, googled Melville before returning the call. They talked about the MAGA media chatter around voting machines, and then Melville said, "I'm going to send you some videos." The clips showed Bartiromo and Dobbs disparaging Smartmatic. Connolly called right back.

"What's your reaction?" Melville asked.

"Well," Connolly said, "I'm assuming none of this is true."

"None of it is true."

"Then you've got a very good case."

■

November 2020 produced a colossal migraine for the United States. The American people had evicted Trump from the White House. The public wanted to hear him get it over with and concede. But Maria Bartiromo was so infected by MAGA brainworms that she believed the public wanted to hear a "path to victory."

On November 29, POTUS was set to call into Bartiromo's Sunday morning show for his first TV appearance since the late unpleasantness. So she texted chief of staff Mark Meadows at 9:21 a.m. to prep for the segment. "The public wants to know he will fight this," Bartiromo wrote. "They want to hear a path to victory. & he's in control."

Trump had never eclipsed 50 percent in approval ratings and won just 46 percent of the vote in each presidential election, but somehow Bartiromo assumed that what he wanted (and what she wanted) was universally backed, and therefore what the *country* wanted.

The host was so determined to help Trump that she even sent questions for him ahead of time to ensure he was well prepared for the broadcast. (According to Dominion, she also scripted answers for herself like "the facts are on your side.") The ensuing "interview" consumed most of the 10 a.m. hour on Fox. Rather than pushing back on Trump's broken-record spiel of propaganda, Bartiromo sat back and encouraged him to lie under the guise of asking for "evidence."

She referred to conspiratorial "dumps" of votes, "big massive dumps" that benefited Democrats. At one point she exclaimed to Trump, "This is disgusting, and we cannot allow America's election to be corrupted."

Trump's lies were also practically scripted. They were predictable and repetitive. For example: "They found ballots in a river with the name Trump," he claimed. "They were signed. And they were floating in a river."

This was so untrue that it had been dismembered by Fox's Jon Decker back in October during a rare White House briefing with Kayleigh McEnany. Every time Decker, a serious reporter for Fox's radio division, pushed McEnany by asking where this river was, she ducked and dodged. "I simply want to know where the river is," Decker pressed. He never got an answer because there was no river.

"Where is the river?" went viral, but it didn't win Decker any fans inside his company. Not surprisingly, he left Fox at the beginning of 2021. On Bartiromo's show, Trump continued to talk about this nonexistent river, and she did not interject, not even once, certainly not to ask for the river's location.

∎

While Bartiromo and Trump were gabbing on the phone, Hannity was in a text chain with Meadows, and like a dutiful soldier, Hannity still seemed to believe all the wild and crazy claims about the election. "I've had my team digging into the numbers," Hannity wrote. "There is no way Biden got these numbers. Just mathematically impossible." He was forgetting a crucial aspect of math: show your work. Biden had just done it, so it was obviously mathematically possible. Hannity then offered up his own contradiction, conceding he needed something valid—something like actual evidence—to prove the concocted charges of fraud: "It's so sad for this country they can pull this off in 2020. We need a major breakthrough, a video, something." Meadows replied one minute later: "You're exactly right. Working on breakthrough."

In this conversation Meadows was the would-be content creator and Hannity was the would-be distributor. "Ok," Hannity responded. "Would be phenomenal."

On CNN, immediately following the Trump interview, I said the president was delusional and Bartiromo was aiding in his delusions. What a disservice it was, to the Republican Party, to democracy, to reality, to have the president on the phone and allow him to deceive and damage viewers. The ratings report for Sunday showed America's rupture: Of the 50+ cable news telecasts that day, the Bartiromo-Trump show was #1 and the *Reliable Sources* dissection of it was #2. The political system was approaching a treacherous point, a point where the peaceful transfer of power could not be taken for granted.

Bartiromo and Trump chatted after the broadcast and Trump said he was happy with how it went. But Bartiromo was doubting herself. She texted Abby Grossberg and said "I hope I didn't blow it by not asking about Biden," then wondered if they should have "just stayed the extra 5 minutes and talked about peaceful transition."

"To be honest," Grossberg told her, "our audience doesn't want to hear about a peaceful transition. They still have hope. And the vouchers"—I think she meant vultures—"would have declared it a concession."

"Yes agree," Bartiromo replied.

One more time the ghost of "Do the Right Thing" had made a visitation, only to be sent packing.

In the TV biz, anchors and producers often crave a segment that can "make news." A guest who "makes news," who says something that gets picked up elsewhere, with credit flowing back to the show, is considered a big win. That morning Trump made a lot of news even though what he said was drivel in a can. "It was the first time he acknowledged Dominion was bad," Bartiromo commented proudly—and ominously.

The two women proceeded to insult the Fox exec in charge of weekend coverage, David Clark, calling him a moron. Clark knew Trump's claims were gibberish and supported afternoon anchor Eric Shawn in saying so. Shawn recapped Bartiromo's interview by saying Trump "doubled down on his claims of widespread voter fraud in the 2020 election, even though local and national election officials, as well as federal and state courts in multiple states, and in some cases the Trump campaign's own lawyers, have said there is no evidence to prove that. And experts say such claims are simply unsupported falsehoods that are not backed up by any facts." See, that's the kind of thing Bartiromo should have said to Trump directly. But speaking truth to power wasn't her style.

Someone sent Grossberg my tweet about Shawn's excellent segment. Grossberg shared it with Bartiromo and called it "pathetic and also not a good look for Fox" because it "perpetuates the narrative of post-election failure and infighting." There *was* infighting—between folks who accepted reality and those who opposed reality.

■

Trump's lying spree on Fox—particularly his statement that the Justice Department was "missing in action"—pushed Attorney General William Barr to publicly break with Trump. The baseless claims (by his boss!) that the DOJ had ignored evidence of fraud "got under my skin," Barr admitted later. "It was time for me to say something." So he invited Associated Press reporter Mike Balsamo to lunch on Tuesday, December 1. That's when Barr said, for the first time, that "we have not seen fraud on a scale that could have affected a different outcome in the election."

Balsamo immediately filed an alert for the AP wire. When Trump learned about it, mid-meal in his private dining quarters right off the Oval Office, he hurled his lunch across the room in a fit of rage. White House aide Cassidy Hutchinson famously testified about the "ketchup dripping down the wall" afterward.

Barr's statement to the AP is what fully convinced Rupert Murdoch that the Trump camp's allegations of fraud were utterly bogus. "That just closed it for me," Rupert said. He moved on, just like a growing majority of the public. But the outgoing POTUS remained addicted; he was still jonesing for steady doses of slavish devotion, and if he couldn't get that relentlessly from Fox, he would look elsewhere. So he changed the channel to OAN, where he was still the man, and where the hosts continued to wish upon a star that he might remain in power. When Barr went to see Trump shortly after the AP interview, he noticed the TV in the dining room was turned to OAN, which was featuring a Michigan legislative hearing full of pro-Trump fraud fantasies. Trump publicly pressured Fox to be as irrational as OAN with tweets like this:

> *@FoxNews daytime is not watchable. In a class with CNN & MSDNC. Check out @OANN, @newsmax and others that are picking up the slack. Even a boring football game, kneeling and all, is better!*

Some of his later tweets promoting OAN and Newsmax coverage of lie-filled election fraud hearings were roped into the Fulton County, Georgia, racketeering case in 2023.

Despite Trump's best efforts, OAN's audience was minuscule. Fox, even in its weakened state, was still dominant. Even with reality-based Republicans like Barr affirming that Trump's bellyaching about fraud was all inert gas, Fox's coverage still took Trump seriously. Sammon texted Stirewalt on December 2, while watching Bret Baier's *Special Report* newscast, and grumbled, "More than 20 minutes into our flagship evening news broadcast and we're still focused solely on supposed election fraud—a month after the election. It's remarkable how weak ratings makes good journalists do bad things."

Stirewalt called it a "real mess" and said "what's most worrisome is that there doesn't seem to be much conflict. Everybody is lazily paddling ahead of Niagara."

Both men were about to be swept up in a post-election house-cleaning. Stirewalt was "restructured" out of a job. Sammon was "retired." The decisions were actually made in November. Rupert wrote to Scott back then, "Maybe best to let [Sammon] go right away and make acting appointment. Also the other guy. Next few weeks will be very sensitive and we can't have sneering at events. And [it would] be a big message with Trump people." Fox scored a respect-the-audience home run by forcing out the men who called the election correctly. Stirewalt spoke out against the "political operators and their hype men in the media" who tried to "steal an election or at least get rich trying."

■

Hannity ignored Barr's "we have not seen fraud" statement and instead dedicated most of his Tuesday show to people he called "election whistleblowers." His guest Kayleigh McEnany called them courageous and implored the rest of the media to follow up. But the dogged Eric Shawn did just that the next day and found no "there" there—or anywhere. An account on Hannity's show from a truck driver who said he carted hundreds of thousands of mail-in ballots from New York to Pennsylvania fell apart under even mild scrutiny. The office of the Pennsylvania secretary of state told Shawn that "continuing to repeat these falsehoods only harms our democracy." When Shawn reported this during a 7 p.m. segment with MacCallum, Scott snapped. "This has to stop now," she wrote. "This is bad business and there clearly is a lack of understanding [of] what is happening in these shows. The audience is furious and we are just feeding them material. Bad for business."

Fox PR later tried to claim that Scott's objection was "not about fact checking—the issue at hand is one host calling out another." But

I rewatched the segment—Shawn didn't mention Hannity at all. Scott was really saying that rebutting Team Trump's antidemocratic lies was "bad for business." And it *was*. The Fox Nation streaming service registered tens of thousands of cancellations in November. Scott's tenure as CEO was riding on expansionist dreams like Fox Nation. This was personal for her.

So while Scott was morally wrong she was technically correct: The audience really was furious, still, a full month after the election. On December 7, Newsmax beat Fox in the ratings for the first time. It was for a single hour, 7 p.m., and in a single demographic, twenty-five- to fifty-four-year-olds, but it was a landmark moment for both channels. I called Chris Ruddy's cell phone to hear his reaction and wound up breaking the news to him. (I had received the overnight ratings in my inbox before he did.) "We're here to stay," Ruddy said. "The ratings are showing that."

Fox execs had derided Newsmax as a "joke" but now the punch line had a new victim. Fox was the one with the bloody nose.

■

On December 7, Fox board member Paul Ryan texted Lachlan, "I think we are entering a truly bizarre phase of this where [Trump] has actually convinced himself of this farce and will do more bizarre things to delegitimize the election. I see this as a key inflection point for Fox, where the right thing and the smart business thing to do line up nicely. A solid pushback (including editorial) of his baseless calls for overturning electors, etc. will undoubtedly accrue pushback and possibly a momentary ratings dip, but will clearly redound to our benefit in terms of credibility."

Ryan had no way of knowing that the very same day, December 7, when he was warning about a possible plot based on "overturning electors," Trump was in fact asking his legal cronies for research into whether a scheme to submit fake electors in the Electoral College tally for president was possible. The idea had been suggested in an email—also that same day—from a Phoenix lawyer, Jack Wilenchik, to Trump aide Boris Epshteyn, proposing that what Wilenchik himself called "fake" electors be submitted from Arizona. (In a subsequent message he concluded "alternate" electors might be a better term than "fake," attaching a smiling face emoji. In a courtroom that would pass for "consciousness of guilt.")

The plot expanded from there to include seven targeted states. The special counsel's indictment said Trumpworld used "dishonesty, fraud, and deceit to organize fraudulent slates of electors and cause them to transmit false certificates to Congress." The intention was to set up Vice President Mike Pence, in his capacity as the official in charge of certifying the Electoral College results on January 6, to refuse the Biden electors in favor of the fake Trump electors, at least creating enough confusion to throw the election into the House, where Trump would prevail.

A "truly bizarre phase," indeed. All Ryan knew was that Fox needed to resist any and all attempts to "delegitimize" the election. "Trump is going to wear thin and look crazier by the day," Ryan texted Lachlan. "Let him cleave off the fringe for his [direct-to-consumer] venture and we can keep the largest pool of people (the center and center right). Fox is stronger than he is now and later."

■

There was a countervailing view, namely that Trump's people knew how to make things very uncomfortable for Fox people. Case in point: When Chris Wallace interviewed outgoing Health and Human Services secretary Alex Azar and Azar called Biden "vice president" instead of "president-elect," Wallace interjected, "he's the president-elect, sir." That was the upstanding, professional thing to do; but Meadows turned it against him, sending an article about Wallace to Hannity and writing, "Doing this to try and get ratings will not work in the long run, and I am doubtful it is even a short term winning strategy."

The suggestion that Wallace would make such a minor word correction in pursuit of ratings betrayed how skewed the thinking was in the Trump White House. Wallace did it because it was true, not because it would boost his audience. That was hardly likely, with his audience largely Trump fanatics. It was about the simple truth: Biden was president-elect. But Meadows couldn't admit that.

"I've been at war with them all week," Hannity replied to Meadows, before unveiling his own self-oriented power play. "Also if this doesn't end the way we want, you me and Jay [Sekulow, an attorney for both Hannity and Trump] are doing 3 things together." Hannity had a list for the former North Carolina congressman:

1- *Directing legal strategies vs Biden*
2- *NC Real estate*
3- *Other business*

In other words: We'll partner up and cash in. Hannity's helicopter didn't fuel itself, after all.

Carlson's greed was equally evident, though the topic was quite different. He flagged Greg Kelly's ratings victory for Wells and Mitchell to advance his long-running campaign to discredit Martha MacCallum, his "lead-in," in TV-speak. To understand a "lead-in," picture TV hosts as runners in a relay race, grabbing the baton from the person before them and handing it off to the next host. Carlson wanted a faster, stronger hand-off. He believed the relatively weak ratings for MacCallum's 7 p.m. newscast hurt his total at 8 p.m. and he wanted her replaced.

Wells was on his side since the ratings affected both of them. If MacCallum ended her hour with 2 million viewers, and Carlson was such a ratings magnet that he ended his hour with 3 million, then how much more popular would he be with a better lead-in? "Martha is basically taking a bat to Tucker's knees" every night, Wells texted. "It's been four years," Carlson added. "She will never work in that hour. They know that. They're too afraid to do anything about it." Mitchell disagreed: "They do know." The C-suite was actively contemplating another big change that would benefit Carlson.

"Slipping away"

Sean Hannity felt like a complete and utter failure.

For "3 years we expose the deep state, what happens? Nothing," he wrote in a late-night text to Mark Meadows on December 11. "The Media protects Joe and Hunter. They steal an election. What am I missing Mark? We r so F'd as a country."

To Meadows, Hannity wasn't sending a drunken post-show rant, he was spouting the truth. "I am afraid you are not missing anything," Meadows replied. "The evil prevails for a time and they are rejoicing. But we must continue to fight."

Hannity was more inclined to pout. Invoking the looming January 5 runoffs in Georgia, he said "these 2 senate seats are slipping away." Then, offering explicit political advice to the White House, he said Trump "has to make this about him. I'll make a deal with you, If you [elect] 2 R's to the senate, I'll run again in 2024."

Meadows concurred that "the seats are slipping away. I agree that he has to give some hope for the future. Connect the future to these candidates." But Trump never really did so, possibly because he wanted to punish Georgia Republicans for refusing to simply hand over the votes he'd needed to win the state. As Carlson put it in an earlier text to Hannity, Trump "is sitting back and letting them lose the Senate. He doesn't care."

Despite the private sulking, Hannity showed a public smile. Nearly every weeknight in December he booked McEnany, and together they looked like two crazy kids clinging to a dream: how to keep Trump in office. They sometimes coordinated talking points ahead of time. On December 14, she texted him, "Where are you on Congress choosing the Trump elector slate over the Biden one? I don't want to give people false hope but just wanting to get a sense of whether you plan on mentioning that. It's constitutional but extremely unlikely."

This was a loyal Trump operative, one with a Harvard law degree, no less, just casually floating a modest little proposal past the White House's favorite media friend. A feeling-out, more or less: *There's a little light coup-plotting getting kicked around down here in D.C. Interested?*

The fake elector scheme ultimately became, in the words of the special counsel's indictment, a "corrupt plan to subvert the federal government function by stopping Biden electors' votes from being counted and certified."

Lest anyone like Lou Dobbs cling to the idea that Trump's fraud allegations were not fully scrutinized, the Trump machine filed sixty-plus cases in battleground states to undo his defeat. Most of the complaints were dismissed quickly for lack of standing. But one lawsuit made it to the Covid-era equivalent of a courtroom—a filing in

Milwaukee, Wisconsin, that claimed local officials illegally expanded absentee balloting.

The district judge overseeing the matter, Brett H. Ludwig, was a Trump appointee. He admitted from the get-go that "this is an *extraordinary* case," emphasis his. Not only was the plaintiff the sitting president, but the defendants were the Wisconsin governor, secretary of state, and nearly twenty other officials. This meant that dozens of lawyers were involved—including a team from Susman Godfrey, a top-flight trial shop that showed up on "Most Feared Plaintiffs Firms" lists with regularity. The team was working pro bono to defend election officials. "We were very involved in election protection legal work in the lead-up to and then, to our surprise, in the wake of the 2020 election," partner Davida Brook told me.

When Ludwig held a one-day hearing in early December, Brook, pregnant with her second child, spoke to the Zoom courtroom from her living room in L.A. along with colleagues in Seattle and New York. Ludwig quickly ruled against Trump, and it registered as more than an ordinary legal victory, Brook said, because it was about "defending the integrity of the election."

The goal, she said, was "simply to defend the truth. Not your truth, not my truth, but *the* truth."

■

Dana Perino spoke for a few isolated Fox voices—but also hundreds of millions of people—when she said to a friend in late December, "I am just living for Jan. 21!" Trump's reign was almost over and the savviest players at Fox were relieved.

Even Tucker Carlson couldn't hold back his excitement at the prospect. He wrote to a colleague on January 4, "We are very, very close to being able to ignore Trump most nights. I truly can't wait."

Carlson and Perino seemed to have scant awareness of the fuse that had been lit.

Someone was aware though, and he was preparing a show-stopping, live-on-television finale. Something big was going down in D.C. on January 6, he told his followers on Twitter. "Be there, will be wild!"

PART THREE

"Destroying everything"

On the evening of January 5, 2021, Donald Trump was finally, fleetingly, happy. His outbursts and all-caps rants had rattled Washington and the democratic world for four years, and in the weeks after he lost the election he had turned especially foul toward his own staff. Officials like Kayleigh McEnany actively avoided him. Hope Hicks, his loyal, longtime aide, said "he didn't want to hear what I had to say." Even his most reliably obsequious Fox wingman, Sean Hannity, was skewering him behind his back. But on the evening of the 5th, "he was in a fantastic mood," deputy press secretary Sarah Matthews said. "And he was so excited." So excited for one last shot at stealing the presidency.

Inside the Oval Office, Trump could hear people—*his* people—blasting country music at an impromptu gathering outside on the Ellipse, where he planned to speak the next day. Trump swung open a door to the Rose Garden to let the cheers, and the frigid air, pour in. "It was so loud that you could feel it shaking in the Oval," Matthews recalled. The entire White House press team was summoned in to see Trump. It was so unusual, and Trump was so uncharacteristically jolly, that McEnany asked the team to pose for a group photo. Trump beamed. To the extent there was any agenda for this meeting, it consisted of Trump wondering how to get the "RINOs" to "do the right thing" the next day. Some aides claimed not to know what he meant, and urged him to put his energy into his speech prep, but he was clearly talking about how to muscle his party into blocking Biden's certification.

Most political minds were focused on Georgia that Tuesday evening. Congress certifying the vote in D.C. was always a mere formality; the big unknowns were the Senate runoff elections down South. But Trump cared only about the certification. The "lunatics," to borrow Hannity's word for the advisers pouring sweet nothings into Trump's ear, had led him to believe he could still prevail. "I do NOT see January 6 happening the way he is being told," Hannity had texted Meadows back on New Year's Eve. Hannity was serving in his self-appointed role as shadow chief of staff and he was sweating about potential resignations in every corner of the administration in its waning days. "We can't lose the entire WH Counsel's office," he wrote.

Hannity felt compelled to repeat his warning to Meadows on January 5: "I'm very worried about the next 48 hours." Even Lou Dobbs privately rained on Trump's charade: "It's been 8 weeks," he texted a colleague, and none of the Trump brain trust "has produced anything tangible or verifiable. And now he wants thousands of his supporters to go to DC without shelter or food to demonstrate." Was either man moved to do the honorable thing and share their view with viewers? No. The doubters stayed quiet while the fantasists continued to scream at the top of their lungs.

Jeanine Pirro (who was getting emails from Trump-aligned lawyers with harebrained Biden-stopping scenarios) invoked the Revolutionary War on air and, desecrating that noble cause by equating Trump with America's founding principles, wondered if anyone in Congress was "willing to battle for the America that those soldiers fought for, the one that you and I believe in." Mark Levin gave a fifteen-minute-long speech on his weekend show and said "if we don't *fight* on January 6 on the floor of the Senate and the House . . . we're done." Any Republican "who doesn't stand up" and object to the results, he bellowed, will be "shredding the Constitution" right along with the Democrats. Trump's campaign posted the entire speech to YouTube.

Another Fox face, Pete Hegseth, turned up in Washington Wednesday morning, along the National Mall, wearing an American flag ball cap and promoting the "March to Save America" rally. He was more or less indistinguishable from the participants. On *Fox & Friends*, he likened D.C. to a "constitutional tinderbox." "We believe the president will take the stage at eleven . . . and then the big show continues on Capitol Hill with the fight over the electoral college," he told viewers.

There was no legitimate "fight" over the Electoral College, only a (literally) trumped-up one, but hosts across right-wing media had been promising a showdown in D.C. for weeks, even though realists like Hannity—and even Rupert!—didn't see any promise in such a challenge to the inevitable. Rupert sent Scott a revealing email on Tuesday, exactly twenty-four hours before Trump's Ellipse speech, saying "it's been suggested that our prime time three should independently or together say something like" the following:

> *The election is over and Joe Biden won. We are all disappointed, but it happened. We love America and have to turn the page.*
>
> *We will now be the loyal opposition criticizing every liberal mistake the new administration makes. Their declared policies . . . are naive at best, or worse, retreads of the failed Obama years.*
>
> *And first, let's wear masks and unite to defeat the COVID plague.*

The suggestion came from his pen pal Preston Padden, the former Fox Broadcasting exec. Words along those lines, Rupert said, "would go a long way to stop the Trump myth that the election [was] stolen. And the basis of his 2024 campaign." (Already there was the assumption that, like the Terminator, Trump would be back.)

Rupert's email was a moderate conservative's dream—which is why it never came true on his far-right network. Scott forwarded the email to Meade Cooper and said "I told Rupert that privately they are all there"—meaning Carlson, Hannity, and Ingraham all knew Biden won and were turning the page. But, conscious of how intractable Trump's support was among Fox's audience, she also told Rupert that "we need to be careful about using the shows and pissing off the viewers."

Recognition continued to slowly seep into the consciousness of Fox executives, recognition of how their own coverage had impacted the people who watched it. The word for it was radicalization. Rupert's propaganda machine of a network had deeply radicalized its viewers. Some employees knew it: I spent the morning of January 6 on the phone with a Fox host who felt like they didn't belong at the network anymore. This particular host was getting bashed by the audience and even her own colleagues for saying Biden won. "We've made Ronald Reagan Republicans into extremists," she said. She worried that Fox was undermining democracy; she worried it was getting dangerous; and she was right. A portion of the political base shared by Fox and Trump had been juiced up on far-right steroids, persuaded to "do your own research" into ludicrous conspiracy theories, trained to reject any and all fact-checks as fake, primed for a fight, and the inexorable result was coming: a bloodstained riot based upon lies.

As I spoke with the distressed Fox source, her network was showing Donald Trump Jr. addressing the "March to Save America" at the Ellipse. Fox skipped Giuliani's call for "trial by combat" and co-conspirator John Eastman's screed about rigged machines, but once the president stepped on stage, Fox, inevitably, went wall-to-wall. Excoriating that decision was completely justifiable. How could any network defend live coverage of an address that amounted to an hour-long stream of reality-denying, self-exalting trash talk? But there was another consideration: The speech was essential context for the events that followed. If you heard Trump's testaments and vows—"we won this election" and "we will stop the steal" and "we're going to walk down" to the Capitol—then you couldn't be all that surprised by the ensuing violence.

At 1 p.m., right after Trump told the crowd "if you don't fight like hell, you're not going to have a country anymore," the Fox control room cut away from Trump and started to show the congressional ceremony.

The bigger story was happening outside, where masses of Trump supporters were breaking through security barricades. From the Capitol Police's perspective, the situation was already out of control. At 1 p.m., "I'm watching my people getting slammed," chief of police Steven Sund recalled later. At 1:09, Sund called for the National Guard. The violent confrontations worsened. At 1:30, police officers standing along the steps on the West Front of the Capitol were overwhelmed, and protesters charged up the steps. The attackers, Sund said, "came with riot helmets, gas masks, shields, pepper spray, fireworks, climbing gear—climbing gear!—explosives, metal pipes, baseball bats." At 1:40, Brit Hume said on Fox that some people are "trying to storm the building."

I want to timestamp this moment, 1:40, because it was so alarming. Fox was *ahead* of other major networks in focusing on the unrest. At 1:43, correspondent Griff Jenkins reported from the Mall that the rallygoers were "very upset." At 1:48, Bret Baier said two Capitol office buildings were being evacuated. At 1:55, correspondent Rich Edson showed tear gas blowing in the wind.

The live shots on Fox were mostly from a distance, showing people waving flags and hanging out on the Capitol steps, looking, for the moment, more like a concert than a coup attempt.

But anyone watching Fox in the 1 p.m. hour could tell that something wicked was coming this way.

This is relevant because the White House was relying on Fox for information. Multiple witnesses later told the House's January 6 committee that Trump was glued to Fox from 1:25 onward. McEnany testified too that "I was learning about events as I was watching Fox." She then tried to claim that as late as 2:23, Baier was saying it was "peaceful" at the Capitol. She was being disingenuous. In reality, Baier had for some time been relaying reports of injuries and disputing others who were portraying the melee as peaceful. McEnany *also* suggested that Trump was watching Fox on a time lag, through his TiVo-like box, after hitting pause during Ted Cruz's earlier speech on the Senate floor. The implication was that Trump had been delayed in learning about the Capitol attack. But even if that's believable, Cruz's speech was at 1:49—after Fox had signaled several times that a crisis was unfolding on Capitol Hill.

The first lesson of crisis management is that every minute counts. On January 6, more than an hour was wasted. Trump disciples pushed and smashed and mauled their way into the Capitol. By the time panic set in, around 2:30, as lawmakers fled for their lives, it was too late to avoid calamity. Carlson's right-hand man messaged Trump's right-hand woman:

Justin Wells: "Oh, boy. This won't end well."

Hope Hicks: "As predicted. I'm not there. So dumb."

Fox's John Roberts wrote to McEnany at 2:33 and asked, "You folks have anything to say about the protesters laying siege to the Capitol?" McEnany did not immediately answer. She was in the president's private dining room as Trump watched the riot show. Some aides pushed him to tweet something to calm the crowd. He contemplated that for a few minutes. What he came up with, at 2:38, was "please support our Capitol Police and Law Enforcement. They are truly on the side of our Country." At his daughter Ivanka's urging, he added the words "stay peaceful," even though the peace had been shattered nearly two hours earlier. McEnany replied to Roberts and said "see POTUS tweet," and he wrote back with an all-time great understatement:

"Got it. Between you and me, seems a little mild given what's going on."

Fox's pundit class was more explicit. "Hey Mark," Laura Ingraham had texted Meadows at 2:32 p.m. "The president needs to tell people in the Capitol to go home." She added a few seconds later: "This is hurting all of us." Ingraham continued at 2:33: "He is destroying his legacy and playing into every stereotype . . . we lose all credibility against the BLM/Antifa crowd if things go South." She added: "You can tell him I said this." Meadows didn't respond, so Ingraham resorted to Twitter, offering her view in public: "The president should order US troops to secure the Capitol immediately."

Many others messaged Meadows as the siege worsened. ABC's Jonathan Karl asked him at 2:53, "What are you going to do to stop this? What is the president going to do?" Donald Trump Jr. wrote at 2:58, "They will try to fuck his entire legacy on this if it gets worse."

Bloomberg reporter Nancy Cook wrote at 3:04, "Are you with POTUS right now? Hearing he is in the dining room watching this on TV . . ."

■

At 3:06, House Republican leader Kevin McCarthy called into Fox in a clear bid to get his point through the president's thick head. His earlier call to Trump, around 2:30, had been a failure; the president seemed intoxicated by the live pictures of the attack and only half-listened to McCarthy's plea for help. In the half-hour since, the situation had worsened, and McCarthy was desperate for Trump to call off the mob. So before he called into CBS, before he called into ABC, or anywhere else, he called into Fox. "People are getting hurt," McCarthy told anchor Bill Hemmer. "Anyone involved in this, if you're hearing me, hear me very loud and clear: This is not the American way. This is not protected by the First Amendment. This must stop now."

McCarthy tried to explain that no matter how bad the armed occupation looked on live TV, it was actually even worse. "I watched barriers being broken. I watched people breaking windows," he told Hemmer. "I watched people running into a building." The violence, he said, was un-American.

Hemmer asked McCarthy if Trump needed to say and do more, and then the anchorman made a very off-brand quip about "the law-and-order president" shortly before McCarthy's cell phone signal faded out. One minute after the interview ended, at 3:13, Trump tweeted a more effective condemnation of the attack, echoing Hemmer's words, saying "I am asking for everyone at the U.S. Capitol to remain peaceful. No violence! Remember, WE are the Party of Law & Order." Once more, Fox, an ostensible news network, had turned into a mediator, a crisis-intervention cop with a megaphone, talking the perp out of continuing some violent act. But it wasn't nearly enough. Not yet.

At 3:30, the recently resigned Trump aide Alyssa Farah texted a friend who was still at the White House, Ben Williamson, and said Trump "should call into Fox and tell them to stand down and leave the Capitol." Williamson replied that he had told Meadows exactly that twenty minutes earlier, adding, "hoping it breaks through. God almighty." At 3:31, Hannity texted Meadows much the same thing: "Can he make a statement. I saw the tweet. Ask people to peacefully leave the capital." At 3:36, Meadows replied, "On it."

At this point, it had been more than an hour since Ingraham texted Meadows. Scores of police officers—a group Trump claimed to support—had been injured. Fox's stars had no way to defend this. Trump was totally off-narrative, standing back and standing by while the seat of American democracy was being sacked. Brian Kilmeade swiped open his phone and started to text every Trump aide he knew. "How is he not on TV demanding they evacuate? This is a disaster," he texted Hicks at 3:56. "Please get him on TV telling them to evacuate. All the good is going out with this scene," he texted McEnany at 3:57. This is "destroying everything you have accomplished," he wrote to Meadows at 3:58. Kilmeade could have said "everything *we* have accomplished."

■

The Capitol attackers, with their Confederate flags, nooses, and actual pitchforks, were so confident, so emboldened, so brainwashed by the MAGA media, that some livestreamed themselves mid-crime. Many attackers were not shy about identifying their favorite media sources. Yvonne St Cyr, who was later convicted of six criminal counts in connection with the riot, so believed Tucker Carlson that she was confident he would protect her. "If we ever make it to sentencing," she later said on Facebook Live, "I think the truth will come before then. . . . So just keep watching Tucker, keep spreading the truth."

Right-wing media swag was visible throughout the crowd. One guy waved a One America News flag. Another protester, Derrick Vargo, wore a T-shirt with Carlson's face and the words "TUCKER IS MY HOMEBOY" while he scaled one of the walls of the Capitol and tried to breach a police line. An officer shoved him off the wall and he was carried out on a makeshift stretcher.

Eventually, in the 4 p.m. hour, Trump recorded a video in the Rose Garden urging the rioters to go home—though he couldn't help fanning the flames even as he talked about dousing the fire. "This was a fraudulent election, but we can't play into the hands of these people," he said. "We have to have peace. So go home. We love you. You're very special."

The president clearly recognized his own fans were at fault, but the occasion called out for a new conspiracy theory to be born. Trump aide Jason Miller texted McEnany at 4:29 with ideas for two potential tweets from @realDonaldTrump's account. They were:

"Bad apples, likely ANTIFA or other crazed leftists, infiltrated today's peaceful protest over the fraudulent vote count. Violence is never acceptable! MAGA supporters embrace our police and the rule of law and should leave the Capitol now!"

"The fake news media who encouraged this summer's violent and radical riots are now trying to blame peaceful and innocent MAGA supporters for violent actions. This isn't who we are! Our

*people should head home and let the criminals suffer the conse-
quences!"*

Miller was later asked by the House's January 6 committee why
he proposed bringing up antifa. He claimed there was "significant
traffic on social media" about the possibility. "It was just unbelievable
that people who were MAGA supporters would be engaging in violent activities," he said, in spite of the fact that performative violence
was a foundational part of Trump's appeal. McEnany, under oath,
similarly called the day "unimaginable," even though the riot was
predicted by some stakeholders in advance. Fox execs imagined that
it could get even worse, which is why Lauren Petterson, the head of
Fox Business, blocked Trump from calling in to *Lou Dobbs Tonight*
during the riot. The two men had privately huddled by phone earlier
in the day, so Trump, absorbed by the live coverage of the Capitol
attack, sought to speak during Dobbs's show, but Fox said no. "I
thought it would be irresponsible to put him on the air," Petterson
testified.

Finally, at the nadir of the Trump presidency, came a speck of
responsibility—and recognition among some at Fox that this creature they had adopted, fed, and raised had gotten loose and was
actually hurting people—not to mention the country.

"It is not your fault"

At eight o'clock on January 6, Tucker Carlson asked the key question: "Why?"

The answers were inconvenient and ultimately ignored by Carlson's
audience. But the question was spot on. Why did Americans like
Ashli Babbitt, an Air Force veteran and small business owner, travel

all the way from California and invade the Capitol? Carlson asked: "What can we learn from this?"

Babbitt was fatally shot by a Capitol Police officer when she tried to break into the Speaker's Lobby, steps from the House chamber, where dozens of lawmakers were holed up, fearing for their lives from the madding mob outside. The officer, Lieutenant Michael Byrd, said he had no choice but to fire—to "save the lives of members of Congress and myself and my fellow officers."

Byrd's and Babbitt's names were not known when Carlson delivered his monologue five hours later, but video clips of the shooting were circulating on the internet. Carlson encouraged viewers to imagine that Babbitt was their daughter: "The last time you spoke to her, she was heading to Washington for a political rally. Now, she's dead. You'll never talk to her again."

Carlson, unsurprisingly, did not invite viewers to step into the shoes of the African American police officer who, under what looked like mortal threat, stood his ground, and who, in the coming months, would endure racist insults and death threats. He was solely focused on the woman who wore a Trump flag as a cape.

"She did not look particularly radical," Carlson said. "She bore no resemblance to the angry children we have seen again and again wrecking our cities—pasty, entitled nihilists dressed in black, setting fires, spray-painting slogans on statues. She didn't look like that." She "looked pretty much like everyone else. So why was she there?"

That's how Carlson began the transmogrification of Babbitt from a trespasser into a martyr. It was a typical example of Fox jumping for a narrative its viewers longed to be true: Just an innocent girl, an Air Force vet, backing her president, a patriot, standing up for her good conservative beliefs, cut down by a brutal defender of the corrupt regime.

But the thirty-five-year-old was something else: a Trump dead-ender. If she was a victim of anything, she was a victim of the network of lies.

"Today we save America from the tyranny, collusion and corruption," Babbitt wrote on Election Day in 2016. "You are my fave," she tweeted to Carlson a couple of months later. She was a Fox fan, for sure, judging from her retweets and replies. During the Trump years, "she became more obsessed with baseless online propaganda—all while her professional life collapsed," *The Washington Post* reported. She went full-QAnon in 2020 and posted dark, dangerous screeds about imagined pedophile rings and conspiracy plots. She also turned into a Covid denier: In December, when VP-elect Harris posted about the incoming administration's plan to "ensure Americans mask up, distribute 100M shots, and get students safely back to school," Babbitt replied, "No the fuck you will not! No masks, no you, no Biden the kid raper, no vaccines . . . sit your fraudulent ass down . . . we the ppl bitch!" On New Year's Day, she replied to a friend who asked "When do we start winning?" and said "Jan 6, 2021."

Carlson said Babbitt didn't look radical, but it was wishful looking. She ticked just about every box in the radical profile.

∎

"Millions of Americans sincerely believe the last election was fake," Carlson said the night Babbitt died. "You can dismiss them as crazy. You can call them conspiracy theorists. You can kick them off Twitter. But that won't change their minds."

Nothing would, not at this point, not after months of poisoning. They weren't just misinformed, they were scared, and Carlson said they *should* be scared: "What happened today will be used by the people taking power to justify stripping you of the rights you were born with as an American," he declared. He predicted a crackdown on civil liberties. Then he finished the monologue with a message that I will never forget. "We got to this sad chaotic day for a reason," Carlson said. "It is not your fault; it is their fault."

You're innocent, they're guilty. That's what Carlson's entire show was about. Every segment, every night, every year. Us, the patriots, versus them, the elites and eggheads and propagandists and perverts. It was never more important than on January 6, when members of a movement claiming to defend America and "back the blue" beat police officers and desecrated the Capitol. At a moment of guilt and suspicion, Carlson offered absolution. *The riot was not your fault.*

Of course it was their fault, not yours. It could never be your fault, or Trump's fault, or the fault of anyone on the right. Excuse-making remained a chief function of conservative media. Fox was good at it; Carlson excelled.

Later in the hour, he called the rampaging horde "kind of solid Americans," preemptively, presumptively, while the police were still trying to regain control of Capitol Hill. In a text thread with Wells during the broadcast, producer Alex Pfeiffer expressed concern about that line, and he criticized the earlier monologue, bemoaning that Carlson was "just beating around the bush." Wells's response was nothing if not honest: "Some days we have to get on the air."

After the broadcast, Pfeiffer scrolled through all the negative tweets about the show and observed that "we had a lot of people hatewatching tonight."

"Good for us," Wells said. "More attention."

Pfeiffer seemed frustrated that Carlson wasn't calling out Trump for fooling millions of people, leading some of them to pillage the Capitol. Wells, with the Arizona call still haunting him and his network, replied, "We're threading a needle that has to be thread because of the dumb fucks at Fox on Election Day. We can't make people think we've turned against Trump. Yet also call out the bullshit. You and I see through it. But we have to reassure some in the audience."

Reassuring meant redirecting the blame. A guest on Carlson's show brought up the "rumor" (better word: hallucination) that "Antifa insurrectionists possibly could have infiltrated" the crowd and "maybe instigated some of this." Later in the evening, Hannity implied the "radical left" could have been behind the riot, and Ingraham said "they were likely not all Trump supporters, and there are some reports that antifa sympathizers may have been sprinkled throughout the crowd." It was the same fever dream Miller tried to spin up earlier in the day. Trump's allies obviously wanted to pin the insurrection on their political enemies—or at least provide some cover for their heavily implicated followers—reality be damned.

Vox's Sean Illing later observed that "the fantasy-industrial complex gave us the Capitol Hill insurrection," and that same complex pushed the "Antifa did it" fantasy even though many of the attackers who were prosecuted later freely admitted to their Trump fandom, with many saying they had followed Trump's marching orders. After all, he had literally told them, "We're going to walk down to the Capitol."

On the air on January 6, Hannity obsessed over voter fraud and cried about double standards. Off the air, he sounded like a completely different person. He wanted to salvage what was left of the Trump administration's legacy. On January 7, one day post-insurrection, he told Kayleigh McEnany that he had a "great call" with Trump's son

Eric, daughter-in-law Lara, and son-in-law Jared. The "key now," Hannity wrote, is "no more crazy people." Somehow, the awareness that so many people in Trump's ear were "crazy people" never led to any self-questioning.

With the knowledge that even Fox wouldn't let him speak live on TV, Trump recorded a two-minute-long video that denounced the Capitol violence and admitted for the first time that "a new administration will be inaugurated on January 20th." He also chatted with Hannity by phone. Afterward, Hannity texted McEnany talking points:

1 – No more stolen election talk.
2 – Yes, impeachment and 25th amendment are real, and many people will quit.
3 – He was intrigued by the Pardon idea!! (Hunter)
4 – Resistant but listened to Pence thoughts, to make it right.
5 – Seemed to like attending inauguration talk.

McEnany clicked the heart button to respond. "Love that. Thank you," she wrote. "That is the playbook. I will help reinforce."

They were both thinking about their own futures as well as the country's. Fox was taking its share of the blame for the insurrection, and the prime-time players were being called out by name. "The mob that stormed and desecrated the Capitol on Wednesday could not have existed in a country that hadn't been radicalized by the likes of Sean Hannity, Tucker Carlson and Laura Ingraham," *Washington Post* media columnist Margaret Sullivan wrote.

"We're going to get more of this," Rupert said when he read the column. Weeks later, he momentarily criticized Hannity to Scott, noting that Hannity was privately "in despair" about Trump, but "what did he tell his viewers?" Rupert seemed aware that the same people who were acting like "guardrails" in private, trying to guard against Trump's worst behavior, helped to crash the car in public.

Hannity wanted to be one of the proverbial Adults in the Room now. So did McEnany. Right after Election Day, she had held talks about joining Fox, but the discussions were "paused," a Fox source said, as she descended the "rigged" rabbit hole. It was time to dig out.

When Hannity spoke with Trump by phone on Sunday, January 10, the president sounded only-one-oar-in-the-water delusional. Poor Sean was close to giving up. But he tried texting Meadows afterward. "Guys, we have a clear path to land the plane in 9 days," Hannity wrote to Meadows and Congressman Jim Jordan after the call. But Trump "can't mention the election again. Ever." *(So much for that!)* Hannity continued, "I'm not sure what is left to do or say, and I don't like not knowing if it's truly understood." He was admitting that Trump could not comprehend his basic attempts to aid him.

That's what those post-riot days were like. Trump teetered close to being completely drummed out of public life. Gone forever. A second impeachment looked inescapable. Carlson, on the air, described Trump as "elderly and retiring," which, according to his texts, is exactly what Carlson wanted: for Trump to disappear. Fox veteran Brit Hume said Trump was "a dead duck politically." Rupert remarked to a friend that Fox was "very busy pivoting" away from Trumpism. "We want to make Trump a non person," he wrote.

Rupert, like many others, wondered if Trump might resign the presidency and get Pence to pardon him. Anything seemed possible during those chilly, eerie January days. "This week was like 3 weeks crammed into 1," Jay Wallace commented to Bret Baier.

On Friday, January 8, Trump was deplatformed, banned from

Twitter, due to what the company called "the risk of further incitement of violence." Naturally, his second-to-last post was a quasi-quote of what he heard guest Alyssa Farah say on Fox that morning. After calling the riot un-American, Farah said Trump's America First policies "gave a voice to people who felt voiceless in our country," so he tweeted: Those people "will have a GIANT VOICE long into the future."

Maybe. But at this moment, in the immediate aftermath of the Capitol attack, Trumpism was in tatters. Fox Corp board members were urging Rupert and Lachlan to distance the company from the rioter-in-chief. "Trump has willfully incited acts of violence and desecration, as he has trampled human decency and the public good, all the way to the inner sanctum of our democracy," board member Anne Dias, the French CEO of the investment firm Aragon, wrote.

"It would have been unthinkable just a few days ago that Fox News would be called upon to explain what represents abuse of power and what is unacceptable in a democracy," Dias continued. "Yet, considering how important Fox News has been as a megaphone for Donald Trump, directly or indirectly, I believe the time has come for Fox News or for you, Lachlan, to take a stance. It is an existential moment for the nation and for Fox News as a brand. I do not believe that the company can stay silent on this matter."

"Dad, let's discuss," Lachlan wrote to Rupert, signing the email with "love you."

Rupert said Lachlan should tell her that "we have been talking internally and intensely along these lines, and Fox News, which called the election correctly, is pivoting as fast as possible.

"We have to lead our viewers"—which, he added, is "not as easy as [it] might seem."

The truth is that the network did little to "lead" the viewers or convey the gravity of Trump's attack on democracy. The weekend after January 6, while CNN and MSNBC were showing special live coverage of the ongoing crisis (More resignations? More riots? No one knew what was next), Fox was back to airing Greg Gutfeld's smirking comedy show on tape.

New videos emerged of the violence day after day, but Fox and other right-wing networks mostly ignored the evidence. I fast-forwarded through all three hours of *Fox & Friends* on Monday, January 11, to confirm what I suspected: Fox showed *none* of the new videos of Capitol violence. The show, always conscious of how well it played to portray conservatives as victims, spent far more time on social media sites "censoring" conservatives than the bloody aftermath of the riot. The hosts might have resembled the three wise monkeys who covered their eyes, ears, and mouth to see, hear, and speak no evil.

■

Dias was not the only board member who wanted Fox to "lead" viewers past Trump. She exchanged messages with Paul Ryan, the former House Speaker, and discovered they were saying the exact same things to Rupert and Lachlan. "Great minds," Ryan wrote to Dias. "I told them this is a huge inflection point to keep Trump down and to move on for the future of the conservative movement. The last thing we should be doing is [breathing] life back into Trumpism when it is at a new low and can stay there. Both Rupert and Lachlan agree fully." But agreeing was one thing, executing it on the air was another.

Ryan did not hide his eagerness to move on from Trump, though it was telling he considered that course imperative for the future of "the conservative movement" not "the country."

On January 12, Ryan forwarded Rupert and Lachlan an article

from *The Dispatch*, the sane-conservative site cofounded by two long-time Fox contributors, Jonah Goldberg and Stephen Hayes. It was titled "the alternate reality machine." It "captures the dynamic we are contending with quite well," Ryan commented.

The Dispatch's article said the "pro-Trump media and punditocracy" (i.e., Fox) operates this way: "Reflexively stake out a position opposite whatever the 'mainstream' one is, make unverified claims that affirm what their viewers or readers want to believe, and then attack 'mainstream' outlets fact checking the inaccuracies as biased or suffering from 'Trump Derangement Syndrome.' It's good business, but bad journalism. And as we've seen, it has dire consequences for the country." The writers added that "the problem appears to be as much on the demand side as it is on the supply side."

The analysis was dead on, but Rupert didn't acknowledge that. Rupert spoke more like a color commentator than a coach, calling January 6 a "wake up call for Hannity, who has been privately disgusted by Trump for weeks, but was scared to lose viewers!" Rupert also made this view clear: "The events of last Wednesday and Trump's behavior overwhelm everything. But I don't believe a majority of the 74 million voters believe the conspiracy nonsense." *Bad leader, good people.* That's how Rupert perceived it. I wanted to share his sanguine outlook, that most voters were people of good faith—but on his "majority" claim, numerous polls in 2021 and 2022 showed that a majority of Republicans *did* subscribe to the Big Lie. Most Trump voters seemed willing to believe almost any Trump-derived nonsense. They trusted Trump even more than their own family members and friends.

Rupert and Ryan went back and forth, with Ryan urging action: "The sooner we can put down the echoes of falsehoods from our side, the faster we can get onto principled loyal opposition. I truly hope our contributors, along with Tucker, Laura, and Sean get that and execute." Rupert responded that he had just talked "at length with Suzanne Scott. Everything changed last Wednesday. She thinks everyone is now disgusted and previous supporters [are] broken hearted."

There are three things to observe about the rest of Rupert's reply. One, his exclamation points—and confidence—about Trump's apparent doom:

> *Trump's troubles multiplying. His businesses now ruined! Who is going to throw a party at one of his golf clubs or hotels? Let alone a tournament. So he has more than just legal problems, bad though they are. The brand is now poison! Who wants Ivanka's fashion lines, jewelry, etc?!*

Second, his shortsightedness. By 2022, *lots* of people were throwing parties at Trump's properties again. Carlson, who had called Trump a "destroyer," was photographed standing next to Trump and grinning at a LIV golf tournament event at Bedminster. Based on his experience with Trump, and his long experience with how hard-core conservatives could be, Rupert should have seen this coming.

Third, his mistaken assertion that January 6 changed everything. By 2023, when this email was made public, it was clear that Rupert (and perhaps Scott) didn't really understand their network's audience, nor the role Fox had played in making the viewers too angry, resentful, and aggrieved to accept reality.

Or . . . maybe they just couldn't bear to look it in the face.

"Uncontrollable forces"

Sean Hannity ended 2020 on the top of the cable news heap in overall viewers, for the fourth straight year, but Carlson beat him for the first time in the twenty-five- to fifty-four-year-old demographic. In 2021 Carlson pulled ahead among total viewers too, topping 3 million many nights. He clearly had the momentum.

This mattered because Carlson, who was nothing if not savvy about how to connect with and manipulate his viewers, led a shift from "pro-Trump" to "pro-Trump-supporter" in the weeks after the riot. He portrayed Trump boosters as downcast and discriminated against. His question—"where's their defender?"—doubled as an answer: *I'm right here.*

On January 13, Carlson pressured Mitch McConnell not to support the impending impeachment: McConnell, he said, should be focused not on the future of Trump but instead "the tens of millions" of Trump voters. As apocalyptic as ever, Carlson claimed Trump fans had been "redefined as domestic terrorists" in the wake of the insurrection. (The rest of us must have missed that particular FBI bulletin.) He said Republican lawmakers should "stop talking about Trump" and "start talking about his voters."

Later that same evening, Laura Ingraham said impeachment was actually an attempt to "impeach the Americans who support his policies." One of her guests, Ben Domenech, said that voting for impeachment was akin to telling Trump voters, "CNN's right about you." (What could be more humiliating than that?) Another guest, the disgraced former *60 Minutes* correspondent Lara Logan, imagined a new "war on terror" targeting Trump supporters. Her word choice was interesting, considering the actual terror that lawmakers and aides and law enforcement officers felt that day. (Logan hosted a show on Fox Nation for two years but was "pushed out" in 2022, she said, claiming "they don't want independent thinkers." In reality, she was blacklisted by Fox because she embarrassed the network by likening Dr. Anthony Fauci to the evil Nazi doctor Josef Mengele.)

The Justice Department launched a sprawling federal investigation to identify riot suspects. On paper a homegrown terror probe would have been catnip to Fox's programmers. But because it was about right-wing terrorism inspired by Trump, they had to stuff it down the memory hole as forcefully as possible. Thus, in the span of just one week, January 6 started to be reframed. It was no longer a coup attempt, but a conspiracy against conservatives. Carlson promised that "it was not your fault." Now Trump fans were the "victims."

■

In mid-January James Murdoch was set to speak with the *Financial Times* about his latest digital venture in India, so he was asked about the insurrection, of course, and he was resolute in his answer. "The sacking of the Capitol is proof positive that what we thought was dangerous is indeed very, very much so," he said. "Those outlets that propagate lies to their audience have unleashed insidious and uncontrollable forces that will be with us for years."

James didn't utter the word Fox, nor did he need to. He was communicating to his father and brother through the interviewer: "I hope that those people who didn't think it was that dangerous now understand, and that they stop."

After the interview, James and Kathryn decided to say more, drafting a joint statement that said "spreading disinformation—whether about the election, public health or climate change—has real world consequences. . . . We hope the awful scenes we have all been seeing will finally convince those enablers to repudiate the toxic politics they have promoted once and forever."

They would have had better luck hoping for a unicorn. Fox was about to make yet another capitulation to the "toxic politics" of the right. In the words of one Fox staffer: "Newsmax won." Carlson won too. Remember, he had long been agitating for a change at 7 p.m. and once Newsmax's Greg Kelly emerged as a real rival at that hour, he got what he wanted. In mid-January, as part of a day-time face transplant, MacCallum's newscast—which, while clearly right of center, was not far *enough* right to satisfy the base—was replaced by an opinion show led by talent To Be Determined. Kilmeade and Bartiromo were the first two hosts to try out in the time slot.

MacCallum was moved to the much lower-rated 3 p.m. time slot. (It was the same step-down Shepard Smith had taken years earlier, from 7 p.m. to 3, before he resigned altogether.) MacCallum played along with the shift in public, but she was deeply disappointed that she wasn't given more time to prove herself. Carlson celebrated, though he knew exactly what it felt like to be downgraded by a TV executive. After *Crossfire* was shifted to 4:30 p.m., he wrote, "Some things are simply impervious to spin or euphemism: Death. Imprisonment. Having your show bounced from prime time to the late afternoon. It's bad. There's no pretending otherwise."

Look, a source said to me when I asked about the 7 p.m. revamp, "The viewers want opinion. That's their opinion." Nearly every change at Fox was about having less news and more opinions-about-the-news. It was like a history teacher being shouted down by the drunk at the end of the bar. I could see how the incentives favored the boozehound: Opinion hosts who activated identity threats (like "the southern border is being invaded") developed a much more intense bond with the audience than news anchors who told them about all the complexities of immigration. Unfortunately, "identity-reinforcing information that is empirically inaccurate can satisfy our needs for comprehension, control, and community," professor Dannagal Young wrote in the 2023 book *Wrong*. And Fox was in the satisfaction business.

Some Fox staffers who couldn't see that, or didn't want to admit it, had gripes about the schedule adjustments. Scott suspected that's what drove a *Daily Beast* story claiming her job was in jeopardy. Carlson, seeing a prime opening to suck up, told her, "Fuck the Daily Beast. We are grateful you're in charge." "Ha!" she replied, professing not to care about the leakers. "I made changes and [I'm] making more. Some ppl unhappy so be it." Carlson responded: "Amen!"

The next change was a right-wing answer to left-wing late-night comedy. Just as Fox News itself was designed by Roger Ailes to appeal to conservatives' resentment of news coverage they felt was slanted left, this new show was born of the conservative sense of victimization by late-night comics, virtually all of whom made Trump the butt of their jokes. It would star Greg Gutfeld, the jokester on *The Five*, which was a roundtable show like *The View* but with four right-of-center combatants and one left-of-center opponent. There was some undeniable magic to *The Five*, both in the banter and in the daily reassurance that the right was right. In 2020—the year of Covid, George Floyd, and the Big Lie—Scott told Gutfeld she wanted to add 11 p.m. to his plate. "People need a reason to laugh," she said. Gutfeld hesitated at first, but Carlson convinced him to say yes. *Gutfeld!*—the first figure on the right who decided he needed his own exclamation point since Jeb!—was a hit right away. Its one and only theme was owning the libs, stopping the "woke," which was the fix conservative audiences had a bottomless jones for. In a right-wing echo of Conan O'Brien being elbowed aside by Jay Leno, Shannon Bream saw her 11 p.m. newscast bumped to midnight to make room for put-down jokes. It was another step in the minimizing of news and the mushrooming of Fox as an all-encompassing cultural brand, an identity, a way of life.

■

Trump managed not to incite any further insurrections in January. On the morning of the 20th, he boarded Air Force One for the final time and watched his plane take off via a TV monitor tuned, naturally, to Fox News. Fox hosts praised him on the way out; MacCallum claimed he "worked hard in the past 48 hours to finish this on a more gracious note." In reality, Trump refused to attend Biden's inauguration; refused to even shake the new president's hand and welcome him to the White House; refused to even pretend that he respected the peaceful transfer of power. That's why he was on the plane before noon.

During the flight, his skeleton staff announced one literally last-hour addition to the long list of pardons he had granted the night before. The surprise name was Albert J. Pirro Jr., aka Judge Jeanine's ex-husband, who had been convicted on conspiracy and tax evasion charges in 2000. Pirro had been so bonkers on the air that Cecily Strong's impression of her on *Saturday Night Live* seemed almost tame; but her loyalty to Trump was unmatched. She had broadcast Trump infomercials for four straight years. So—divorced or not, father of a "love child" or not, tax-evader or not—she was outraged when Albert's name wasn't on the final pardon list (the one that included Steve Bannon) overnight. She lobbied Trump early on inauguration morning, and around 9 a.m., aides were told to get it done—throwing a wrench in final-day plans.

By the time Trump touched down in West Palm Beach, Pirro Jr., who had been out of jail for almost twenty years, was a pardoned man. Insiders gossiped about the possibility of a quid pro quo. Whether there was or not, Trump's final act in office was a favor to his Fox friend.

"A semi conscious corpse"

Washington sparkled on Inauguration Day. The inauguration was a national sigh of relief . . . except on *Fox & Friends*, of course, where Ainsley Earhardt said Trump voters have "a hole in their heart this morning."

Biden's Inauguration Day address took aim straight at the divided country Fox had fostered—and cashed in on. "Recent weeks and months have taught us a painful lesson," he said. "There is truth and there are lies. Lies told for power and profit. And each of us has a duty and responsibility, as citizens, as Americans, and especially as leaders—leaders who have pledged to honor our Constitution and protect our nation—to defend the truth and to defeat the lies."

Then Biden confronted a root cause of the lies. "I understand that many Americans view the future with some fear and trepidation," he said. "I understand they worry about their jobs, about taking care of their families, about what comes next. I get it. But the answer is not to turn inward, to retreat into competing factions, distrusting those who don't look like you, or worship like you do, or don't get their news from the same sources you do. We must end this uncivil war that pits red versus blue."

Shortly afterward, *Fox News Sunday* moderator Chris Wallace said it was "the best inaugural address I have ever heard," and the remarks about defending truth and defeating lies were "a call to all of us, whether it's us on the air, on cable or broadcast, whether it's us on social media, on our Twitter accounts, understanding that we have to deal from facts."

Wallace, the son of *60 Minutes* legend Mike Wallace, embodied the political and journalistic establishment. If Biden's anti-MAGA mission was to "make America sane again," well, Wallace could get on board with that. Thus, he was increasingly uncomfortable at Fox, even though he rarely had to cross paths with the network's radicals who despised him. (As Carlson wrote in November, "We devote our lives to building an audience and they let Chris Wallace . . . wreck it.")

Ailes's old rule, no "shooting in the tent" between hosts, was still supposedly in effect at Fox, but Greg Gutfeld felt powerful enough to openly mock Wallace on the air a few hours later. "I'll even go further than Chris Wallace!" he shouted. "It's the greatest inauguration I will ever see! I think we should just stop the inaugurations!"

This was not a suitable environment to accept Biden's talk about ending the "uncivil war." This was where the war raged. Incivility and wars of words amounted to the business Fox News was in.

■

Well before Inauguration Day, Fox began to tell a tale about Biden that proved the network was even more anti-Democrat than it was pro-GOP. Carlson, for one, was a staunch critic of the GOP establishment. But he and the other Fox stars were united in a campaign to tear down Biden and VP Kamala Harris.

In a text to Meadows, Hannity called the new president "a semi conscious corpse" who "will be controlled by a very radical left wing element." (This despite Biden having won the Democratic nomination largely because he was much more a politician of the center than rivals like Elizabeth Warren and Bernie Sanders.) Hannity and his colleagues' anti-Biden messaging absolutely worked: By 2023, six in ten Americans said Biden did not have the mental sharpness or physical strength to serve effectively as president.

Internal docs from Fox showed a deeper hatred of Biden too. Fox Business president Lauren Petterson mocked the president: "Joey is going to unite the country. Let me know when that happens." Fox's mission was to make sure it didn't. On Inauguration Day, a banner on Tucker's show said "PARTY IN POWER IS DEMONIZING HALF OF THE COUNTRY." At the same time, on all the other major channels, Tom Hanks was hosting a Biden-Harris inaugural telecast called "Celebrating America." *All* of America. Tucker dismissed it as an "infomercial." He resisted airing any of it, even the new president's short remarks from the Lincoln Memorial, until his control room was told to briefly show Biden. Carlson wore the anger on his face and went back to his regular rage programming immediately afterward. (Fox viewers missed out on a spectacular D.C. fireworks show.) Later in the evening, Hannity said the president was "weak" and "cognitively struggling" and accused his family of running a "crime syndicate." (The "Biden crime family" became a GOP catchphrase.) And not to leave Laura Ingraham out, her show said "BIDEN'S DIVISIVE POLICIES SACRIFICE OUR FREEDOM."

Before the election, during one of Carlson's typically specious essays about liberals destroying free speech, he said, "What do you think they plan to do to Fox News if they take power?" His implication, silly, and calculated to push his viewers' buttons at the same time, was that a Biden White House would crush poor little Fox. The brand-new president, though, went out of his way to show respect. When he was about to wrap up his first news conference on January 25, he saw Fox's White House correspondent Peter Doocy trying to ask a question, and said, "Wait, wait, wait. I know he always asks me tough questions, and

[they] always have an edge to them, but I like him anyway. So go ahead and ask the question." Doocy's question was "dripping in bad faith," as one liberal commentator put it, but Biden gamely fielded it anyway—an obvious gesture toward a genteel-in-public relationship with Fox, one that the network would never reciprocate.

Behind the scenes, the Biden White House was cognizant of what was going on. The president assessed Fox "as one of the most destructive forces in the United States," Jonathan Martin and Alexander Burns reported in *This Will Not Pass.* According to the book, Biden told an unnamed associate in mid-2021 that Rupert was "the most dangerous man in the world." But Biden never mentioned Rupert or Lachlan in public, for fear of poking the proverbial bear—or because he actually believed what he'd said on Inauguration Day.

■

From the very first days of the Biden presidency, segments about the fallout from the Capitol attack, and Trump's role in it, were minimized on Fox while segments about the "BIDEN BORDER CRISIS" and "BIG TECH CENSORSHIP" were scheduled twice an hour. Management even ordered special "censorship" graphics packages. The anti-tech crusades conveniently lined up with Rupert's corporate interests, namely, to force Google and Facebook to pay for the content he generated. It also aligned with the priorities of his biggest star, Carlson, who broke with standard GOP views and favored greater structural intervention into the marketplace.

Fox remained in full-on "respect the audience" mode, which in practice meant "lots more Tucker." The network increasingly revolved around his opinions. *Fox & Friends* and the daytime shows were instructed to make liberal use of clips from Carlson's show. Entire segments were framed around what Carlson said sixteen or eighteen hours earlier—which meant his isolationist, paleo-conservative ideology was suffused across the network in a way that, say, Hannity's more traditional unabashedly pro-GOP boosterism was not.

Carlson, always on the hunt for self-aggrandizing opportunities, did not let the post-Arizona crisis go to waste. He had pitched an expansion of his mini-empire inside Fox: a "new line of content" called *Tucker Carlson Originals* with long-form interviews and documentaries produced by a "prime time reporting team." It could "reestablish trust with our viewers," he wrote to Scott, and he would promote the new content on his 8 p.m. show. Carlson mentioned Fox Nation, the network's nascent streaming service, and that's exactly where *Originals* launched in February 2021. He had successfully parlayed Fox's post-election panic into more airtime and attention for himself.

"Respect the audience" was in effect in other ways too. Producers fought with each other to book the subset of conservative guests whom viewers loved—media bashers like Mollie Hemingway and shouters like Dan Bongino—while ignoring more rational Fox contributors like Jonah Goldberg and Stephen Hayes. "Fox is a really different place than it was pre-election," a network commentator remarked to me. No one wanted "another Arizona," so the network became even less news-driven and even more mission-driven.

The reality was that Fox *preferred* having Biden in office. When Republicans held power, Fox sat at the table with the defense. When Democrats were in charge, Fox could join the prosecution and pound the table, a much more enjoyable role to play. As Rupert analyzed it, "We always do better as the opposition." He was right insofar that the base gravitated back to Fox in early 2021. Memories of Arizona faded. A new fragile peace was achieved. Fox was further to the right—or as journalism scholar Jay Rosen put it, "further from the real"—than ever.

"Seeking to kill us"

J. Erik Connolly, the A-list lawyer retained by Smartmatic shortly after Thanksgiving of 2020, welcomed complex and challenging cases. Some of them got press attention: a beef producer's defamation claim against ABC News, which cost the network a lot of sirloin to settle, at least $177 million (one of the largest defamation settlements in history), and a *Real Housewives of Beverly Hills* star's attempt to squelch rumors she was a madam, which landed Connolly on the syndicated celebrity gossip show *TMZ*. He was happier working behind the scenes, managing mind-numbingly complicated contract and tort disputes. Smartmatic's case against Fox wasn't in either category. It was beautifully straightforward. It turned on one uncomplicated, incontestable fact about the city of Los Angeles.

All winter long, as Trump's coup attempt was repelled and Biden took office, Connolly's team at Benesch, Friedlander, Coplan & Aronoff drafted an astonishingly detailed lawsuit, 285 pages long, accusing Fox and the Wild Bunch—Dobbs, Bartiromo, Pirro, Giuliani, and Powell—of "a conspiracy to spread disinformation about Smartmatic." The firm's associates watched hundreds of hours of Fox coverage and produced a five-week-long timeline of the nationally televised propaganda that had cast Smartmatic as a clear and present danger to America. ("I had to pay them hazard pay," Connolly joked to a colleague about the assignment he'd given the young associates.)

Like Dominion, with its flotilla of "Setting the Record Straight" emails, Smartmatic made a protracted, good-faith effort to put a stop to the smears long before filing suit. On December 10, Connolly's firm sent retraction demand letters to Fox, Newsmax, and OAN, charging all three networks with a "concerted disinformation campaign against Smartmatic." The next day, Fox's Brain Room brain-stormed a potential rebuttal. Smartmatic "is claiming that we didn't challenge the narrative" about fraud, exec VP Tom Lowell wrote to the group. "Sometimes, we didn't," he admitted. "But we are looking for the times we DID."

As a legal and a practical matter, saying "beware of dog" occasionally does not absolve you of all the times you said "Sic 'em, Fang."

But Fox tried it anyway. Lowell worked with Fox's legal and PR departments to cook up a peculiar response. It was described by *New York Times* media columnist Ben Smith as "one of the strangest three-minute segments I've ever seen on television." The segment consisted of a guy named Eddie Perez, a voting software expert, debunking the anti-Smartmatic innuendo that had proliferated on Dobbs's, Pirro's, and Bartiromo's shows. Fox management slotted the segment into the rundowns of all three shows, and the hosts were told not to say anything to undermine it. The segment was clearly intended as a shield against Smartmatic's legal threats; a way to say *"we aired your side of the story."*

With an implied: *"so you got nothin.'"*

The interview with Perez happened so belatedly, however, that it arguably weakened Fox's case. As Connolly's lawsuit noted, Fox was essentially trying to close the door after the horses had already befouled the barn, saying Fox "could have put Mr. Perez on the air at any time prior to December 18." Additionally, Dominion's lawyers later, inevitably, used Fox's fact-check about Smartmatic to question why Fox didn't afford Dominion the same consideration.

The Perez segment also weakened Fox's standing within MAGA world. Steve Bannon texted Bartiromo about it, alarmed, as though she had suddenly turned into a traitor to the movement. Viewers tweeted their disgust. "Who got to @MariaBartiromo?" one of her fans asked.

On the air, Bartiromo was still spinning like a break-dancer, conjuring up a vast conspiracy to defraud the United States—one morning on Fox Business, she said there's "an intel source telling me that President Trump did in fact win the election," and no one even blinked. But attached to just a whiff of concession, even *she* could enrage the base.

■

Connolly's legal team compiled all the misinformation and then turned to motive. When Trump lost, they wrote in the lawsuit's opening pages, Fox and Giuliani and Powell "needed a villain. They needed someone to blame. They needed someone whom they could get others to hate. A story of good versus evil, the type that would incite an angry mob, only works if the storyteller provides the audience with someone who personifies evil." So they teed up Smartmatic.

Smartmatic CEO Antonio Mugica said he had "no choice" but to sue. "For us, this is existential," he said when the suit was filed in New York on February 4. The smears were spooking potential customers; subjecting employees to death threats; and, Mugica argued, jeopardizing the company's very survival. The suit sought a blood-curdling (for Fox) $2.7 billion in damages.

So what gave Mugica and Connolly so much confidence? Bizarrely: La La Land. The defendants (the right-wing networks) repeatedly referred to "swing states" like Arizona and Georgia in connection with their accusations against Smartmatic. But their research was apparently as incompetently executed as the entire "rigged election" scam. Mugica's company provided election software to just one locale in the U.S. in 2020: Los Angeles County, California. "Nowhere else," the lawsuit emphasized.

Thanks to that devastating fact, "I can prove everything they said was a lie," Connolly told me. "I've been doing this for a long time and that might be the easiest way to demonstrate falsity that I've seen."

Proving that Lou Dobbs et al. *knew* the truth was a higher bar to clear—but Fox did something the next day, February 5, that gave Smartmatic even more conviction about the power of its case. Fox fired Dobbs.

The move seemed to come out of nowhere. While Fox Business was low-rated, the thing about Dobbs was, feeble as his numbers were, he was that channel's highest-rated host by far. Sometimes he would double the performance of the show before his—a demonstration of how much of a draw Dobbs was for men of a certain age and political affiliation. When I went live on CNN from my Covid-era home studio to analyze the news of Dobbs's sudden defenestration, anchor Erin Burnett asked, "Can you remember a network canceling its highest-rated show?," and I said the closest analogy was Fox's ouster of Bill O'Reilly in 2017.

In this instance, technically, Fox canceled Dobbs's show and sat him on the bench. (It was the same "pay or play" treatment that Carlson would receive in 2023.) The Smartmatic lawsuit was undoubtedly a factor in the abrupt cancellation, but sources insisted to me that the plan predated the lawsuit; Dobbs's contract was too fat, his show struggled to turn a profit, and he had pissed off management one too many times, so he wasn't worth the headache anymore. Scott later said "I had a plan in place, in my mind . . . for a year, where I was ready to make a change with Dobbs." She said she had "spent many months navigating a path to make a change with Dobbs."

And she reached the end of the path, magically, exactly one day after Smartmatic demanded $2.7 billion. Go figure. (But bring a calculator.)

I found it startling, and telling, that Rupert in his deposition claimed to know almost nothing about Lou Dobbs. Rupert was the one who wanted to launch Fox Business in the first place, back in 2007, and Roger Ailes only reluctantly agreed. Yet Rupert was hands-off: "Mr. Ailes was running the show completely," he said, and Ailes hired Dobbs in 2010 to strengthen the business channel—"which I don't think worked anyway," Rupert added.

When compelled to testify on the matter, Rupert was borderline nasty about Fox Business: "I never watch," he said, "and I certainly never watch Lou Dobbs," who "had very few viewers." Very few, but still far more than any other personality on the channel, so something just didn't add up. NPR's David Folkenflik, the author of *Murdoch's World*, proffered the best explanation of Dobbs's departure: He told me it was reminiscent of the way Rupert handled the phone hacking scandals at his British tabloids ten years earlier, when "they would throw somebody over the side and see if that was enough." Folkenflik said the surprise cancellation seemed like "an effort to cauterize the wound, to distance Fox from this feverish conspiracy theory."

Staffers wondered what, if anything, Dobbs's disappearance said about the future of the Fox brand. Dobbs's producers speculated that he was canned for being "ultra MAGA" in a media marketplace that seemed, for the moment, to be post-Trump. "Lou was reckless," Carlson told a colleague. "But I think this will give energy to CNN and other forces seeking to kill us. So we should be as aggressive and tough as we can be."

■

Fox still had to pay Dobbs's legal fees due to the cooperation agreements that are standard in TV contracts. But Dobbs's ouster was the first signal that the Big Lie—and the campaign inside Fox to substantiate it—was going to have long-term consequences.

The lawsuits added up fast: On January 8, two days after the riot, Clare Locke, Dominion's legal strike force, filed the first of the company's lawsuits, a $1.3 billion claim against Powell. There were numerous other offenders to pursue: Giuliani, Lindell, Fox, Newsmax, and OAN, to name a few. "It was clear that we were going to need a whole bunch of skills," partner Tom Clare said. And Dominion's owner, Staple Street Capital, wanted to signal that it had the wherewithal—the resources—to see the case through. Enter Susman Godfrey, the firm that played a key role in post-election litigation, including Trump's big legal spanking in Wisconsin. "Susman Godfrey decided to go after the biggest fish first," an insider said, and that was Fox. Partners Justin Nelson, Davida Brook, and Stephen Shackelford would be the three lead attorneys.

As they examined possible avenues of attack in January and February, "we thought we could win based just on the public statements," Shackelford told me. The statements came in two flavors: the stark raving mad claims made about Dominion on Fox's airwaves, and the authoritative comments from government and judicial officials in both parties debunking the craziness. "It helped that Dominion had sent so many 'Setting the Record Straight' emails to Fox," Shackelford said. "The truth was in Fox's inbox."

Dominion's resulting 137-page complaint was a scorcher. The suit enumerated four categories of lies and listed twenty times those lies were advanced on Fox. Three of the TV segments (by Dobbs and Bartiromo) managed to incorporate all four poisonous varieties of lie: that Dominion rigged the election for Biden; that its algorithms manipulated vote counts; that Dominion was owned by a company founded in Venezuela; and that Dominion paid kickbacks to government officials. There were scores of other Fox segments alluding to fraud, some even citing Dominion by name, but "we wanted a clear case," Brook said. "We were disciplined." The reasons would become clear later.

On March 26, the day the suit was filed, Fox trotted out the same defense that it did against Smartmatic, stating that it was merely covering newsworthy matters involving the highest officeholder in the land. I put that to Shackelford in an interview on CNN and he shredded it. "Fox was not reporting the news with these reports that are outlined in our complaint," he said. "Fox was not giving voice to some grand political debate. Fox was repeatedly stating as fact . . . all of these lies about Dominion . . . even while they were being told the truth over and over again."

Hearing that, it was reasonable to ask: Could Fox mount any believable defense?

Viet Dinh thought so. Dinh, as a former assistant attorney general under George W. Bush, crafted the post-9/11 PATRIOT Act. Then he founded a boutique law firm with an emphasis on Supreme Court litigation. Dinh, born in Saigon, and an immigrant to the U.S. when he was ten years old—three years after his native city fell to the communists—had an exceptional academic record (Harvard, both undergrad and law), top-notch conservative credentials, and very powerful allies, including, by 2004, Lachlan Murdoch, who brought Dinh onto the Fox board of directors. In 2018 he came off the board to become Fox's chief legal and policy officer, reporting directly to Lachlan. His compensation package—cash and stock and perks—routinely topped $12 million.

Dinh's colleagues described him as relentless and frenetic— often "on two cell phones at any one time," a friend said. He was once dubbed "Viet Spin" for his "opportunistic politicking" in D.C. At Fox, his portfolio encompassed legal, compliance, regulatory, and government matters. He moved his family to Los Angeles for the job, with an office just steps from Lachlan, and within two years there was chatter that Dinh was the true leader of Fox Corp, that he was much more hands-on than his boss, that he was doing the heavy lifting. Dinh said the aggrandizement was false. The perception did not abate though; it was further fed by Lachlan's decision to move his family back to Sydney, Australia, in March 2021. "They've wasted no time settling back into Sydney life," a local columnist wrote two months later. Lachlan's wife, Sarah, "goes to the ballet and takes the kids to fun parks. Meanwhile Lachlan zips around town in his shiny $400,000 Maserati." He promptly paid $30 million for a boat shed in a pricey Sydney neighborhood.

Lachlan's people said he was still working American hours even though Sydney was seventeen hours ahead of L.A. When Lachlan occasionally dipped into Fox editorial meetings on Zoom, staffers snarked behind his back that he might be on his yacht. In *The New York Times*, Ben Smith labeled Dinh "a kind of regent" at Fox. So, the expectation inside the corporation was, if anyone was capable of steadying the American ship, it was Dinh.

Smartmatic had already sued, and Dominion was just days away from filing, when Dinh spoke with legal journalist David Lat in March 2021. "I'm not at all concerned about such lawsuits, real or imagined," Dinh said. Why? Because Trump's post-election challenges were so "newsworthy." Fox News "did its job," he said, "and this is what the First Amendment protects." That's what he told the Murdochs too. Sit back, relax, and let the Bill of Rights sort this out.

"New war on terror"

The House of Representatives opened a formal investigation into the January 6 insurrection. Which meant Fox had a big problem.

Trump's supporters had mounted an attack on the nation's constitutional system; an attack that included overt deadly threats to members of Congress—of both parties—and even Trump's own Republican vice president; an attack that turned so violent it resembled scenes from *Game of Thrones*, with brutal hand-to-hand fighting and makeshift weapons like flagpoles and hockey sticks; an attack that played out live and in color on national television, for hours, and was augmented by months of up-close, blood-and-guts video footage of even more ferocious assaults on Capitol police officers. But Fox fans did not want to see it, did not want to hear it, did not want to face it.

I could see this in the ratings over the summer. When the House Select Committee investigating January 6 held a pivotal July 27 hearing with some of the heroes of the riot, such as police officer Michael Fanone, who was assaulted and suffered a traumatic brain injury, Fox aired the proceedings in full—and viewership fell nearly in half. The viewers only came back for the antipolice commentary at night.

Antipolice commentary? On Fox? I never thought I'd see the day. But Carlson found a way. He snickered at Fanone's account of the "psychological trauma" endured by officers. Later in the evening, Ingraham outright mocked Fanone—a regular cop trying to do his job—awarding him "most exaggerated performance" from the hearing.

It was sickening. But, as Carlson, Ingraham, and Gutfeld proved constantly, cruelty was never costly on the right. Fanone noticed that the hate mail he received used the exact same phrases Ingraham used. One of the many trolls asked him if he wanted an Emmy or an Oscar and proceeded to call him the full compendium of English-language slurs. Hosts like Carlson and Ingraham "inspire people who are already prone to, or have a propensity for violence, to commit violence," Fanone said.

■

The whitewashing of January 6 demonstrated how the network-of-lies effect works. The scrubbing of history happened not just on Fox, but on Newsmax and Breitbart and Steve Bannon's *War Room* show and dozens of other MAGA media destinations. The effect was to make the lie seem omnipresent and obvious and indisputable. Republican elected officials caught the drift. Mike Pence—the subject of "hang Mike Pence" chants in D.C., complete with faux gallows—went on Hannity's show in October and minimized the insurrection as "one day in January." Pence's distortion rightly received head-scratching reaction from CNN and other news outlets afterward. Fox's shows didn't follow up at all.

But downplaying or deflecting the reality of the riot wasn't enough for Fox News Republicans. They hated the established January 6 narrative: that loyal backers of Trump—as in, people just like them—had stormed the Capitol in pursuit of an out-and-out political coup that would undermine every principle of American democracy. They hated that the protesters were being portrayed as seditionist villains instead of flag-draped patriots who had stepped up to block the certification of a "rigged" election. They hated being in this defensive crouch. And they needed their media leader to go on offense.

So that's what Tucker Carlson did. The host who said on the night of the insurrection that "it is not your fault" set out to prove it. And by "prove," I mean, construct a Potemkin counternarrative and seed so much doubt about the attack that people would believe just about anything—or nothing at all.

In the fall, Carlson found his theme: Why believe the government version of the riot? Maybe, just maybe, it was the government's fault. Maybe the assailants were false flag operatives, antifa, or even the FBI. "We still don't know how many federal agents were involved in the event," he remarked. As for the actual provable, self-admitted Trump adherents in the crowd, Carlson exonerated them: "They don't look like terrorists, they look like tourists." It was another familiar "us" versus "them" story—us innocent protesters versus those government agitators.

Carlson took the story to its incendiary extreme with *Patriot Purge*, a three-part documentary-style series that cast January 6 as a "false flag" operation meant to entrap Trump fans. On October 27 he announced that his blistering counterattack would stream on Fox Nation in November. Carlson, stroking his ratings results like Bond-villain Blofeld stroking his white kitty, had basically big-footed Fox executives into giving him that second sandbox to play in, although he was filling the box with a different substance. *Purge* was the highest-profile project the service had yet produced, though it was not entirely warmly embraced in Fox's executive offices. Reporters who did not make explicit that this was a streaming product, detached from the cable lineup, were likely to get a call from Fox PR alerting them to go back and make that distinction. Maybe the PR people were trying to protect the flagship cable channel brand—or maybe they were just trying to sell more Fox Nation subscriptions.

Regardless, the show was promoted on cable, including on *Fox & Friends* and by Carlson on his own show of course, where he previewed what his fans would see: "We believe that it answers a lot of the remaining questions from that day," he said. "Our conclusion:

The U.S. government has in fact launched a new war on terror. But it's not against al Qaeda. It's against American citizens."

If that wasn't enough to get MAGA blood boiling, the cinematic trailer for the series included an interview subject saying "the left is hunting the right" and alluding to the Guantánamo Bay prison camp.

In the actual series, Carlson, lit from below and looking like he was speaking through the smoke of battle, opened with his prevailing take: "January 6 is being used as a pretext to strip millions of Americans—disfavored Americans—of their core constitutional rights." He used images from the war in Iraq—torture, waterboarding, even beheading—to illustrate what American citizens were allegedly potentially facing from their own government.

"They've begun to fight a new enemy in the war on terror," Carlson said on the show. "Not, you should understand, a metaphorical war but an actual war. Soldiers and paramilitary law enforcement, guided by the world's most powerful intelligence agencies, hunting down American citizens, purging them from society and throwing some of them into solitary confinement." Are you shivering in fear yet? Because you were supposed to be. But to be clear, most of the people swept up in connection with the January 6 attack were released soon after their arrests. A small number of defendants were kept in jail—not by "soldiers," but by federal judges—mostly because they posed flight risks or were charged with especially odious crimes.

The series included an interview with Elijah Schaffer, a podcaster for Glenn Beck's The Blaze, who had posted video from inside Nancy Pelosi's office during the siege. The people who raided Pelosi's office and the rest of the building were, Schaffer claimed, mostly moms and dads "who were mad about what they saw to be an election that they thought was unfair, rigged, fortified, stolen . . . and a lot of them just got caught up in the frontlines of chaos."

That declaration of innocence was absurd. But *Patriot Purge* worked. Carlson succeeded in shifting the Overton window (a concept that explains how unthinkable ideas move into the mainstream). When the series was picked apart by critics like the carcass of a genuine turkey, Carlson fans blasted the critics. Fact-checks that said Carlson's theories were "debunked" galvanized distrust of the fact-checkers. Fox's Geraldo Rivera watched the *Purge* promo video and tweeted, " 'False flags!?' Bullshit," which just gave Geraldo haters more confidence in the bull.

"Tucker's wonderful, he's provocative, he's original, but—man oh man," Geraldo told *The New York Times*. "There are some things that you say that are more inflammatory and outrageous and uncorroborated. And I worry that—and I'm probably going to get in trouble for this—but I'm wondering how much is done to provoke, rather than illuminate."

Fox penalized Geraldo for speaking out. Suffice it to say, he did not get his own three-part documentary about the truth of January 6.

Admirably, two of the network's best-known paid pundits pulled the cord and leapt off the Fox train. "I'm tempted just to quit Fox over this," Jonah Goldberg texted his friend Stephen Hayes when he saw the *Purge* trailer at the end of October. "I'm game," Hayes replied. "Totally outrageous. It will lead to violence. Not sure how we can stay."

The two men said they had hoped that Trump's ouster from office would normalize Fox, but "for us, the release of 'Patriot Purge' was proof that waiting for Fox to get back on track would be like waiting for Godot."

To the surprise of no one, Carlson laughed off the resignations. "Great news," he said. "Our viewers will be grateful."

■

Prior to the *Purge*, Carlson made a rare return to D.C. for a celebratory dinner at Cafe Milano, the see-and-be-seen restaurant on Prospect Street in Georgetown, where Fox Corp liked to convene from time to time. Lachlan was at the center of a long rectangular table in a private dining room. Carlson was to his right, logically, given the 8 p.m. host's sway. Perhaps more surprisingly (in terms of rank, not political viewpoint) Chris Wallace was to his left.

Wallace's contract was coming due at the end of 2021. He was certain that he wanted to leave. But Fox was making a good-faith effort to keep him in the fold, because, it seemed, Lachlan liked this seating arrangement: Carlson sowing conspiracies on one side and Wallace safeguarding Fox's credibility on the other. One senior staffer called it a "double or triple game" that the Murdochs play—making money from the opinion operation but reaping other rewards from the news outfit. What troubled Wallace was not so much the extreme Carlson-type content, but the way the news side mirrored it, becoming more and more propagandistic and disinclined to fight it.

The dinner was emblematic in another way: Carlson and Wallace barely exchanged any words at all, according to an attendee.

It's an overstatement to say that *Patriot Purge* was a key factor in Wallace's exit. His mind was already made up. He struck a deal in November with CNN boss Jeff Zucker to host a signature interview series for the ill-fated streaming service CNN+. "I spent a lot of 2021 looking to see if there was a different place for me to do my job," Wallace said later. He said "I'm fine with opinion: conservative opinion, liberal opinion. But when people start to question the truth—

Who won the 2020 election? Was Jan. 6 an insurrection?—I found that unsustainable."

Wallace gave notice to Fox management on Thursday, December 9. Scott was taken aback. The next day Wallace's agent Larry Kramer told him that the execs weren't giving up yet. They wanted to know: "Is there anything we could offer that would change your mind?"

"Nothing," Wallace replied.

For the *Fox News Sunday* staff, December 12 was just another normal Sunday; before the show, they joked about Wallace's love of blueberry muffins. Wallace had drafted his on-air goodbye in secret, looping in only his executive producer, who back-timed the rest of Sunday's hour to fit his script. The script wasn't even loaded into the teleprompter until the show was halfway over, lest anyone find out prematurely. Thus there were audible gasps across Fox's D.C. bureau when Wallace announced, "After 18 years, this is my final 'Fox News Sunday.'"

The shrinking band of journalists left at Fox hated to see Wallace go. One producer at the bureau likened it to "a death in the family." I thought about it more like a purge—no, not the Carlson kind. Political scientist Brian Klaas observed that "when organizations radicalize, the moderates either get purged or purge themselves." Wallace pushed the eject button himself to escape the suffocating fumes of Fox's radicalization.

A version of this was happening all throughout the Republican Party too. Mainstream voices in the GOP were being squeezed out and were barely represented by the party's media apparatus. There was little content for them or about them. All the energy was at the extreme, at the edges, where Carlson thrived. Rupert and Lachlan's channel, sadly, was programmed more for reactionaries, cranks, and conspiracists than for moderate Republicans and politically exhausted independents.

In his sign-off, Wallace alluded to a "new adventure" but said nothing about CNN because the rollout plan called for CNN PR to announce his new gig on Monday. But someone at Fox leaked the CNN news minutes after Wallace signed off, making his big move even bigger: He was not just quitting Fox, he was fleeing to the network that punctured Fox's propaganda at every opportunity.

When the cable news wars began in the mid-1990s, when MSNBC and then Fox challenged CNN for every available viewer, the channels were more alike than they were apart. MSNBC emphasized tech news more, Fox highlighted middle America more, but the story lineups were by and large similar.

No more. By the early 2020s, the channels no longer covered the same topics, save for rituals like elections and certain emergencies like mass shootings. This was the single greatest change I tracked in twenty-plus years covering cable news. It's tempting to say this was a positive development—less duplication and more diversity across the dial—or to turn it into a punch line—hey, while Fox was hyperventilating about Dr. Seuss, CNN was interviewing actual doctors about Covid. But it wasn't funny at all. It was a serious transformation, a symptom of a country coming apart, a country full of people unable to see what they have in common while they stare at screens that separate them further.

This tearing of reality was asymmetric: It happened much more severely on the right during the Obama and Trump years. And it ultimately eroded some Republicans' commitment to the basic tenets of democracy. Ron Brownstein, a political analyst with a keen eye for demographic changes, said it all came down to "demographic eclipse." This was distinct from Carlson's "demographic replacement" conspiracy theory because the "eclipse" was visible to the naked eye. The rise of a majority-minority society panicked portions of white Christian America. Trump's election and the coup plot and the Capitol riot and the cover-up of the riot were all downstream from that panic, Brownstein said. "The fundamental dividing line in American politics," he told me, "is between those who welcome and those who fear the way America is changing." What many people saw as progress, others registered as loss. Fox was programmed for the latter—and often reinforced that sense of anger and mourning. They're "feeding that sense that you are under threat, that elites disdain you, and immigrants and minorities are coming to kill you," Brownstein said. *Your* America is gone. *Their* America is here, and it's terrible. "That is the drug that they offer their audience," he said, "and it's increasingly become the message of the Republican party over time."

Fox had two settings for an unwelcome story like the January 6 investigation: Attack and ignore. Tucker Carlson usually attacked, as seen with *Patriot Purge*. When Trump ally Steve Bannon was indicted for refusing to testify to the House's January 6 committee, Carlson's show portrayed it as "DEMS USING JAN 6 TO CRUSH POLITICAL ENEMIES." But oftentimes the default setting was hands-over-the-ears. When the morning shows on NBC, ABC, CBS, and CNN all led with Bannon's indictment, *Fox & Friends* only mentioned it for fifteen seconds. When the January 6 committee revealed that Fox stars like Hannity and Ingraham begged Mark Meadows to have Trump call off the mob, the network barely touched it. Ditto when the committee asked Hannity to cooperate with the probe. (Hannity refused. He still, to this day, has not shared with his viewers what he knew about Trump's state of mind in the days before and after the attack.)

Frustration with Fox's story-snubbing occasionally erupted on the air. "You don't want to deal with the news!" liberal panelist Juan Williams exclaimed when *The Five* downplayed Trump's post-insurrection impeachment—as though it was an event of little consequence. In the 1990s, the impeachment of Bill Clinton was the top story everywhere, of course. But audience incentives and producing instincts changed. And those who disagreed were unplugged. (Williams was off *The Five* within a few months.) At Fox, you got ahead not by covering the story better than the competition, but by not covering the story at all, and then mocking the competition's coverage. "All they care about is January 6," rising star Jesse Watters whined. Laura Ingraham said "the entire January 6 campaign has become one of revenge and defamation." It was actually about accountability—including for the network of lies.

■

At the end of the year, Fox got creamed and Dominion got the thumbs-up to proceed to trial.

Dominion's defamation lawsuit was filed almost two months after Smartmatic's, but was heard in court much sooner, due to some crucial decisions by Susman Godfrey. Instead of filing in New York, where the state courts were backlogged in part due to Covid, Dominion filed against Fox in Delaware, where the companies were incorporated. "We wanted both for our client and the country to get to resolution as quickly as possible," Stephen Shackelford, one of Dominion's lead lawyers, said.

Fox's lawyers implied that Dominion was forum shopping, but the Delaware court judge assigned to the case, Eric Davis, took umbrage at that insinuation. When Davis initially had to rule on Fox's motion to dismiss, he had to assess whether it was possible Dominion would ultimately prove defamation "by clear and convincing evidence."

In other words: Did Dominion even stand a chance? Some pundits doubted it did because proving "actual malice" by a news organization was considered a legal Mount Everest—almost an impossible hill to climb. Furthermore, some observers anticipated a quick settlement, since Dominion was owned by a private equity firm, which would see a 2x or 3x return as a welcome victory. But this case would not be won through dollars alone. On December 17 Judge Davis rejected Fox's motion to dismiss and said Dominion could try to prove actual malice. Davis seemed persuaded by Dominion's arguments at every turn, which should have been a glaring warning sign to the Murdochs. Both sides were now subject to a full-blown document discovery process. It was, in the words of lawyer Davida Brook, "full steam ahead."

"Hire some Trump people"

When Fox was at its lowest point, post-Arizona, Jesse Watters thought he knew what management should do. "Wallace, Cavuto and other [*sic*] have got to go," he wrote in a text to Carlson. "Need some fresh blood. Should hire some Trump people."

Like Christopher Walken laying on excessive cowbell in the memorable *SNL* sketch, Fox's pushy prankster was calling for extra helpings of Trump. But hiring more "Trump people" was difficult in the wake of Rupert's post–January 6 desire to make Trump "a non person." He didn't even want the man mentioned on the air. Fox's solution in 2021 was to add Trump son Eric's wife, Lara Trump, and former press secretary Kayleigh McEnany as commentators. Former Trump aides who couldn't abide the Big Lie looked askance at the hirings; McEnany "knew we lost the election, but she made a calculation that she wanted to have a certain life post-Trump that required staying in his good graces," Alyssa Farah said, explaining "the big lie amplification that I saw her doing on Hannity and elsewhere."

"I think she saw that as a moment to kind of, like, 'if I do this one last public-facing stand for Trump, I'm going to be set. This is going to work out for me.' And, I mean, it did. She got her Fox News gig," Farah said. "It worked out precisely how she'd always planned for it to. But she knew better." Farah was describing the classic trajectory of the suckerfish—in politics they're known as presidential aides—who attach themselves to a passing whale hoping to benefit from the free ride.

McEnany's payoff was a cohost seat on *Outnumbered*, Fox's lunchtime chat show. She exemplified how Fox endeavored to be Trumpy without Trump: Give the Trump aide the platform. Fox viewers would see the familiar face and feel some level of Trump bliss. Watters was a different spin on the same thing: the implacable loyalist, who understood the audience's slavish devotion to Trump and supplied it without reservation. After trying out various yakkers for a full year, the Fox exec squad asked Watters to lead the 7 p.m. hour, effective in January of 2022.

Age forty-three at the time, though he came across as still of towel-snapping age, Watters would be Fox's youngest top-tier host and its closest approximation to a walking, talking in-your-face troll. Charlie Sykes, editor in chief of *The Bulwark*, said "the arc of Fox News is bending toward more clown car, more recklessness, more extremism." Watters heard that on MSNBC, chortled, and decided to pin the clip to his chest during his debut episode. "I'm so extreme!" he bragged, knowing that it showed Fox viewers that he was opposed by "the right people."

Maybe Watters was precisely the "fresh blood" he said Fox needed. Although his guest list was anything but fresh, it was exactly what the viewers wanted: pro-Trump fixtures like Kellyanne Conway, Stephen Miller, Sarah Palin, and Newt Gingrich. To give the show a righteous cause, Watters obsessed over conservatives' crime fears, with nightly segments like these:

AMERICANS FACE RECORD HIGH VIOLENT CRIME
LIBERALS RUN CITIES INTO THE GROUND
NO ONE FEELS SAFE IN BIDEN'S AMERICA

During one early episode Watters pushed the hysteria dial to full throttle, declaring that crime was "totally out of control in America." He then went full-parody, bringing on noted amateur MMA aficionado Sean Hannity to share self-defense tips. It was like some host of a Green Bay sports-talk cable-access TV show, based in his wood-paneled basement, suddenly getting a gig on ESPN and bringing on his old Pop Warner League coach to discuss how pathetically the Packers were playing. Consider: This time slot used to belong to Shepard Smith, who sought to broadcast an hour of impartial facts, viewer feelings be damned. Now the hour was entirely *about* hyperpartisan feelings with no time for facts at all.

■

Growing up at Fox, under Bill O'Reilly's sneak-attack tutelage and then as a cohost of *The Five*, Watters saw that slithering along behind Trump was the path to fame and fortune. He played the Trump loyalist, through thick and thicker, and in good log-rolling etiquette

Trump fired off a statement in mid-2021 endorsing his book. (Most of the statement was copy-and-pasted straight from Watters's about-the-book webpage.) The book debuted at #1 on the *New York Times* best-seller list.

But the mutual-admiration society membership only went so far during the Trump-embargo period at Fox. Trump barely existed in the universe of *Jesse Watters Primetime* and Fox's other signature shows in early 2022. Yes, Eric and Don Jr. were invited guests on the shows, but where was the patriarch? Still non per-soned. Trump rallies, once deemed automatically newsworthy by the network, no longer merited dog-to-master attention. The official line, transparently lame, was that he wasn't a candidate for anything anymore, so he didn't warrant incessant live coverage. But in the shattered hearts of Fox watchers, he was "The Real President," so many of them took the Trump snub personally. More than a few Fox producers did too. One griped to me, "You know that expression about leaving money on the table? We're leaving ratings on the table." Newsmax was lucky to draw fifty thousand viewers on a normal Saturday night, but with wall-to-wall coverage of a Trump rally, the channel attracted an insane multiple: 1.5 million. Newsmax sold special ads to run during the rally, taking up almost half the screen, turning Trump's free con-tent into quick cash.

Still, Trump was mostly invisible on Fox News, and across major outlets like ABC and NBC. When I pointed this out during a CNN segment, Farah offered a prescient note of caution. "Yes, the former president has lost steam in legacy media," she said. But the fringier networks and livestreamed rallies still counted for something. "We are going to regret it," she said, "if we think that he is not coming back and we don't prepare accordingly."

■

At his January rallies, Trump attempted to complete what Carlson began one year earlier: the beatification of Capitol attacker Ashli Babbitt as martyr in the Church of Conspiracism, and the reframing of January 6 as an unholy attack *on* Trump supporters.

Bartiromo nudged the process along when she interviewed Trump in July 2021, before the officer who shot Babbitt had identified himself. "Who shot Ashli Babbitt? People want to know," Trump said. "I want to talk about that," Bartiromo said, calling Babbitt a "wonderful woman" who was shot as she "tried to climb out of a broken window." Somehow Babbitt was now a victim of a life-threatening conflagration, forced to bust out through a window to save herself. As gross distortions of events go, this was a hall-of-famer. Babbitt was trying to break *into* the House chamber. But Bartiromo continued: "Her family has spoken out. Her family has been on Tucker Carlson, and they want answers." Translation: They'd gone to the mountaintop; how could they be denied?

Trump regularly invoked Babbitt's name in public—because, as rhetoric professor Roseann M. Mandziuk stated, Babbitt represented "the right's New Lost Cause into corporeal form." She was being exalted as this Lost Cause's Stonewall Babbitt. In January Trump, pushing the "brazenly false" meter way into the red zone, said she was shot "for no reason." He also dangled pardons for accused rioters (simultaneously tampering with potential witnesses against him) "because they are being treated so unfairly." Carlson's influence was manifest in multiple ways.

On the first anniversary of January 6, Carlson ridiculed people who cared about the anniversary; paid tribute to Babbitt; and served up several conspiracy concoctions about the coup attempt. Then, because he knew a defenseless punching bag when he saw one, he punished Ted Cruz for saying at a Senate hearing that January 6 was "a violent terrorist attack on the Capitol."

"It was definitely not," Carlson stated, leaning into the camera and addressing Cruz directly: "So why are you telling us that it was?" He said "you're making us think maybe the Republican Party is as worthless as we suspected." It was Carlson stepping in to ensure that nobody, not even a regular political ally, was going to threaten his control over the narrative directed at minimizing the meaning of January 6. He had to intervene. He had to put Cruz down, like, as Trump might have put it, a disloyal dog.

Cruz, shaking in his Texan snakeskin boots, texted Carlson immediately. He asked to come on the next day's show. Carlson agreed—but continued to flog this U.S. senator and onetime presidential candidate the whole time. The banner said "WHAT ON EARTH WAS TED CRUZ THINKING?" It was Cruz's most humiliating moment since he Twitter-liked a threesome video, *Dick for Two*, then claimed a staffer "accidentally hit the wrong button." (Don't look it up unless in private.)

When he came on, Cruz told Carlson, "the way I phrased things yesterday, it was sloppy and it was frankly dumb."

Carlson, whose undeniable talents included a special skill for twisting the knife in some hapless carcass, interjected: "I don't buy that!" He had receipts. Cruz had said January 6 was a "terrorist attack" at least a dozen other times previously. See, Cruz, who was fighting far out of his class in the ring with Carlson, was operating from an outdated assumption that the GOP was still the tough-on-crime party. He said he routinely called anyone who assaulted a cop a "terrorist." *That's* who he was talking about, he argued desperately—not the rest of Trump's mob.

Carlson slashed back, interrupting again, this time to say that a cop-basher is a criminal but not a terrorist. "Why'd you use that word?" he asked. "You're playing into the other side's characterization." And Carlson knew that for the viewers he revved up night after night, that was the real crime, right? Aiding the enemy?

Cruz practically prostrated himself pleading for forgiveness. His word choice was a mistake, he said, reaching deep into the familiar right-wing bag of excuses, and pulling out the conventional words, "Democrats" and "the media." Because "we've now had a year of Democrats and the media twisting words and trying to say that all of us are terrorists," he said. "Trying to say you're a terrorist, I'm a terrorist." (I must have missed that year of news coverage.) Cruz said the January 6 protesters were trying to "defend this country" and—don't forget—he was *there* helping: "I was standing on the Senate floor objecting to the election results."

Carlson was unconvinced. But his blood lust was satisfied. It was obvious to everyone that Carlson had won the joust convincingly and Cruz had lost humiliatingly; the unelected, radicalized TV host put the duly elected senator in his subservient, far less consequential place. Both men knew that a "terrorist attack" was a crime committed to advance a political or otherwise ideological agenda. There was little dispute that January 6 was an example of domestic terrorism, except among people too cowed, too delusional, too willing to deny their own rationality—and eyesight—to admit that. People like Carlson and Cruz.

This mismatch of a lightweight bout was destined for the history books (I mean, here it is!) because it demonstrated who had the power in the GOP and what party members were supposed to think—and say. Carlson v. Cruz was one of the fiercest internecine fights of the nascent 2020s, widely discussed and dissected everywhere, *except* for Fox. The network, as it did with most events that could irritate the psyches of its viewers, pretended it never happened.

Because it was about what happened on January 6, and why—a topic Fox did not want to confront.

But Kayleigh McEnany didn't have that luxury. She was subpoenaed by the January 6 committee and took a day off from *Outnumbered* to testify, which meant she went head-to-head with Liz Cheney.

One decade earlier, Cheney occupied a perch quite like McEnany's, analyzing politics as a paid commentator on Fox. Cheney's evolution from Republican family royalty and Fox employee to snake in the GOP grass illustrated the party's capitulation to Trump's alternative facts. Cheney agreed to be the panel's vice chair, making the House committee genuinely bipartisan despite many Republican efforts to the contrary. She recognized that she would likely lose her seat in Congress as a result of her fact-finding mission.

The House investigators quizzed McEnany about her many texts to Hannity about fraud allegations. They asked if anyone from Fox ever followed up with her to fact-check the info. (Of course not.) And they asked, "Do you think that the stolen election talk contributed to the events of January 6?" "I don't," McEnany said, playing innocent to the point of incognizant.

Then Cheney squinted as if to say "really?" Cheney took over for the staffer and interrogated McEnany herself. She asked: "Ms. McEnany, have you read any of the filings . . . where hundreds of defendants make clear that they came to the Capitol, and in many cases, decided to breach the Capitol, because of the claims that the election had been stolen that were being made by President Trump and others?"

"I have not read those filings."

"So given the fact that the defendants have themselves said that they were here at the Capitol because of the claims made by President Trump, does that change your view?"

"No."

She hid behind the argument that individuals who commit violence are solely responsible for their actions.

McEnany's testimony played like the vague murmurings of a glassy-eyed cult member out in the real world for a day to give an account of events to legitimate secular authority, someone who was mainly interested in getting back to the cult as soon as possible. But she was a Harvard-trained lawyer. The incongruity seemed to underscore the separate cognitive universe Trump was leading—and Fox was exploiting.

■

When Russia violated international law and attacked Ukraine in February 2022, Fox crews were there, in Kyiv and beyond, right alongside CNN and NBC. But attention always boomeranged back to the opinion-slingers in their warm, cozy studios. On the night Russia began its invasion, when the focus should have been solely on the flak-jacketed reporters in the field, Laura Ingraham wasted time by pumping up Trump on the phone. Trump, beginning to sound like an animatronic figure in Disney World, routinely derided Biden and repeated the "rigged" election lie because that button was pushed again. Ingraham then tossed in an unexpected curveball, mentioning a report that "U.S. officials are looking at a potential amphibious landing now in Odessa, Ukraine." She meant that Russian forces were possibly invading from the Black Sea. The report was fog-of-war bogus. As if that wasn't bad enough, Trump, who often was only half-listening if the topic wasn't directly about him, misunderstood what she was saying and thought the U.S. was now somehow invading Ukraine.

"You told me about the amphibious attack by Americans," he said, chastising Ingraham. "You shouldn't be saying that because you and everybody else shouldn't know about it. They should do that secretly." Ingraham jumped in, trying to stop him from embarrassing himself further, and said, "Those are the Russian amphibious landings." For Trump, this was a staggering show of geopolitical ignorance. Even if Trump innocently misheard her, how could he possibly think that U.S. troops were launching an amphibious attack on Ukraine? (Did he have a secret Pentagon attack plan on Ukraine beside his old golf shoes in a box in his Mar-a-Lago bathroom?)

The episode was telling for Ingraham as well. She was trying to save a political figure from revealing, at a minimum, how dense he was about potential military operations, or at worst, how massively unqualified he was to be commander-in-chief, rather than questioning why he would believe such an attack was even possible.

■

The Russian blitzkrieg failed, and the courage and skill of the Ukrainian people inspired and united the democratic world. It was a monumental story, one worth taking risks to cover. In mid-March Fox correspondent Ben Hall, veteran cameraman Pierre Zakrzewski, and a local producer, Oleksandra Kuvshynova, drove out of Kyiv to report on fighting northwest of the capital. Their car came under fire, apparently by Russian forces, and Hall was catastrophically injured. Both his crewmates were killed—the first war zone deaths in the twenty-six-year history of Fox News. Hall lost both his feet, one leg, and sight in one eye. Evacuating Hall from Ukraine and assisting three grieving families was a 24/7 project for Scott and her executive team. Journalists around the world stood in solidarity with Fox. Yet when it came to Russia's war in Ukraine, what was Fox best known for? What garnered the most attention? Tucker Carlson's strikingly pro-Putin monologues. He downplayed the conflict as a "border dispute," criticized Ukraine ceaselessly, and parroted Kremlin propaganda, so much so that Russian state TV shows ran clips of his rants. Other Fox hosts had drifted toward pro-Putin commentary (because, after all, Biden was supporting Ukraine and Putin had supported Trump so the line between good guy and bad guy was not so definite for them), but Carlson's open disdain for Ukraine and defense of Putin commanded the most attention—just the way Carlson liked it. Mediaite, a website that covers the best and worst of cable news, had more than 5,430 headlines with the word "Tucker."

In mid-2022 a high-ranking source at Fox told me Carlson was "getting away with murder" internally. I knew the person well enough to discern that they weren't wielding the word "murder" in any literal or hyperbolic sense. They meant that Carlson was doing whatever he wanted, whenever he wanted, however he wanted. He could at this point get away with anything. He could murder the facts, for sure, and no one could stop him. The implication was that Carlson had tested the Murdoch family's limits, found them feeble, and intentionally pushed *past* those limits in order to assert himself and gain even more power. It was not unlike turning the screws on Ted Cruz.

"They are lying"

More than 20 million Americans watched as the House Select Committee to Investigate the January 6th Attack held its first made-for-prime-time hearing. The date was June 9, 2022. The committee chair, Representative Bennie Thompson, introduced himself to viewers as a native of Bolton, Mississippi, "a part of the country where people justify the actions of slavery, the Klu Klux Klan, and lynching."

"I'm reminded of that dark history," he said, "as I hear voices today try and justify the actions of the insurrectionists on January 6th, 2021."

Fox's viewers didn't hear any of that because the chief justifier refused to air it. Carlson declared that the "ruling class" (surely his audience didn't know he was tweaking them by using a term from Marxist ideology) was delivering "yet another lecture about January 6." He said "they are lying and we are not going to help them do it." There were much more urgent stories, he added, like the economy "careening toward a devastating recession" (which did not materialize) and the U.S. being "at the brink of a full-scale war with Russia" (which didn't happen either). Instead of letting his imagination run wild about that, Carlson showed the muted House proceedings on the right side of the screen and minimized the "vandalism" of the Capitol with a clique of alt-reality counterprogramming guests. Most tellingly, he never mentioned that Fox was providing live coverage of the hearing over on the Fox Business Network. Normally an on-screen graphic would have guided curious viewers to the sister channel, but Carlson wouldn't tolerate that. He wouldn't allow anything to undercut his political agenda—or to suggest in the interest of being well-informed citizens his viewers might want to check out the most significant congressional hearings since Watergate. He never even took a commercial break because he wouldn't give viewers any reason to turn on any of the channels that were taking the hearing seriously.

Overriding the hearing sounded like Carlson's call but it was actually Scott's. It was a very visible instance of "respecting the audience," based upon the conviction that Fox had committed corporate seppuku in 2020 by allowing the "news" people to tell them the truth about Arizona, the truth about Trump being a loser.

"JAN 6TH COMMITTEE FLOPS IN PRIMETIME," Laura Ingraham's show declared after the hearing wrapped. But how would Fox's base have even known? They didn't see it. The Fox Business broadcast of the hearing barely netted 200,000 viewers while Carlson reached 3.3 million.

The fact-free zone only extended to prime time, however. Carlson accused other networks of "colluding" with Democrats to air "propaganda"—yet, four days later, Fox did air the House committee's second session live. The only difference was that this presentation was during the day, when Fox's ratings were always lower and Fox's "news" reporters were theoretically in charge.

Still, the familiar pattern repeated itself: Fox viewers steered clear of anything that questioned (or might undermine) their established convictions. Every time the committee held a daytime hearing and Fox televised it, its audience tuned out en masse. On a Tuesday in July, Fox had 1.9 million viewers in the hour before a January 6 hearing . . . and only 723,000 viewers by the end. When *The Five* came on at 5 p.m., and talked about happier topics like the fentanyl epidemic, the Covid pandemic, and "liberal city decay," things they could blame on Democrats, Fox sprang back to 3 million.

The ratings were the best, the most convincing data I had ever seen about the radicalization of the right. All those breast-beating avowals by conservatives about cherishing law and order? Being pro-police? Being anticrime? They were all blown to bits by this transparent hypocrisy about January 6. The House committee members, particularly Cheney, pointedly and repeatedly hit on Fox's role in the Big Lie. "We cannot abandon the truth," she said, "and remain a free nation."

∎

While the House investigation progressed on live TV, Dominion advanced its suit against Fox far out of public view. It was as if two probes were happening on parallel tracks, bringing down on Fox, in different ways, that rare and dreaded enemy, accountability.

"We had to fight for the emails. We had to fight for the texts. We had to fight for the texts from personal cell phones," Dominion lawyer

Davida Brook told me. "Every single thing that Fox could fight about, they did. We had to just keep, keep, keep up the pressure."

Judge Davis appointed a special master, a separate official who reported to him, to handle a maze of document disputes. "We compressed 3 years worth of discovery into a 6 to 9 month period," Stephen Shackelford recalled. At the outset, Fox only handed over a small number of emails and texts. And in April 2022, the company claimed it was done handing things over altogether. Dominion flipped out—and attacked legally. It was a key moment because the special master ruled that Fox had to produce *every* document that hit on a specific search term, like "Dominion" or "fraud," instead of deciding for itself whether each document was relevant, and not just from work cell phones, but from personal phones too. Now Dominion's lawyers were truly on the inside of Fox, Roto-Rootering through years of memos and missives and chats, starting in the summertime, as they prepared to depose executives and hosts. "The case just kept getting stronger as we received more material," Shackelford said. Judge Davis penciled in a trial date: April 17, 2023.

Not every ruling was in Dominion's favor—far from it. The special master ruled that the plaintiffs themselves had to provide documents dating back as far as 2010. Fox was looking for financial figures, evidence to undercut Dominion's enormous damages claim, among other things. Document production "went on and on and on and on," said Dan Webb, the Winston & Strawn attorney retained by Fox in July 2022, at a First Amendment Salon after the case was settled.

Webb's law firm promotes him as one of the country's "most distinguished and sought-after trial lawyers," so his arrival meant Fox wanted to fight, not beg to settle out of court. But it was also a sign of trouble. Fox had initially retained the Texas law firm Jackson Walker, but the lawyers wound up disagreeing with Dinh so often about defense strategy that Dinh replaced them with Webb.

Webb was assigned to be the lead trial litigator, while Dinh retained Clement & Murphy, the firm cofounded by his Harvard Law School classmate and former colleague Paul Clement, to handle the inevitable appeals. Clement was legal royalty, having argued more than one hundred cases before the Supreme Court. "On our side of the aisle," Webb said, "there was a strong belief that the appeal could very well be as important, or more important, than the trial itself," due to the First Amendment implications.

So it seemed that Dinh was plotting a strategy several steps past Judge Davis, placing his faith—and maybe a billion-plus of Rupert's chips—on a favorable ruling from the conservative, partially Trump-filled majority on the Supreme Court. This misplaced confidence trickled down to the rest of the legal team. Abby Grossberg said that the Fox lawyers who prepared her for deposition pooh-poohed Dominion's chances: "It's a slam-dunk First Amendment case. The whole thing is so stupid."

∎

Contrary to some contemporaneous news accounts, Dominion wasn't desperate, or even willing, to settle at this stage either. Hootan Yaghoobzadeh, the cofounder of Dominion's owner Staple Street Capital, said "settlement" was a curse word. Something more was at stake for Dominion. "We were not willing to settle until the reams of information that we were able to gain through the discovery process had an opportunity to see the light of day," Yaghoobzadeh said. And the lawyerly way to do that was, as Attorney General Merrick Garland once said, to "speak through its court filings."

First they had to find out what to say. It was time to put Fox's lineup under oath.

Take it from me: Being deposed is a nerve-racking experience. You're being quizzed about conversations and decisions that happened years ago and you're well aware that the questioner wants to use your answers against you. You're not allowed to bring any notes or other material. You may feel like the other side is far better prepared than you are. You might spend multiple days talking through your recollections with your lawyer—but that only magnifies the stress. More than one of the Fox employees deposed by Dominion described the experience to me as "brutal." Carlson said of the lawyer who deposed him, Tom Clare, that "the hate that I felt for that guy" was "unhealthy."

The first deposition of a Fox host was a breeze, though. It was on July 26, and the deponent was afternoon host Dana Perino, who never indulged any part of Trump's coup plot. She said she thought the smears about Dominion were "nuts." The allegations of fraud were "not good for America."

At the same time Perino was testifying via Zoom, Trump was reminding everyone that the Big Lie was not a past-tense topic, it was a present-tense and future-tense personal crusade. He was still selling the story to gullible audiences. Trump made a lollapalooza of his traveling to D.C., for the first time since slinking out of the White House, and delivered a ninety-three-minute speech with election-denying applause lines. Trump's trip was—inevitably, because it was Trump stirring the pot—a top story almost everywhere ("Trump is still a vibrant threat to democracy as he returns to DC," one of CNN's headlines said) but Fox turned an icy cold shoulder. The network showed exactly 0 minutes of his policy speech even as Newsmax hung rapt on every word. (And with a ninety-three-minute speech, that's a lot of rapt.) Rupert's "non person" posture was still in effect. Could anything shake it off?

■

Trump wanted—maybe *needed*—to believe that Fox "would die without me." That's what he wrote on his lonely, you-could-hear-an-echo-in-here Truth Social platform on August 4. But it was plainly untrue. Fox had shown enough right-wing leg to fully rebound from the post-Arizona turmoil and (to reduce complex political calculations to crass dating analogies since that's ultimately what all of life is about) had started to hook up with other people. "Inside Fox News, DeSantis is 'the future of the party.' And he's taking advantage," the *Tampa Bay Times* put it in a prescient 2021 headline. The news outlet used public record laws to obtain hundreds of emails between the Florida governor's office and overeager, sometimes outright pathetic Fox staffers. "The governor spoke wonderfully at CPAC," one starry-eyed producer wrote. He's "the future of the party," another producer gushed.

The best example of this heavy-breathing flirtation came early in the Covid vaccine rollout, when DeSantis was still championing the shots, months before his cynical sellout turn toward vax-skepticism. The governor's office staged a vaccines-for-seniors event exclusively for *Fox & Friends*; other media was kept out. Afterward, *Friends* booker Bridget Gleason wrote to her DeSantis contact, "I honestly think he could host the show with the chops we saw from him at the vaccine site."

This DeSantis-Fox collaboration was sealed in January 2021, just three days after Rupert emailed Scott and said words Republican politicians remained terrified to utter: "Trump insisting on the election being stolen and convincing 25% of Americans was a huge disservice to the country. Pretty much a crime. Inevitable it blew up on Jan. 6th."

"Best we don't mention his name unless essential and certainly don't support him," Rupert added.

Enter DeSantis—a new leading man for Fox—younger than

the former president, savvier, and not nearly as orange. Every word DeSantis uttered came with a wink, nod, and wave of jazz hands toward the 2024 presidential race. Many of those words came through the Fox loudspeaker, where the governor was the grand prize with a big red bow in an all-out booking war—*Fox & Friends* versus *Special Report*, Maria Bartiromo versus Martha MacCallum. The DeSantis team favored the more malleable, more opinionated, more slavishly adoring shows, of course. When a news producer was turned down, she exclaimed to a DeSantis aide, "He made time for Tucker last night!" Nothing played better on Fox than unabashed hero worship, of whoever qualified as the latest caped crusader for (right-wing) truth, (right-wing) justice, and the (red state) American way. DeSantis was the paragon now.

Trump, by contrast, was barely ever welcome on Fox anymore. His phone interview with Sean Hannity on April 13 was the last time he'd be on for five months. Hannity, who still had Trump's mug tattooed on his heart, stuck his neck out to make the interview happen. He knew DeSantis was Fox's favorite at the moment. Heck, every time Trump spoke, Fox execs cringed—partly because they feared further legal exposure. There were political calculations too. Both current GOP electeds like Mitch McConnell and formers like Paul Ryan continued to urge Rupert to ice Trump out. McConnell made the case to Rupert directly: "We will not win again," he said, meaning the GOP will not take back the Senate (all McConnell ever really cared about) if Trump is front and center.

Many of Fox's heavy-hitters were still 100 percent in Trump's corner—they supported him on air, they cheered for MAGA candidates, they opposed Biden even for breathing—but Fox as an institution was trying to break away from their old hero. One executive described it as a "soft ban"—like no shoes, no service at a boardwalk pizza joint. Nothing about it felt soft to Trump; in another missive on Truth Social, he assailed his longtime-favorite show *Fox & Friends* because, he claimed, they "just really botched my poll numbers, no doubt on purpose. That show has been terrible—gone to the 'dark side.'" The morning show had highlighted a poll that showed De-Santis gaining ground against Trump in a hypothetical 2024 primary.

But then came a surprise, and in the state of DeSantis no less: The FBI executed a search warrant at Trump's Palm Beach estate.

Trump as victim? Victimization, the gold-standard conservative narrative? The ban was reversed for at least a few nights. As CNN media analyst David Zurawik wrote, "We thought Murdoch's news outlets were abandoning Trump. Then the FBI searched Mar-a-Lago."

Jesse Watters's outburst on *The Five* spoke for MAGA media reaction as a whole. "I'm angry. I feel violated. The whole country feels violated. This is disgusting. They've declared war on us, and now it's game on." The message from Fox was clear: Hey, he may be a non person, but he's *our* non person. Hands off.

"They must be stopped"

Whenever I touched base with people in and around Fox, gossip greased the conversations, as at any other white-collar institution. *"Sean and Ainsley are spending the weekend together in Florida."* That would be evening host Hannity and morning host Earhardt, who were dating semi-secretly. *"Greg is trying to deport Geraldo again."* That would be Gutfeld and Rivera, sparring partners on *The Five*, which was starting to eclipse *Tucker Carlson Tonight* as the network's highest-rated show. Relatedly: *"Tucker is panicked about* The Five.*"* There was no end to the scuttlebutt about intramural ratings rivalries. "There was a lot of concern" about Carlson's 8 p.m. hour coming in second place behind the 5 p.m. chatfest, a senior source admitted to me. A Carlson staffer said the word came down that "we need more animal segments." Cute kittens and puppies, stat.

On the occasions I steered these source chats in a more serious direction, toward the impact of Fox-fueled disinformation on society and democracy, staffers turned cagey or dismissive. Some resorted to whataboutism and pointed out the flaws of other networks. Others said the Biden-era narrative about defending democracy against demagogues like Trump was just a front, liberal virtue-signaling, and a way to score points against the GOP.

Introspection, like accountability, was always in short supply at Fox, a tone that was set at the top, by Rupert, who advised Suzanne Scott to "ignore the noise." Scott said she tuned it all out: "If I wasted any time reading stories about myself or social media posts or what have you, I wouldn't be able to get my job done. And you know what I always say? I sleep well at night." On a MyPillow, quite possibly.

But a tug-of-war was under way between people of good faith and all parties who wanted to protect American democracy, and those on the other side of the rope who tugged in an authoritarian direction. Carlson's unapproved trip to Hungary in 2021 was surely in the latter category. Carlson whipped his show up into an infomercial for Viktor Orbán's increasingly autocratic, patriarchal nation. (He was supposed to return there when the Conservative Political Action Conference, putting its imprimatur on Orbán-style strongman tactics, held a special gathering in Budapest in 2022, but someone at Fox, I was told, reined him in, and he merely sent a videotaped message.) Orbán praised Carlson and said "programs like his should be broadcasted day and night. Or as you say 24/7." With each passing month, Carlson seemed like a Macy's Parade balloon, floating on high in the firmament, looming over the network where he worked. And now a national leader was calling for 24/7 Tucker Carlson Channels.

Back in the U.S., President Biden tried to make the 2022 midterms a referendum on Trumpism. "Equality and democracy are under assault," he said in a prime-time speech on September 1. "We do ourselves no favor to pretend otherwise." Biden's advance team turned Philadelphia's Independence Hall into a stage set; the building was bathed in red and the tree canopy was illuminated with white lights. Biden walked to the podium right on schedule, 8:01 p.m., but Carlson was already way ahead of him. Carlson obviously wasn't going to cede his time to the commander-in-chief; no, he'd summarize the speech instead, and by summarize, I mean lie—extravagantly.

Carlson said—before the event began—that Biden's message was, "the single gravest threat to America today is Republican voters, all 75 million of them. They are Nazis and destroyers of democracy. They must be stopped. That is the message."

No, it was not. I drove to Philly for the speech. I heard it for myself. I noticed that Biden drew a dividing line between "MAGA Republicans" who disregarded democratic norms and the mainstream "majority of Republicans." He did it at the outset:

"Donald Trump and the MAGA Republicans represent an extremism that threatens the very foundations of our republic. Now, I want to be very clear—very clear—up front: Not every Republican, not even the majority of Republicans, are MAGA Republicans. Not every Republican embraces their extreme ideology. I know because I've been able to work with these mainstream Republicans. But there is no question that the Republican Party today is dominated, driven, and intimidated by Donald Trump and the MAGA Republicans, and that is a threat to this country."

In person it was a nuanced attempt by Biden to cleave the radical right away from power; naive, maybe, but well-intentioned. On Fox, specifically on Carlson's show, it was portrayed as a bloodthirsty war cry. "Tonight he declared . . . that anyone who disagrees with him is a threat to the country," Carlson claimed, queuing up a clip of Biden, the only segment of the speech that he would allow his viewers to hear. The video showed the first and last sentences of the part I extracted above, cutting the key part that "not every Republican, not even the majority of Republicans, are MAGA Republicans."

It was a little like editing the Gettysburg Address to say, "Four score and seven years ago, our fathers brought forth . . . a new nation . . . dedicated to the proposition that . . . all . . . government . . . shall . . . perish from the earth."

As Biden's voice echoed off the buildings around Independence Square, I could hear why Carlson did not want his viewers to hear the rest. Biden said MAGA Republicans "promote authoritarian leaders" and "fan the flames of political violence"; he said they portray the January 6 mob as "patriots"; they "look at America and see carnage and darkness and despair"; they "spread fear and lies" for profit and power. It was a provocative speech, to be sure, but Carlson wildly misrepresented it. "THIS IS BY FAR BIDEN'S MOST SHAMEFUL MOMENT," one of his hyperbolic banners proclaimed.

From outside the hall in Philly I heard anti-Biden protesters with bullhorns shouting "Let's go Brandon," conservative code for "Fuck Joe Biden," somewhere outside the Secret Service perimeter. The protesters were not silenced. They were not beaten. They were not hauled off to Gitmo as in some *Patriot Purge* nightmare. Biden acknowledged them and said, "They're entitled to be outrageous. This is a democracy."

It was Biden's defense of democracy that led two members of the Murdoch family to throw open their home to him. In October James and his wife, Kathryn, agreed to host a Democratic Senatorial Campaign Committee fundraiser at their Upper East Side townhouse. Biden spoke for about twenty minutes and once again delineated between mainstream Republicans and extremists who "don't like the system the way it is."

The donor confab went unmentioned on Fox, but among those who were in the know, it was a *Succession*-worthy juxtaposition: James raised money for Biden and the Democrats while Lachlan and Rupert plotted to restore Republican control.

"Wackadoodle"

A woman by the name of Marlene Bourne who believed she could talk to the wind wound up providing one of the most important pieces of evidence in *Dominion v. Fox.*

As Dominion's legal team reviewed hundreds of thousands of emails and texts unearthed from the bowels of Fox, they zeroed in on a uniquely zany missive dated Saturday, November 7, 2020.

Bourne wrote that she was "told" to send the email, titled "Election Fraud Info," to Trump lawyer Sidney Powell, Lou Dobbs, and pro-Trump activist Tom Fitton (who was later identified as a co-conspirator in the Georgia indictment). Because Powell was booked on Bartiromo's show the next morning, Powell forwarded it to Bartiromo, as if to prep the host on the hysterical hijinks she planned to unleash.

Parts of the three-page email were, by Bourne's own admission, "wackadoodle." She claimed to be "internally decapitated"; she described having visions; she said "The Wind tells me I'm a ghost." She said some things that were easily debunked: For example, that Roger Ailes and other "owners of the major US media outlets secretly huddle most days to determine how best to portray Mr. Trump as badly as possible." It was a supremely well-kept secret, indeed, since Ailes died in 2017—and he hadn't *owned* Fox, he'd just acted like he did. The email also asserted that Supreme Court justice Antonin Scalia "was purposefully killed at the annual Bohemian Grove camp . . . during a weeklong human hunting expedition."

These laugh lines should have led Bartiromo to click the delete button, as well as the one that opens a trap door under the chair of deranged guests. Instead, she shared it with her producing partner Abby Grossberg, and she clicked reply, telling Powell that "I just spoke to Eric and told him you gave very imp info"—a reference to Eric Trump.

Bourne's "wackadoodle" email was germane for two reasons: It was chock-full of equally loony claims about Dominion, and it was the *only* message referencing Dominion in Bartiromo's and Grossberg's inboxes prior to Powell's live shot on their show. In other words, it was Patient Zero in the coming contagion that would infect all of Fox.

Powell didn't send Fox any legit evidence of wrongdoing before smearing the company on national television. Bartiromo didn't contact Bourne before going ahead with the segment. Grossberg didn't conduct any due diligence about her guest's apparent source. It was the Fox paradigm in all its glory: shoot first; don't ask questions at all.

If any of them had followed up with Bourne, they might have learned, as *The Daily Beast* did, that "she based her now nationally prominent ideas about election fraud on a wide variety of sources, including hidden messages she detects in films, song lyrics she hears on the radio, and overheard conversations she hears while in line at the supermarket checkout."

The existence of the crazed email was a gift to Dominion's lawyers since Bartiromo and Powell's November 8 cross-talk was the first alleged instance of defamation. Davida Brook grilled Bartiromo about it during her early September deposition. The host kept saying she didn't know Bourne, but admitted the email was "kooky." Yet on the November 8 broadcast Bartiromo looked down, as if at a printed sheet, and repeated some of Bourne's bogus email almost word for word. This rip-off has not been reported before; review it for yourself:

> *Bourne:* "Don't you find it curious that Nadeam Elshami, Nancy Pelosi's longtime chief of staff, is a key executive there, and that Richard Blum, Senator Feinstein's husband, is not only a significant shareholder of that company, but in Avid Technologies as well?"
>
> *Bartiromo:* "I also see reports that Nancy Pelosi's longtime chief of staff is a key executive at that company; Richard Blum, Senator Feinstein's husband, a significant shareholder of the company."

Bartiromo's use of the word "reports" gave away the game; it's a cheat word for sloppy cable news hosts, used to allow inclusion of some unverified claims, but to offload responsibility for one's words. But it couldn't work in this case. To make matters even worse, Bartiromo "never reported on the existence of this email," Dominion pointed out. Nor did she disclose to viewers that she was acting as a liaison between Powell and the Trump family.

One week after Bartiromo's deposition, it was Grossberg's turn, and Grossberg's stomach was in knots. When she later sued, she alleged that Fox's legal team "coerced, intimidated, and misinformed" her during multiple days of depo-prep. She said she was given the impression that she couldn't tell Dominion's lawyers that Bartiromo's show was "severely under-staffed" or that she felt stretched too thin as a result. When confronted with Bourne's "kooky" email during the interrogation, Grossberg kept saying "I don't recall" and "I don't know."

Grossberg was also questioned about Carlson—which was notable because she had just transferred over to his show team and become Carlson's head of booking. Grossberg had been functioning as the executive producer (EP) of Bartiromo's Sunday show but without the title or respect (or money), and saw *Tucker Carlson Tonight* as a way out. (Bartiromo texted her, regretfully, that "I tried hard to get them to make you an EP.") The Carlson booking job was vacant because the previous booker moved to Fox Business. A source claimed that Carlson's team wanted to poach "one of theirs" to get even. It didn't quite make sense, and some Carlson loyalists had serious reservations about Grossberg from the get-go, according to emails I obtained from sources. But Justin Wells hired her anyway—to his and Carlson's eternal regret.

Grossberg, a Johns Hopkins grad, was not a Fox lifer like many of her colleagues. She worked at all the major networks—CBS, CNN, NBC, and ABC—before joining Bartiromo's show in 2019. She started her newest job on Carlson's staff in September and quickly learned, according to her lawsuit, "that she had merely traded in one overtly misogynistic work environment for an even crueler one." She said the office was plastered with oversize photos of the octogenarian Pelosi in a "plunging bathing suit revealing her cleavage." She said staffers openly debated which women politicians were "more fuckable." She made the place sound like a retrograde hellhole. Sexist comments were commonplace, Grossberg said, and a senior producer had a mirror with the word "cunt" scrawled on it. But when she was deposed by Dominion and shown text messages between Carlson and Wells referring to Powell as a "cunt," she kept all that to herself. Dominion attorney Davida Brook asked her if the texts made her feel uncomfortable and Grossberg said no. Brook must have sensed that Grossberg was withholding. Grossberg's lawsuit later said she responded "as she had been conditioned" and "knew full well that Mr. Carlson was very capable of using such disgusting language about women."

Grossberg said later, regarding the deposition, "When I went into the office the next day, people were very curious. I told them Tucker had come up, because I was asked if he did. I said I protected him, and they rewarded the staff with lunch." It was dubbed "Abby Day." A feast for a cover-up well done.

But Fox staffers were foolish to think that the depositions were proceeding in their favor. Hour by hour—Dominion was granted about seven hours per witness—the hosts and producers were contributing to the ultimate case against the Big Defamation. "We thought their strategy was to pin the blame on the hosts; to say the executives had no responsibility," an insider said. "But then the execs confessed to their responsibility."

While Bartiromo might well convince a jury that she truly believed all of Trump's bullshit, and thus wasn't guilty of actual malice, Dominion could counter with David Clark, the exec in charge of weekend programming, who was supposed to oversee Bartiromo's show. Clark "never believed it," Shackelford told me. "His state of mind mattered because he could have stopped it from airing. But he didn't."

Clark and Meade Cooper provided crucial testimony because they both described the chain of command and undermined any argument that Bartiromo et al. were just babbling on air without any checks and balances. In fact, when MSNBC's Chris Hayes said one night that Fox's hosts "don't really seem to have bosses exercising any kind of judgment at all," Cooper was so offended that she flagged the segment to Scott and said "Our enemies hope this narrative takes hold. I hope we are fighting back against that smear."

Clark testified that "we have a process of vetting guests" and "would correct any errors . . . as quickly as we can." Yet Bartiromo's and Dobbs's shows were routinely rebroadcast later in the day—including on the weeks Dominion was being pummeled. "That presented an extraordinary and unique opportunity to argue malice," Tom Clare said. "Because one of the things that Fox was saying in their papers was like, 'Oh, we had no idea what these people were gonna say when they went on the air . . . And we would never put them on the air if we had known that their evidence was nothing.' Well, this was a controlled experiment, right?" Because when Powell appeared on a show, said crazy stuff, and Fox aired it again *later*, "they made an affirmative decision," he said. The rebroadcasts usually happened automatically, but Dominion could argue that the executives failed to intervene.

At the same time, the discovery process and the depositions *did* show the limits of exec oversight. On the day Biden became president-elect, Clark emailed Bartiromo and said, "Maria, I am asking that we reconsider the Rudy Giuliani booking tomorrow." Clark attached an article titled "Giuliani releases bizarre video claiming Fox News won election for Biden." The election was over; why book a conspiracy theorist to say otherwise? Because, Bartiromo said, "it was our show." Carlson wasn't the only host who believed he was bigger than the Fox brand.

But consequences were coming—and not just for Carlson. Numerous investigations into the 2020 coup attempt were making steady, secretive progress. Prosecutors kept finding new evidence of how the network of lies' words led to potentially criminal actions. In Georgia, for example, Trump allies traveled to rural Coffee County and breached sensitive voting equipment in an ill-fated bid to find fraud.

The machines were made by, you guessed it, Dominion. The digital intrusion played prominently in the eventual RICO case against Trump in Georgia. But even as the courts began to achieve accountability, echoes of 2020 harmed the victims. Vice reporter Elizabeth Landers went to Shasta County, California, after the county terminated its contract with Dominion as a result of the lie brigade. She asked: "Did Fox News melt this county's brain?"

"I have no freaking idea"

"First, the good news," Carlson declared as he started his show on November 2, 2022, one week before the midterm election. The Democratic Party, he said, is "about to suffer a humiliating repudiation."

He was right about the humiliating repudiation, but it was going to happen to a party much closer to home.

Carlson giddily reported that Democrats will likely "lose both houses of Congress." He predicted "overwhelming losses." He channeled conventional wisdom of a "red wave" *and* tried to help it crest. He said "New York, of all places, could have a Republican governor," and then chatted with that candidate, Lee Zeldin, almost willing him into the executive mansion.

The Fox host explicitly endorsed some of the Republicans running for office, like Blake Masters, a hard-line nationalist candidate for Senate in Arizona. Carlson booked them on TV and promoted them at greater length on his Fox Nation streaming shows. "Being able to get on Tucker for free and have him say, 'I hope you win, I agree with what you're saying,' was really important," Joe Kent, a far-right House candidate in Washington State, told *The New York Times*. Well, maybe not *that* important. Kent lost. So did Masters. So did Zeldin. So did Kari Lake in Arizona, Doug Mastriano in

Pennsylvania, Tiffany Smiley in Washington, Don Bolduc in New Hampshire. Of all the candidates Carlson hyped, the only one who prevailed was J. D. Vance, now a senator from Ohio.

Carlson, by his own admission, "got it wrong up and down the board." But why? Why had he misled his viewers, and himself, so thoroughly?

■

People often asked me if Carlson really believed all the crazy stuff he spouted on TV. My answer was that he did, but with a caveat. He wasn't always this doctrinaire. For decades he was a writer; then a performer; and now he was an end-of-days preacher. What some of his associates reckoned, and what I thought too, was that once he saw how it played on TV, Carlson talked himself into being a true believer.

And he did *so* much talking. Night after night, he played his own version of the "Mad Prophet of the Airwaves," telling viewers that the Democratic Party was hell-bent on death and destruction. "They have run this country into the ground," he said, "wrecking our economy, desecrating our military." He said "no group in American history has done a worse job running this country than the neoliberals currently in charge." They're vicious, intolerant, and incompetent, he said. If this was your frame for the midterms, then how could the Democrats earn a single vote? But of course it wasn't the average person's frame. Far from it. Times were tough, in a country slowly coming out of a once-in-a-lifetime pandemic, but most people didn't recognize the dystopian picture Carlson painted.

In Carlson's defense, almost every other show on Fox also massively overstated the GOP's midterm chances. Hosts and guests hyped the impending "red tsunami" with giddy glee. When Biden expressed concern about Republicans running for office who "won't commit to accepting the results of elections that they're running in," and called that attitude un-American, Jesse Watters came on and said "no one is going to question the results of this election, Mr. President, because it's going to be a blowout." That's the type of fallacious commentary that aired hour after hour: people in a hard-right bubble, talking only to themselves, like a sports bar devoted to the rowdy fans of one team convincing themselves their boys are so good they can never lose. They were priming the base to be shocked and appalled when it was *not* a blowout.

By Monday, November 7, Carlson said Democrats were "about to be crushed." He seized on random news stories from sites like *Politico* and imparted greater meaning onto them, asserting that Democrats were peddling "conspiracy theories" to preemptively shift the blame for the losses they were about to endure. But sometimes a cigar really is just a cigar.

As another Tuesday bad-news election night turned into Wednesday's walk-of-shame postmortem, reality started to break through on Fox. Commentator Marc Thiessen called the midterm results "an absolute disaster for the Republican party." He urged the party to look in the mirror, reject "radical candidates," and rally behind the likes of Ron DeSantis and Ohio governor Mike DeWine. That's what many others at Fox were privately thinking, as well.

There was little direct criticism of Trump and how he'd hurt the party by endorsing fringe-to-lunatic candidates, but there was plenty of praise for DeSantis and his huge reelection in Florida. When the only things actually crushed on Election Day were the hopes and dreams on the right, DeSantis provided a much needed way still to "own the libs." Kayleigh McEnany, previously best known for her staunch Trump defenses, said DeSantis's victory speech clips were positive, sunny, and forward-looking, and that "needs to be the future message for the party"—i.e., the opposite of Trump. She said

Trump needed to put his 2024 announcement plans "on pause" until after the Senate runoff in Georgia.

No way. Just one week after the midterms, Trump announced his reelection bid. His prime-time speech at Mar-a-Lago was timed for Hannity's 9 p.m. show, but after forty minutes, Hannity bailed out in favor of his Trump-boosting panel of guests. It was a familiar Fox impulse: *"We can sell you better than you can sell yourself."* Post-announcement, Fox largely kept Trump off the air; he was running for president again, but Murdochworld believed he was the party's past, not its future. At least that's what they *hoped*.

∎

Unlike Trump, Carlson *did* reflect on what went wrong with his midterm forecasts. He said (more clearly on podcasts than on his own show) that he made a mistake by making predictions and endorsing candidates. He mocked himself for thinking that a Republican would win the governorship in New York. "I was huffing my own gas," he admitted in a conversation with conservative activist Charlie Kirk.

Carlson said his "hatred" of liberals, particularly what he called an "anti-human movement that's sweeping the west," clouded his judgment and caused him to believe in the red-wave-that-wasn't. "I was like, 'I dislike these people so much.' What they're doing is so wrong. It is helping so few people and hurting so many. It's so immoral on every level that I just want it to be repudiated . . . I wanted that so much, not because I like the Republicans—I really dislike them more than I ever have—but I dislike the other side more."

Researchers have a term for this: negative partisanship. Political "teams" were ever more defined by disdain for the opposition. When Trump—himself sounding astonished as much as anyone else—joked in 2016 that "I could stand in the middle of 5th Avenue and shoot somebody and I wouldn't lose voters," it showed that, intuitively, he grasped the growing power of negative partisanship better than the average political analyst.

"I did learn that, like, I have no freaking idea what goes on in American politics," Carlson told Kirk. "That's what I learned." He never articulated the logical conclusion that applied to his show and the rest of Fox: that he was too blinded, too consumed by his own ideological agenda, to see the country writ large.

Indeed, a (shrinking) wing of the GOP knew that the Fox machine was a big part of the reason why Republicans kept losing. Some in this wing even worked for Fox: As former South Carolina congressman turned Fox commentator Trey Gowdy said in a candid on-air moment in 2021, "Most of the voices in the conservative movement have never held political office before. . . . Fox has much more influence over Republican primary voters than anyone who's elected."

Let that quote sink in. A bunch of tanned and bronzed entertainers who sat in front of mics all day spouting a predetermined narrative had more power than the actual politicians. Gowdy was right, and any honest assessment of the midterm results had to start there.

It was the right-wing media, for example, much more than the right's electeds, that turned critical race theory into a bogeyman and semantically bleached the word "woke" into a catch-all for any and everything the right despised about the left—especially things like tolerance and diversity. "Wokeness" became seen, by conservatives, as a threat to their place in American society, their rank, their status. *Vox*'s Aaron Rupar rightly identified it as a grievance-stoking programming strategy: The GOP's media wing, he wrote, has "leaned into so-called 'cancel culture' as a way to make the case against Democrats without having to discuss policy or really anything of substance at all." One day they complained about Dr. Seuss books being outlawed. (They weren't.) Another day they raged about Mr. Potato Head being "canceled." (He wasn't.) Even if this was good TV, which is very much debatable, it was definitely not the stuff of healthy civil discourse. While Fox's hosts ginned up the audience about a toy potato's pronouns (and parts), angry viewers (including a certain former president) "woked" themselves up into a frenzy, because they actually believed this stuff.

Tellingly, Trump never used the word "woke" while in office, but he caught on by March 2021; in a phone interview with Fox's Harris Faulkner, he said the Democrats "are destroying our country . . . they're destroying it with 'woke.'" Trump was permanently Fox-brained. And as a master of short simple slogans and buzzwords, he understood in his gut that "woke," a word with overtones of compassion and social justice and undertones of hipness, would fuel the deeply ingrained far-right narrative that liberalism is not an ideology about progress for all, but rather a social and cultural crusade to embarrass and isolate conservatives. DeSantis got it too, and tried to out-woke Trump, which delighted his terminally online fans but barely registered with normal people.

The anti-"woke" movement also stirred a moral panic about transgender Americans in 2022 and 2023. Hyperbolic claims about "groomers" and gender-affirming care spread all across the network of lies—part of a backlash to gay and transgender rights that had been brewing for years. "SCHOOLS BECOMING TRANS INDOCTRI-NATION CULTS," Fox blared during one of hundreds of segments on the subject. A transgender teacher in Orange County, California, said they were targeted by Fox for posting TikTok videos about the school's queer library, and received multiple death threats in the ensuing weeks. Similar onslaughts were reported across the country.

The subject caused divisions inside Fox. Some of Carlson's staffers felt personally attacked when Fox's news division produced a heartwarming Pride Month report about a transgender teen. "It was a pointed rebuke of our perspective," a member of the Tuckertroop said. Carlson responded a few months later with a two-part "documentary" claiming "transgender activists are targeting America's children" and featuring "detransitioners."

The MAGA base devoured transphobic content in 2022 the same way it gobbled up anti–Black Lives Matter material in 2020. Trump actually seemed taken aback by the level of rage. When he mentioned "transgender insanity" to a crowd in North Carolina in 2023, the crowd went buck wild. Many attendees stood up and cheered. "It's amazing how strongly people feel about that," he said. "You see I'm talking about cutting taxes, people go like that"—he pretended to clap limply—and then "I talk about transgender, everyone goes crazy. Who would have thought? Five years ago, you didn't know what the hell it was."

That was precisely the point. When liberal stalwart Robert Reich listed "the GOP's dangerous distraction ploys," he put these three on top: "Claim everything is 'woke,'" "vilify trans people," and "complain about Critical Race Theory." It's what animated Fox's rundowns and some 2024 campaigns—but it simply didn't translate to the rest of the country. Rupert sometimes objected to the culture war obsessions his network fostered because, his associates said, more than anything else, he wanted to win. Perhaps Carlson did not know best, after all?

■

Undeterred by his midterm face-plants, the 8 p.m. star inserted himself right back into intraparty politics in January 2023 and played kingmaker as Kevin McCarthy fought to win the House speakership.

Carlson had rarely passed up a chance to lambaste McCarthy as a D.C. swamp creature. His 2021 polemic against McCarthy for being roommates with pollster and consultant Frank Luntz left a welt for years. On Tuesday, January 3, when McCarthy came up well short on the first vote for Speaker, Carlson again hooted at him for being in the pocket of lobbyists; but then, sensing an opening on the chess board, he proposed a path forward. To win over recalcitrant House Republicans, Carlson said, McCarthy should "release the January 6 files"—all the surveillance footage that conspiracy theorists thought could prove them right, that the rioters were just Mom and Pop out for some sightseeing—and at the same time "put Thomas Massie of Kentucky in charge of a new Frank Church committee, designed to discover what the FBI and the intel agencies have been doing to control domestic politics." (The Church committee, a Senate Select Committee chaired by Idaho senator Frank Church in 1975 to investigate intelligence abuses, was widely praised for its thoroughness and professionalism. Whether a repeat was possible in the disinformation age was very much debatable.)

McCarthy lost in the voting again and again on Wednesday, so on Thursday Abby Grossberg, now Carlson's chief booker, was asked to pursue him for a live interview that night. "Please tell them that I promise I won't mention Frank Luntz," Carlson told Grossberg in a text. "This interview isn't about that. No one else has stepped forward to challenge McCarthy. He's still the only option."

Carlson, who had been working the phones like a shadow party whip, said, looking to slather on whatever buttering-up substance he could apply, "I keep hearing from people who know him that this process has improved him. I want to give him a chance to make the case that it has. Feel free to screenshot this text for his office."

Grossberg passed it along, but McCarthy's camp was still hesitant. Carlson growled that "he'd be a cowardly idiot not to" come on the show, "which he may be." He typed out another message for Grossberg to screenshot and share. "I really hope he does it," he wrote, flexing his threat muscles now. "I'll be a little mean, because that's who I am. But I won't be too mean. I want to help fix this."

Carlson looked at the landscape (and in the mirror) and decided that he, and only he, could broker a deal to solve the stalemate—live on TV, no less. On Thursday afternoon, Grossberg said later, Wells "came in and he said, 'Here's the plan.' Tucker's going to first have Kevin on. Hear him beg and grovel. Then we'll bring in Matt Gaetz," a leader of the House rebels. Gaetz will "set his terms, then Tucker will set *his* terms that McCarthy has to agree to." The vision, Grossberg said, channeling Wells, was that "we're going to make this whole thing happen on air and save the Republican Party." All hail, Tucker of Arc.

Except—McCarthy refused to show up. So there were no televised peace talks. No Begin-Sadat rerun. But Carlson still had sway: The next day, the host told colleagues, McCarthy called him with good news about the Massie plan. "McCarthy is taking our recommendation and putting him in charge of the new Church committee," Carlson texted Grossberg. "That's a win." Massie wound up only being a member, not the chair, of the less-than-mellifluous "Select Subcommittee on the Weaponization of the Federal Government." Still, the committee would provide a steady stream of accusatory fodder for literally hundreds of Fox segments in the months ahead. McCarthy, who finally became Speaker on the record fifteenth round of voting Friday night, had bought into his Republican predecessor John Boehner's advice: "You gotta feed the alligators, otherwise, they'll eat you." As Andrew Lawrence of Media Matters observed, in the Ailes era, Fox News existed to prop up the Republican Party. Now, though, "the Republican Party exists to prop up Fox News." It was all about the Republican bubble. Lawrence said, "Fox News's influence outside of the bubble, I think, has shrunk considerably." But "inside of that bubble," he said, "their influence, their grip on the base of the Republican Party, has strengthened."

PART FOUR

"They endorsed"

Dominion maintained three goals as it advanced toward trial, Staple Street cofounder Hootan Yaghoobzadeh said: to "make sure the truth got exposed, kept Fox accountable, and that we were compensated for the damages they inflicted."

The judge ordered both sides into mediation back in December, but Fox was still full of bravado and Dominion wasn't close to achieving its goals yet. So in January Susman Godfrey partner Justin Nelson and associate Katy Peaslee boarded flights to Los Angeles to depose the most powerful witness of all: Rupert Murdoch.

■

Fox's lawyers had tried mightily to avoid having to hand the chairman over to this inquisition. When they argued that Dominion was only suing Fox News, not the parent company, Dominion filed a second suit against Fox Corp, thereby ensnaring Rupert and Lachlan. A few days before Christmas 2022, Judge Davis agreed to consolidate the two cases. The parent company avoided a second trial but it could no longer build a border wall between Fox News and the larger enterprise.

Most of the Fox witnesses had appeared via Zoom and most completed the agreed-upon seven hours of questioning in a single day. But Rupert opted to split it up over two days and do it in person, in a spare conference room on the Fox Corp studio lot off Pico Boulevard on L.A.'s Westside.

Nelson was in an enviable position. Countless journalists, attorneys, and activists would have jumped at the chance to question "The Man Who Owns the News," as Michael Wolff titled Rupert in a 2008 book. But that's precisely why the chance never came about; Rupert almost never availed himself of scrutiny. The most recent exception was Wolff's book; Rupert agreed to be interviewed for dozens of hours, and he was so angry about the finished product that he left Wolff "more than a dozen increasingly insistent and irate voice-mail messages." Neither Rupert nor his inner circle had read much of Wolff's past work, the author deduced, so they didn't know that Wolff's pen was oft full of poison. "This might be an information company, but they like their information in the short version," Wolff concluded.

This dynamic benefited Dominion fifteen years later. In the lead-up to the two deposition days, Rupert continued to get overly rosy counsel from Viet Dinh, sources involved in the case said. Perhaps as a result, Rupert did not spend enough time reviewing the documents that Nelson was likely to ask about, the sources said. Days before his deposition, Rupert was photographed in Barbados enjoying the surf with his new girlfriend, Ann Lesley Smith. (Smith and a younger man helped the fall-prone Rupert make it from the ocean to the sand.)

Once the deposition was under way, Nelson started with layups like "do you currently believe Dominion committed election fraud by rigging the 2020 presidential election?"

Rupert's response was startling: "I honestly do not know."

Was Rupert secretly an election-denier? Nelson slowed down and started to ask yes-or-no questions. "Have you ever seen any credible evidence that Dominion software and algorithms manipulated vote counts?" Rupert said no. Have you *ever* believed that? No, the mogul said, "I've never even heard about this until a few months ago." If true, he had abdicated his duty as the head of a major media company.

Nelson methodically asked if Rupert believed any of the "four lies" Fox aired about Dominion. Rupert pleaded ignorance. When the one about Dominion being owned by Smartmatic came up, Rupert said, "I don't know. I never thought about it." Nelson repeated all of the most preposterous theories about Dominion, at times quoting directly from Fox segments, and asked if Rupert believed any of them. "I've seen no evidence." "No." "No." "I said no."

Rupert seemed shell-shocked by Nelson's interrogation, which filled thirty-three entire pages of the court transcript. The self-professed newsman was either staggeringly oblivious or seriously ill-prepared. Nelson felt that he caught Rupert in contradiction after contradiction. When asked about Sidney Powell, for instance, Rupert said "I have never heard of her before." Yet in a November 23, 2020, email to an old pal, Rupert called Powell a "crazy would be lawyer." (And she had been on his network a profusion of times by that point.)

Rupert claimed not to know other key figures in the post-election saga, as well. He said he wasn't aware that the Department of Homeland Security was on the lookout for voting-related disinformation. "I was in England," he said, offering an excuse. "I wasn't following it." Nelson was taken aback by that. "You weren't following the election?"

Rupert claimed that "once I knew the result, that was it." He moved on. But Nelson pulled up emails that showed otherwise, like his mid-November gripes about Rudy Giuliani "damaging everybody."

Nelson left Rupert almost tongue-tied. The witness repeatedly said "I do not read Mediaite," a popular industry news site, and insisted he did not read a specific article about Powell and Giuliani. But then Nelson presented an email indicating he had. "Looks like I looked at it," Rupert admitted.

And that was just day one. Rupert had to come back for another three and a half hours the next day. The break allowed Nelson all the time he needed to get his artillery arrayed on the high ground, fully loaded, and ready to blow Rupert's confused and crumbling Maginot Line to dust.

∎

In person, Rupert, as he had been in most engagements during his storied and stormy career, was disarming and intelligent. The plaintiff lawyers who attended the deposition were asked afterward if he seemed fully "there," fully "with it," in the manner that you'd ask about a ninety-two-year-old relative you haven't visited in a while. Their answers were unequivocal: Rupert showed no signs of being senile.

Since Rupert never gave interviews anymore, the testimony was a rare window into his private life. "I'm a journalist at heart," he told Nelson, or more specifically, a newspaperman, still obsessed with print. "I read my newspapers a lot more than I watch television," he said, naming *The Wall Street Journal*, *The Times* of London, and the *New York Post* as the three he followed. He said he also checked the *Drudge Report*, "to see if I've missed something," and skimmed gossipy sites like the *Mail Online*. "I don't watch Fox News enough, or as much as I should," he volunteered. During the deposition he mixed up the names of hosts; said "I don't talk to Sean [Hannity] very often"; and refrained from talking about Fox's shows except to brag about their high ratings. To hear this billionaire tell it, he was merely a bystander at his own company:

"Sir, when you speak, you understand that, just like EF Hutton, people listen?"

"I don't really think so."

"You don't think that people listen to your voice?"

"I think my influence over other publishers is greatly overestimated."

"Do you think your influence within Fox is greatly overestimated?"

"By the outside world, yes."

But Nelson brought along ample evidence of Rupert's influence: evidence that he banned Steve Bannon from Fox's air; that he mobilized Fox assets to help Republicans win Senate races; that he wanted to tamp down Fox News coverage of the Colin Kaepernick kneeling controversy because of Fox Corp's broadcasting deal with the NFL.

On January 20, during part two of the proceeding, Nelson once again caught Rupert in a contradiction. One moment Rupert said he was "completely unaware" that ex-anchor Shepard Smith aggressively fact-checked Trump's lies; the next moment, when faced with his own email to Suzanne Scott and Jay Wallace, he said "it looks like I have to amend what I said earlier." He had, in fact, sent a July 15, 2017, email criticizing a Smith fact-check segment as "over the top" and adding, "Need to chat to him." Wallace affirmed: "Will call him in Monday." That's how Rupert operated his mostly hidden hand.

Nelson used this extraordinary opportunity to get Rupert on the record about the former president. "Do you believe President Trump was a sore loser?" Yes. A mad egomaniac? Yes. "You agree that the Republican Party is destroying itself on the altar of Trump?" Yes. Rupert seemed happy to get some of this off his chest, one of the people in the room later commented, to show he understood the true nature of Trump. He was fully "with it," except, curiously, about the subject at hand, Dominion's defamation allegations.

To illustrate his hands-off-ness, Rupert proffered that Scott "took away" Jeanine Pirro's Saturday evening show and shifted Pirro to *The Five* without having "any discussion" with him. I found it curious that Rupert said Pirro, who led "the number one show we had on Saturday," was "cancelled" in early 2022, since it certainly didn't play that way in the press. So I looked into the matter further, and found that yes, Pirro's move was seen internally as a demotion. "Pirro was a problem," two sources said, using the same language and citing what Dominion found through the discovery process, namely that Pirro's stubborn, slavish Trumpiness clashed with Fox execs who'd grown tired of her histrionic shenanigans. She submitted drafts of her opening monologue ahead of time, but when higher-ups dared to suggest tweaks, she was liable to accuse them of censorship. She caused headaches week after week. To put it bluntly, "nobody wanted to deal with her," one of the sources said. Her own executive producer called her a "reckless maniac."

Scott had an open conservative seat on *The Five*, so by moving Pirro there, she solved two problems at once. Pirro was far easier to manage on a five-person talk show—she wasn't writing monologues or picking guests anymore. She was also reaching a larger audience, five days a week, than she was on Saturdays. But it was pointed out to me that *The Five* is not the cushiest job for a seventy-something former prosecutor to hold. Pirro was now in the studio five days a week and sharing the stage with the likes of the grandstanding Jesse Watters. Solo-hosting once a week was definitely easier for her—but harder on the managers and lawyers.

Back to the deposition. Rupert's invocation of Pirro gave Nelson an opening. Nelson asked, "Do you know that, in November of 2020,

Jeanine Pirro's executive producer said that she should never be on live television again?" No, Rupert said, "I had not heard that." That piqued Nelson's interest because the Pirro criticism was included in a legal filing that Dominion submitted several days earlier. He asked: "Have you read Dominion's summary judgment motion, sir?"

"No."

"Have you read our complaint?"

"No. I mean, Mr. Dinh has been . . . No, I don't think he's told us in that detail."

■

Throughout the deposition, Rupert insisted that Fox was merely relaying the news. Regarding the bogus anti-Dominion charges, he said, "We only report what was going on. That's all. We didn't state them. They were not our charges."

Newsworthiness. That was Fox's main talking point, the crux of their defense. When the president says something, says anything, "it is news," Rupert said, doing his version of huffing his own gas.

Yet the mogul also emphasized the difference between Fox's anchors and arguers. Pirro "is not involved in reading news," he testified, contra Pirro, who repeatedly called herself a "reporter" and "newsperson."

No matter what you called Pirro, many key Fox figures went far beyond disinterested reporting. They demanded action. They made Trumpworld's charges their crusade too. They endorsed the lies. Could Nelson get Rupert to admit that?

He tried toward the end of day two, asking, "We just looked at examples, sir, of Fox hosts endorsing these lies, correct?"

"No," Rupert said, shrugging it off as "two or three hours."

"Was it wrong for Fox hosts to endorse these lies?"

"If they knew they were lies, yes. If they knew."

Dan Webb was in the room to advocate on Rupert's behalf, so when Nelson completed his cross-exam, Webb spent about fifteen minutes asking his own questions. This is known as "redirect." Webb used it to underline the newsworthiness defense and Rupert's distance from the delinquents in New York. Rupert said he was holed up in the United Kingdom "under Covid lockdown" in November and December 2020, and his TVs were not working well. "I constantly asked our IT people to come out and fix it, and they didn't," he said.

This cop-out was a precursor to the most devastating part of the testimony. Because when Webb opted for redirect, Nelson had the opportunity for "re-cross," that is, re-cross-examine the witness. As one observer remarked to me later, "In the last five minutes, Rupert destroyed their entire defense."

"Sir," Nelson said, "you are aware that, prior to President Trump saying a word about Dominion, Maria Bartiromo aired charges about Dominion on her November 8th, 2020, broadcast?"

"Prior to Trump saying anything?"

"Yes, sir."

Nelson brought up guests like Powell and Giuliani. "You are aware now that Fox did more than simply host these guests and give them a platform, correct?"

Two days' worth of evidence washed over Rupert. "I think you've shown me some material in support of that," he admitted.

And here was Nelson's chance. "In fact," he said, "you are now aware that Fox endorsed at times this false notion of a stolen election?"

"Not Fox, no," Rupert said. "Not Fox. But maybe Lou Dobbs, maybe Maria, as commentators."

Nelson started naming names. Bartiromo? "Yes, c'mon," Rupert said. Pirro? "I think so." Dobbs? "Oh, a lot." Hannity? "A bit."

Then Nelson harked back to a document he showed Rupert earlier in the day titled "Instances of Talent Support for the 'Stolen Election' Narrative and Belief That Congress Would Change Electoral Votes on January the 6th." Irena Briganti's PR team had pulled it together in late January 2021 when Rupert wanted to know if some of his hosts, not just guests, "fed the story that the election was stolen" and that January 6 was "an important chance to have the result overturned."

In asking the question, Rupert appeared to be quoting someone else's assessment—but didn't say whose. My reporting indicates that he was reacting to criticism from his friend Mitch McConnell, whom he was visiting at the time. We're "still getting mud thrown at us!" he wrote to Scott, as if Fox was squeaky clean and unaccustomed to dirt-diving. Then Rupert asked, channeling McConnell, is it "unarguable that high-profile Fox voices fed" the Big Lie?

Briganti sent back seventeen pages of transcripts that implied the answer was yes.

Nelson said the document showed "Fox endorsing the narrative of a stolen election."

"No," Rupert said. "Some of our commentators were endorsing it."

"About their endorsement of a stolen election?"

"Yes. They endorsed."

"Okay. Sir, I appreciate your time."

Nelson had what he needed: the head of the company shredding the company's legal defense. And Rupert knew it. "Are we done?" he huffed. "We are done," Nelson said. "Thank you."

As the phalanx of attorneys prepared to leave the conference room, Dinh reassured Rupert that the deposition went well. "They didn't lay a finger on you," Dinh said, according to an eyewitness.

Rupert knew when a subordinate was blowing smoke in his direction. He pointed at Nelson and said "I think Mr. Nelson would strongly disagree with that."

"Indeed, I do," Nelson said.

■

Fox's stable of talent, at least the A-listers, got a heads-up about what the discovery process dredged up in the Dominion suit. "They're going to call us hypocrites," an exec warned, by juxtaposing private doubts about fraud with public shouts about it. It was likened to "a seven-layer cake of shit." And it would be served through "summary judgment," the final big step before a jury hears a civil case like *Dominion v. Fox.* Each side stepped forward and argued that the other side's case was so weak that the judge should rule in their favor and avert a trial.

For Dominion, summary judgment briefs were the #1 way to force reams of evidence into public view—a key step toward accountability. Judge Davis limited each side to 45,000 words. "They were big briefs, but they could have been even bigger," Stephen Shackelford told me. Dominion included scores of quotes they had culled from internal Fox documents—the cringier, the better—and snippets from the late 2022 depositions. When the first set of documents was made public on February 16, it was a wild free-for-all in the media. Headlines about the filings were exactly the distasteful dessert the exec had expected:

"Fox News Hosts Called 2020 Election Fraud 'Total BS' in Private"
"Off the Air, Fox News Stars Blasted the Election Fraud Claims They Peddled"

*"Tucker Carlson and Fox News Knew Election Fraud Claims Were
Bogus"*

Fox PR pushed back aggressively, saying Dominion had "cherry-
picked quotes" and larded up the filing with facts that were embarrassing for Fox but irrelevant for proving actual malice. (True!)

Carlson, always freelancing, had his own response to the bad
press. It was to reassure viewers that he still genuinely shared their
doubts about Biden's legitimacy. He opened his show by wondering
out loud, in his aren't-I-the-cleverest-little-boy-ever way, how "did senile hermit Joe Biden get 15 million more votes than his former boss,
rock star, crowd surfer Barack Obama?"

"Results like that would seem to defy the laws of known physics and
qualify instead as a miracle," he said. "Was the 2020 election a miracle?"

Carlson knew the Dominion disclosures would keep raining
down during the lead-up to trial—and he had a canny piece of
counterprogramming up his sleeve. Some of his producers were already on Capitol Hill, secretly viewing surveillance footage from the
January 6 attack, courtesy of his new, obsequiously grateful ally: the
freshly anointed House Speaker, Kevin McCarthy.

■

Feeling somewhat freed by the midterm results, and emboldened by
the Dominion filings, the Biden White House began to take some
harder swings at Fox. It was yet another form of accountability—public
shaming. On February 17 Carlson's producers decided to be offended by
White House Press Secretary Karine Jean-Pierre's comment seven days
earlier that newly promoted White House aide Ben LaBolt "will be the
first openly gay communications director, which is very very important."

Carlson researcher Benno Kass emailed Jean-Pierre (a frequent target of Carlson's sneering scorn) and asked, "Can you explain why the administration thinks Mr. LaBolt's sexual orientation is so important? We plan on covering this tonight."

It was a promise of a kick in the teeth, disguised as a request for comment. Jean-Pierre forwarded it to deputy press secretary Andrew Bates, who decided to kick back. He replied three hours before airtime with the following statement:

"As Karine said, over a 20-year career Ben has earned the strongest credentials any person could have to be White House communications director. For much of our history, regardless of their individual excellence, hard-working Americans were legally refused employment and even fired just because of who they were. We believe in breaking barriers. And we stand against discrimination, just like we stand against firing journalists for honoring their responsibility to tell the truth. Apparently, you disagree with us on both counts."

Bates added, "I hope y'all have the courage to use it in full." (Unbeknownst to the White House, Fox PR routinely asked for the same treatment—"please use the statement in full"—when dealing with reporters.)

To no one's surprise, Carlson's show did not quote a single word of the statement; instead, he implied the White House ignored his request for comment and proceeded to mock Biden and anyone else who stood up for the value of representation. His dishonesty, and further disclosures from the Dominion suit, motivated Bates to continue the trolling. Months later, in an exchange with a Fox writer over a story about Biden's advanced age, Bates wrote, "I go back and forth on whether these stories are born out of Fox News executives trying to send a signal to y'all's 92-year-old chairman, or that 92-year-old chairman's frustrations with the political successes of a younger man running an exponentially more complex operation."

People inside the house Rupert built also found humor in the network's incessant "Biden's too old to govern" narrative. When Carlson delivered a Biden-bashing monologue about powerful older men in decline who "get bursts of irrational energy" and make embarrassing decisions (like an ill-conceived marriage) while "raging against the dying of the light," more than one Fox person snickered that it could have been an exact description of Rupert too. By February 27, when the damning quotes from his depo were revealed in another Dominion filing, he was making plans to propose to Ann Lesley Smith. Meantime, his sweetheart's favorite host was on the network he controlled saying that "82-year-old men should not be running countries" because "they're not strong enough mentally or physically." Happy 92nd birthday, Rupert.

"Tell Tucker to stop"

"We're about to show you surveillance footage from inside the United States Capitol," Carlson proclaimed on March 6. Then he began to lie. "Virtually no one in Washington, Republican or Democrat, certainly not in the news media, wanted to see this tape released," he claimed. In fact, numerous news outlets had been petitioning for the tapes for months. Police body cam footage and other vantage points of the attack *had* been released through various court proceedings. Carlson was hyping what amounted to the leftovers.

The result was as predictable as it was pathetic. Carlson cherry-picked some relatively calm scenes from the occupation to deny that an insurrection took place—but no matter how hard he tried, he couldn't erase people's memories. *"Look at these polite protesters"* couldn't negate all the looting and lawbreaking already etched in living color on most Americans' memories.

Carlson's broadcast was almost universally ridiculed, even by some Republicans in Congress; they had lived through the riot, after all, many hiding or running for their lives. The gentlest rapping of Carlson's knuckles, but a smack nonetheless, came from Mitch McConnell, who said Fox's depiction of the riot was a "mistake," as though it was some innocent accident of film editing, not a deliberate distortion of history. U.S. Capitol police chief J. Thomas Manger said more forcefully that Carlson's conclusions were offensive, outrageous, and false. "We agree with the chief," the White House said, and, reaching back for Carlson's most public humiliation, "we also agree with what Fox News's own attorneys and executives have now repeatedly stressed in multiple courts of law: that Tucker Carlson is not credible."

The rest of Fox acted in agreement—other shows almost totally ignored the blatantly deceptive tapes. It was uncanny. It was a sound judgment call though: Carlson wasn't revealing anything new. Still, his "investigation" was newsworthy for two reasons.

First, it showed that the House Speaker really did grovel at Carlson's feet, exactly as Wells had envisioned in January. McCarthy now owed Carlson, and Carlson now owned McCarthy. "The tapes were part of the deal they struck in January," a senior source at Fox told me.

Second, it showed how desperately MAGA media wanted—needed, really—to turn the riot into a "fedsurrection" by government plants, or by the greatest mythic beast since the Great Pumpkin: the deep state. "Tucker was very set on finding an FBI person who was implanted in the crowd," Grossberg said later. Carlson lamented that his footage-review team did not have access to facial recognition software to catch a "fed." Grossberg said she was told to find a lawyer representing a January 6 defendant who would allege such a conspiracy, but she struck out with one attorney who told her, "This is dangerous; tell Tucker to stop." That didn't matter. She said she was commanded by a fellow producer, "Well, find somebody else. Tucker is really intent on this."

A Carlson segment on March 6 recast the so-called QAnon shaman, Jacob Chansley, who pleaded guilty to obstructing the certification of the election, as a harmless, though perhaps a bit eccentric, tourist. Carlson said police officers had "acted as his tour guides." He left out the context that the police were outnumbered 58 to 1 that afternoon, leaving de-escalation as the only realistic option.

Chansley watched Carlson's show and then appealed his case to a federal judge in an attempt to reverse his conviction. He claimed the videos were withheld from his defense attorneys and were "exculpatory." Judge Royce C. Lamberth called that nonsense. "These videos are decidedly not exculpatory," Lamberth wrote in a July ruling that pointed out all the clips that Carlson "conveniently omitted," including Chansley "unlawfully entering the Capitol through a broken door, disobeying orders from law enforcement on more than a half-dozen occasions, screaming obscenities, entering the Senate chamber, climbing onto the Senate dais, sitting in the Vice President's chair, and leaving a threatening message for the Vice President." (Well, Tucker implied he was eccentric.)

Those omissions were more than a mistake by Carlson—they were part of his self-created game: "false flag fraud." Judge Lamberth, a Reagan appointee, lit into the "ill-advised television program," saying Carlson had unfairly questioned "the legitimacy of the entire U.S. criminal justice system with inflammatory characterizations of cherry-picked videos stripped of their proper context."

"In so doing," Lamberth wrote, "he called on his followers to 'reject the evidence of [their] eyes and ears,' language resembling the destructive, misguided rhetoric that fueled the events of January 6 in the first place."

"The court finds it alarming that the host's viewers throughout the nation so readily heeded his command," Lambert added. "But this court cannot and will not reject the evidence before it. Nor should the public." It was a legal way of saying: guilty—and *stop wasting our time.*

■

Carlson would need a lot more than a judge calling him a charlatan to ever reach the level of chastened. He soaked up the media world's attention with his McCarthy tapes, and promised more the next night, March 7. But another story intruded: the release of 556 exhibits that Dominion intended to show at trial. Although the documents were heavily redacted (at Fox's behest) they contained an extraordinary amount of new information. Among the buzzy quotes: Carlson's post-election texts about hating Trump "passionately" and despising Fox's "pathetic" reporters almost as much.

Some Fox staffers believed that Carlson's rollout of the Capitol tapes was not a coincidence, but a smoke screen. Fox's lawyers and execs knew when new tranches of evidence would be made public; presumably Carlson knew too. Fox tried to blunt the impact by delaying document dumps until the end of the business day, 5 p.m., to "game the news cycle," as one source put it, and give reporters less time to read the docs. Carlson, once again one-upping the corporate strategists with his own scheme, played the game his way.

The Fox journalists Carlson derided were mortified both by his egregious journalistic misconduct and the brutal candor in his newly disclosed texts and emails. The combination was a potent poison. Remember Scott's admonition to "respect the audience"? That's what some of Fox's journalists did—to their own career detriment. As correspondent Kristin Fisher said in her deposition, "I believed that

I *was* respecting our audience by telling them the truth." Fisher was sidelined in 2020 after having the audacity to fact-check Giuliani and Trump on election-denying. The March 7 document haul included Fisher's December 2020 text exchange with a fellow correspondent, Gillian Turner, where both women observed that shows like *Fox & Friends* had stopped booking them for live shots. The mornings are "back to being a shit shift again," Turner wrote. "It's a shit network," Fisher wrote back. "I'm 100% being muzzled." She sensed that it was a direct result of her Big Lie debunks. "I'm being punished for doing my job," she wrote. "Literally. That's it."

By 2023 Fisher was long gone from Fox, having landed at CNN covering space, a job that felt to Fisher like the last rocket escaping from a dying planet.

But legitimate journalists like Turner were still at Fox, still striving to make it a place where they could be proud to work. Let's be honest—it kind of sucked to be a reporter with serious intentions at an outfit better known for Republican ragebait and racist great replacement rhetoric. These journalists often felt like they had to suffer for others' sins. Case in point, some producers and writers had to sit through libel law training sessions in January and February, causing attendees to quip that the legal refreshers "came a little bit late." Dominion and Smartmatic were not mentioned by name but, as a producer pointed out to me, "we all knew why we were there." It was like teaching Bill Buckner to stay down on ground balls after the Red Sox had lost the World Series.

Some of the remaining journalists tried gamely but in vain to come up with ways to make a difference. In early March, at least three people in the Fox newsroom called out sick midweek to protest Carlson's misbegotten tapes and management's tolerance of the intolerable. But did management even notice? My impression was no.

However, in a way that's only obvious in retrospect, the Carlson tapes fiasco was a foreshock, a hint of the big shake-up that was coming. Not only did Fox's other shows shrug off the bogus story Carlson hyped, the 6 p.m. *Special Report* newscast actively discredited him.

Senior congressional correspondent Chad Pergram, who was inside the Capitol on January 6, fronted a package about the blowback to Carlson. He included McConnell . . . and the police chief . . . and the Capitol Police's statement that Carlson's show "never reached out to the department to provide accurate context." Pergram knew that this just-the-facts report marked him as an enemy to some of his own colleagues. Carlson was "running around threatening people" before the package aired, a source said. But *Special Report* anchor Bret Baier, who had honed a cordial relationship with Carlson, concluded that Pergram's piece was necessary. Baier, I was told, gave Carlson a courtesy heads-up before it ran. Most strikingly, Baier tagged the package after it aired, saying, "To be clear, no one here at Fox News condones any of the violence that happened on January 6." If you have to specify that, then by definition, you've lost the plot.

■

Ashamed by Carlson's January 6 antics, and wounded by the release of texts showing Carlson and other stars trashing the news side, Fox staffers waited for some confidence boost from management, some rah-rah memo or at least some greasy pizza in the break room. They went hungry. "Our bosses are acting like nothing is happening," one of the perturbed journalists told me. There were perfunctory attempts to smooth things over after the exhibits showed Scott criticizing Fox's journalists for the sin of fact-checking—*"we value you,"* yeah right—but there was no sense of a wartime mobilization. Scott, perhaps shamed into a pillar of salt, stayed silent while the network needed defending, giving her critics another reason to argue that her leadership skills were lacking (or nonexistent). On the other hand, what could she possibly say to raise morale in the face of universal professional scorn?

A settlement with Dominion before the evidence became public would have averted so much ignominy. But only the Murdochs were authorized to write such a prodigious check. Even after Rupert's face-flattening deposition, and with the April 17 trial date rapidly approaching, Murdochworld still could not get serious about settling. Yes, they started to entertain the notion in February, according to a source; but their focus in March was on the summary judgment process. (Excluding Rupert, whose goo-goo-eyed focus was on his engagement.) Dan Webb, the Winston & Strawn lawyer brought in by Fox, and his associates had another chance to persuade Judge Davis at a two-day hearing.

Davis mostly just listened, but when he spoke, he revealed doubts about Fox's case. When Fox cited the "neutral reportage" doctrine to advance its newsworthiness argument, Davis brought up the anything-but-neutral Lou Dobbs and asked, "You're saying he's a neutral reporter?" "There seems to be a Dobbs problem, sometimes," the judge added. The fact that Fox fired Dobbs one day after the first lawsuit had not solved the problem.

When Dominion attorney Justin Nelson presented his arguments before the judge, he said Rupert and Lachlan had to be considered responsible for defamers like Dobbs: "They made the decision to let it happen." Nelson needed to make sure that Fox Corp, not just the Fox News division, was fully liable in the case. He was thinking ahead to the expected trial, where he was very much looking forward to cross-examining Rupert again, this time in front of a jury. Rupert's lawyers were already filing motions to stop that from happening, arguing that making a ninety-two-year-old mogul fly (private) to (gasp!) Delaware was an undue burden (though apparently Barbardos was no problem) and that the previously recorded deposition was sufficient. As a practical matter, lawyers will tell you that jurors tend to tune out videotaped testimony. ("If you play 20 minutes of a deposition, juries start to fall asleep," one of the Dominion lawyers quipped.) So Nelson needed Davis to compel Rupert to get on that Gulfstream, and on the hearing's second day, Davis hinted that he would.

Fox's strongest arguments, if any existed, were about the amount of money at stake. The network took shots at Dominion's "opportunistic private equity owners" at every opportunity. Fox said the damages figure was based on "questionable testimony" from an accountant who predicted Dominion would lose all of its customers in the next decade—even though Dominion landed several big new contracts after the 2020 election. Fox's arguments against the $1.6 billion amount were persuasive, but also inadvertently revealing, because they were reduced to disputing not *whether* Dominion was hurt, but *how badly*.

∎

As I reconstructed the case and interviewed the lawyers, I came to the conclusion that Dominion won three times. The first victory was achieved through the summary judgment motions in February and March, which pushed a vast quantity of evidence into public view, sparking weeks of media coverage of Fox and misery inside the network. The second victory was on March 31, when Judge Davis ruled on summary judgment. He said the case would indeed proceed to trial, but made an all-caps pronouncement in Dominion's favor. "The evidence developed in this civil proceeding demonstrates that [it] is CRYSTAL clear that none of the statements relating to Dominion about the 2020 election are true," he wrote. "Therefore, the court will grant summary judgment in favor of Dominion on the element of falsity."

Dominion's team was overjoyed by that paragraph. A court ruled in all caps that Dominion wasn't the vote-flipping villain that Trumpworld thought it was. Conspiracy theorists might never believe the truth about Dominion, but as a matter of law, it was now settled.

Davis also ruled that the "neutral reportage" defense could not even be argued at trial. He noted that the evidence did not support the claim that Fox "conducted good-faith, disinterested reporting"— far from it. When the ruling came down, a Dominion insider texted me and said, "this is as thorough a loss [for Fox] as you will see." But Fox, incredibly, magically, still believed it could turn up in court with a shoeshine and a smile, holding a hand full of deuces and threes and sevens, and find some other card to play—a press card, maybe.

"I am your retribution"

Donald Trump, known for many things but not his appreciation of American jurisprudence, nor his spelling, claimed to be certain of how Fox could beat Dominion in court. "RUPERT," he wrote in all caps on Truth Social to his erstwhile booster, "JUST TELL THE TRUTH AND GOOD THINGS WILL HAPPEN. THE ELECTION OF 2020 WAS RIGGED AND STOLLEN . . .YOU KNOW IT, & SO DOES EVERYONE ELSE!"

Never mind that he misspelled stolen. Never mind that Judge Davis had studied all the evidence pertaining to Dominion and ruled that Fox *couldn't* cry "rigged," even if tempted. Trump, who never met a losing legal argument that he didn't like, thought it was a sure thing, the way forward. He truthed:

> *IF FOX WOULD FINALLY ADMIT THAT THERE WAS LARGE SCALE CHEATING & IRREGULARITIES IN THE 2020 PRESIDENTIAL ELECTION, WHICH WOULD BE A GOOD THING FOR THEM, & FOR AMERICA, THE CASE AGAINST THEM, WHICH SHOULD NOT HAVE EXISTED AT ALL, WOULD BE GREATLY WEAKENED. BACK UP THOSE PATRIOTS AT FOX INSTEAD OF THROWING THEM UNDER THE BUS—& THEY ARE RIGHT! THERE IS SOOO MUCH PROOF . . .*

This screech was the shoutiest, loud-mouthiest of Trump's comments about *Dominion v. Fox*, but he had been clamoring about it for months. Trump had been in touch with Maria Bartiromo, I was told, which explained why he said the hosts who "got it right" (meaning who got it wrong and spread his lies) "SHOULD BE ADMIRED & PRAISED, NOT REBUKED & FORSAKEN!!!"

"Forsaken?" Bartiromo was still on the air licking his boots.

Trump posted over and over, calling Fox News "the RINO Network"; bashing Fox Corp board member Paul Ryan; and even putting them in the axis of evil next to CNN, saying "they are aiding & abetting the DESTRUCTION OF AMERICA with FAKE NEWS." The proximate cause of all this hair-pulling emoting was Fox's continued promotion of the man Trump name-called "Ron DeSanctimonious."

■

DeSantis wasn't officially running against Trump yet, but as he prepared for his presidential campaign, he made the case to donors that he was younger, less morally compromised, and more results-oriented than Trump; and for a cherry on top, he had a much better grip on the Fox machine. DeSantis told benefactors about his visit to Rupert's ranch in Montana and his regular appearances up and down the network. "I have won the Tucker primary," he told confidants in early 2023, according to a source. His declaration turned out to be embarrassingly premature, but the phraseology was revealing: In past Republican races, reporters paid close attention to what everyone called the "Fox primary"—whom would the network dub their latest champion? But Carlson now superseded all that, at least in the eyes of one top candidate.

DeSantis certainly benefited from slavering promotion across Rupert's media properties: the *New York Post* never passed up a chance to promote the glories of DeSancitified Florida; News Corp's publishing division released the governor's Woke-Warrior brand-burnishing book; and then DeSantis did the full Fox star-junket tour to sell copies. One show mattered more than all the rest. Despite his midterm screw-ups, Carlson was Broadway, center stage, the unique spotlight for the primary process. Vivek Ramaswamy proved it: In February the venture capitalist and another soldier in the anti-woke army traveled to Carlson's remote studio in Florida to announce his (long-shot) presidential bid. Ramaswamy wanted to start his campaign on Carlson's show, in person, paying respect to the host, and seeking the jefe's blessing. Candidates feared winding up like Nikki Haley, whom Carlson derided at length.

In March, in the ultimate flex of Carlson's power, his show sent out a six-part questionnaire to thirteen GOP hopefuls to test their position on Ukraine. It was a clear attempt to pressure them into supporting Carlson's isolationist, anti-Ukraine, pro-Russia position. (Even Carlson remarked on it being "kind of presumptuous for a cable show" to push candidates this way, but of course he was wearing his presumption like an opera scarf.) He noted that Haley and four others declined to play along, but all the top contenders responded. And it was DeSantis who made the most news, by casting the war as a "territorial dispute" that was not in America's vital interests. Carlson rewarded him on the air with clear praise for his positions. But the reality was that Trump was still the hands-down favorite in the "Tucker primary."

■

"Tucker should get a prize," Trump opined from the stage at CPAC in March. Trump was in the middle of one of his standard riffs about the "Russia hoax" . . . and why he was suing the newspapers that won Pulitzer Prizes for exposing his ties to Russia . . . and how right-wing talking heads should get prizes instead. "Frankly, Jesse should get a prize, Jesse should," he added. Everyone in the hall knew which Jesse he was talking about, Fox's Jesse Watters.

This speech made both headline and head-shaking news for Trump's declaration/promise/threat that he would use a second term in office to punish his enemies and seek vengeance. "In 2016, I declared I am your voice," he said. "Today, I add I am your warrior, I am your justice. And for those who have been wronged and betrayed, I am your retribution. I AM YOUR RETRIBUTION."

All that was missing was a crash of thunder and some lightning effect, with Trump standing in a spotlight holding a sword and a scepter. Trump was presenting himself as a god of vengeance, ready to smite the terrible enemies of the simple folk, super-demons like Joe Biden and Nancy Pelosi. Trump's perception of what played to the audience of the right remained unerring. They were eternally afflicted by big media, and Hollywood, and academia, feminists, socialists, humanists, and all those other "ists," the ones preaching tolerance and equality. Trump embraced the permanent victimhood of his followers; they were "wronged and betrayed" by the elites and dark forces. As other voices from another era had summed it up: "stabbed in the back."

But Trump would come back to make them all pay. There would be retribution. That was the ultimate goal of his new campaign. Not a better economy, or peace on earth. Payback.

And, he implied, it would be wild.

These proclamations further tightened the bonds between Trump and his base. Trump's supporters "feel protected by him, but they feel protective OF him," scholar Ruth Ben-Ghiat said, identifying a duality in autocratic leaders that "has been present since Mussolini." Yes, we see you standing on balconies sticking your jaw out, preening like a goose-stepping peacock, but you'll bully the people we don't like, and arrest them when you feel like it. We'll back you to the end. Retribution was exactly what Fox had primed the MAGA audience to crave.

Fox carried the entire Trump speech from start to finish, and it lit up an otherwise dismal Saturday ratings scoreboard. Trump attracted 1.6 million viewers in a time slot that usually averaged 1 million. Trump's aides saw these ratings boosts as signs of strength while I regarded it as a hint of weakness; he couldn't even double Fox's baseline audience.

Still, it had to be scored as a win for Trump. Fox had put the CPAC speech on the air. Trump was looking more like a person on

Fox again, or at least the outline of a person; not back yet in the full embrace of Fox and its friends, anchors, and execs, but within reach of the hug.

Rupert was asked during his deposition about this dynamic, and he revealed, "I have said we shouldn't be covering every single Trump rally. But I didn't say we were barring him." Thus, the "soft" quality of the soft ban.

Sources at Fox told me that a "no phoners" edict came down in 2022. It meant that Trump could no longer call in to chat with his Fox friends in his socks. "He's the former president," an insider said. "He should be on camera." Trump stomped his feet; he felt he didn't look "presidential" doing interviews via satellite, stuffed into a box like any other ordinary B-block guest.

The Trump interview blockade ended when Hannity came to Mar-a-Lago to interview him on March 27. Hannity exchanged a soft ban for soft ball, giving his hero an hour of slo-pitch to show the mighty Trumpy hadn't lost his bat speed. The agenda was easy to discern from the questions: allow Trump to exonerate himself from the criminal accusations swirling around his head.

Too bad for Sean, Trump had other things in that head. The former president was his own worst enemy.

When Hannity offered up a sitting duck of an out for the charges that Trump had pilfered classified documents, hid them in his Mar-a-Lago club, and thwarted polite government entreaties to return them, Trump refused to (or just plain couldn't) see it Sean's way.

"I can't imagine you ever saying, 'Bring me some of the boxes that we brought back from the White House. I'd like to look at them.'" Hannity pitched out the words like lines from a prearranged script. "Did you ever do that?"

Instead of following the obvious cue with "Of course not,

Sean! I follow the law to the letter!" Trump fell immediately into defendant-at-trial mode, saying, "I would have the right to do that. There's nothing wrong with it."

Hannity, still trying to push Trump into a lifeboat, came back with: "But I know you. I don't think you would do it."

That made Hannity a member of a very exclusive club of people who, despite years of experience and myriad examples, still didn't believe or accept that Trump would do whatever the hell he wanted no matter what incidentals like the rules or the law required. So Trump tried to disabuse his acolyte of his delusions.

"I *would* do that," Trump said, as though lecturing a fifth-grader. "There would be nothing wrong."

Hannity's trust in Trump's character was a little like a guy with a pet tiger, stroking his orange coat and saying, "I know you. I don't think you'd turn on me and maul me to pieces . . ."

Days later, Trump was indicted by the Manhattan DA, in one of his other looming cases, the hush money for porn star case. Virtually the entire Republican Party rushed to his defense, crying political foul—and of course, casting Trump as a victim. That was a production Fox simply could not resist joining. He was fully "personed" again.

Picture a rubber band: No matter how hard one side is pulled, the two sides almost always snap back together. That's how I pictured Trump and Fox. Every attempt to pull apart was stymied by physics. With Trump facing arrest, Fox snapped right back into place, both siding with Trump and fully welcoming him back into the fold. There was just one difference from 2020: Trump interviews could not be live. They would always be taped so that anything borderline-defamatory could be edited out before airtime. Fox wouldn't get Dominioned again.

"Search for the truth"

As *Dominion v. Fox* gathered hyper-charged momentum as its trial date approached, lawyers for the voting machine company agonized over every potential pothole and speed bump, not to mention the prospect of a few jurors getting the sniffles. "We're all keeping our fingers crossed that the jury stays healthy," Stephen Shackelford told me on April 6, the day Susman Godfrey's paralegals began to arrive in Wilmington to set up the team's "war room."

A mistrial—whether because of juror illness or some intractable conflict—was a very real concern. Dominion's team believed that Fox was angling for a mistrial by insisting on having only six alternate jurors, rather than the full slate of twelve that Dominion wanted. (Davis eventually decided to seat twelve alternatives anyway, Fox's objections be damned.)

An anomalous damages award—in either direction—was also a concern. What if the jury found Fox liable for actual malice, but one or two jurors—maybe Tucker fans?—were swayed by Fox's arguments that Dominion wasn't worth all that much? Conversely, what if the jury wanted to make a statement against the democracy-degrading effects of the Big Lie, and awarded Dominion even more than $1.6 billion? Anything could happen in the jury room. Davis could feel compelled to knock down the damages total. "We, both sides, knew that damages was gonna be a big focus of this case," Fox's attorney Dan Webb said.

The uncertainties didn't end there. On Dominion's side, Tom Clare said "we knew that Dan and his team were playing for an appeal." It was almost as if Rupert and Lachlan were resigned to a loss in Delaware but reassured, again by Viet Dinh, that they'd win in the end, at the Supreme Court. The judge's ruling about falsity, stripping it from trial, "could have been the card that got this case to the United States Supreme Court," Webb said.

Given all the unknowns, I could see why a guaranteed sum of money now—in the form of a settlement—would be superior to a possibly higher but maybe lower and potentially nullified windfall years later. But Dominion still wasn't quite there mentally. And Fox wasn't ready to guarantee anything yet. So it was time to bring the rolling briefcases to Wilmington.

■

Anyone who's driven through Wilmington, or ridden in by rail on President Biden's beloved Amtrak, knows that "city" is an over-statement for its squat downtown. Law firms handling lengthy trials usually gravitated to the same two hotels, Hotel Du Pont and the Doubletree, and that's how it worked in April—Fox Corp set up camp at the fancier Du Pont and Dominion at the more practical Doubletree, which offered a first-floor legal suite with private offices, workstations, and a conference room. Dominion had at least a full floor of the hotel booked solid for all six expected weeks of trial. Lawyers arrived en masse on April 9 because pre-trial conference hearings got under way on Tuesday, April 11. If you think those hearings sound boring, think again, because Judge Davis used the occasion to disembowel Fox for hiding information from him.

"What do I do with attorneys that aren't straightforward with me?" he wondered aloud. He said "omission is a lie."

See, Fox had neglected to mention that Rupert was, in addition to his well-established positions at Fox Corp and News Corp, officially the "executive chair" of Fox News. That fact would have undercut all the attempts to insulate Rupert from the Dominion disaster—so no wonder it was skirted past for months. Dominion's interrogator, Justin Nelson, had even inquired about it when Rupert was under oath, and Rupert initially said, "No. My son is the chief executive of everything at Fox," then, perhaps remembering he was under oath, changed his answer to "I don't know. It is a separate company. The news network is a subsidiary. I may have had that title in the past. I may have it now, I don't know."

On Easter Sunday, Fox, under pressure from Judge Davis, belatedly disclosed to Dominion that Rupert was, in fact, contractually an officer of Fox News. Davis was incensed. "It has been represented to me more than once that he is not an officer," he said, and had made his rulings accordingly. If he had known the whole truth, he might have given more leeway to Dominion during the discovery process. Nelson hammered that point home at the hearing: "We have been litigating based upon this false premise that Rupert Murdoch wasn't an officer of Fox News!"

Fox tried to say that Rupert's title was merely "honorific," but the company documents said otherwise. Dominion's team believed the other side had been deliberately lying, and the judge seemed to be of the same mind. "You have a credibility problem," Davis said to one of the Fox litigators.

The exasperated judge decided to sanction Fox and appointed a special master to probe whether Fox withheld key documents or misled the court.

Why had Fox taken the risk of alienating the judge and inviting sanctions? Observers concluded that exposing Rupert to further questioning was an even bigger risk.

Grossberg's lawsuit was one more pain point. She filed against

Fox, alleging unlawful discrimination and retaliation, in mid-March, one month after Dominion's summary judgment brief showed her telling Bartiromo in 2020 that "our audience doesn't want to hear about a peaceful transition," among other embarrassing texts. Employees at Carlson's show, and elsewhere at Fox, believed she filed suit to save face—to publicly break from her Trump-indulging past to help her odds of being hired elsewhere. But she claimed she was coerced by Fox to provide misleading testimony and she now wanted to correct the record. At deposition, she was asked, "If someone says something untrue on one of your shows, do you think it's important to correct it?" She said "no." In March she made a court filing to change her answer to "yes," adding, "it was Maria's responsibility to push back against untrue statements with facts or follow-up questions."

After filing suit and changing her deposition answers, Grossberg went on NBC and said the harassment at Fox was so severe that she contemplated suicide and called a crisis prevention hotline. "I thought I could just walk in front of a car and I wouldn't have to go to work tomorrow," she said. Some of my sources at Fox, while dismissing her "coercion" charge, admitted that the claims she made about Carlson's workplace were disturbing. And in an echo of Gretchen Carlson's legal strategy that helped bring down Roger Ailes in 2016, Grossberg said she had tapes.

Grossberg routinely taped her pre-interviews with guests who were slated to be interviewed on TV. Those recordings and others were uploaded to Otter, a web platform for voice transcription. But not all of them wound up in Dominion's possession during discovery, so Grossberg did Dominion a solid by publicizing their existence. She then went a big step further and gave MSNBC some audio snippets, including one of Bartiromo speaking off air with Rudy Giuliani on

November 8, 2020, the day Bartiromo infamously smeared Dominion for the first time.

"What about this software," Bartiromo said, "this Dominion software?" "That's a little harder," Giuliani said, exposing his empty hand. "Seems troubling," she said. "It's being analyzed right now," he claimed weakly.

An impartial observer might conclude that Grossberg's legal filings and interviews and leaks were all calculated to maximize a payout from Fox at a time when the network was maximally vulnerable. But that's often how the legal world works. At the end of June, Grossberg dropped the suits and accepted a cushy $12 million settlement, and Fox stopped disputing her claims against the network. On the twentieth floor of Fox News HQ, where Carlson's former staffers still resided, there were "literally people cursing out loud at their screens" when the payout was reported, a source told me. Hardworking, loyal producers were lucky to land a 1 or 2 percent raise in the current climate. And Grossberg walked away with $12 million because management "wanted the Tucker story to go away," the source said. "It's just such a slap in the face."

The ugly reality for the network was that Grossberg had damning evidence about the poisonous climate at *Tucker Carlson Tonight*, and Fox wanted to prevent yet another potential trial, the same fear that had motivated the $20 million payout to Gretchen Carlson seven years earlier. "You don't pay $12 [million] without serious evidence" against you, Gretchen tweeted.

Inside Fox, Ailes's ghost, dragging chains of sexual transgressions, still haunted the place. Some Fox old-timers argued that the Dominion scandal, which involved a relatively small number of employees but discredited everyone, was proof of a post-Ailes leadership vacuum. "If Roger were still here," one said, "this never would have happened." When I raised this idea with one of Suzanne Scott's allies, they shot back, "Roger was too busy harassing women to lead anything."

The Fox chain of command was important, but Dominion's lawyers were focused on the very top, since Rupert had admitted to culpability—at least by omission—during his deposition. Nelson posited, "You could have said to Suzanne Scott or to the hosts, 'Stop putting Rudy Giuliani on the air'?" and Rupert said, "I could have. But I didn't."

Dominion's lawyers anticipated that Rupert would either repeat what he said under oath, or try to squirm his way out of it, at which point Dominion could show the video of his depo and ask why he was changing his testimony.

"If a jury is sympathetic to an argument that, 'Yeah, this was newsworthy,' but the chairman of the company is admitting that what they did was wrong, then that's a really powerful argument to the jury," Shackelford told me as he prepared to deliver his opening argument.

Since the case revolved around proof of actual malice—meaning "with knowledge that it was false or with reckless disregard"—it all came down to state of mind. "We basically get 20 at-bats," Shackelford said, since the lawsuit identified twenty times Dominion was defamed. "My bet is that the jury is going to get comfortable with some time period when they all had to know." Of course, he thought the date should be November 7, when Bartiromo received the undeniably "wackadoodle" email, but let's say it was November 12, when Dominion sent the first "Setting the Record Straight" fact-check, or November 16, when PR exec Tony Fratto directly appealed to Scott and Wallace and said "this situation is crossing dangerous lines." On that timeline, Dominion could still prevail on nearly twenty counts. And Fratto was going to be the first witness at trial. Nelson and Peaslee were already preparing the questions.

Shackelford called Fratto's early intervention "one of the most amazing facts" of the case: "Here's a guy saying 'please stop this' to the CEO and they still let it go on for weeks and weeks? That was crazy to me."

The second witness was going to be Rupert, and the third was going to be Carlson, not because a blue state jury would recoil in horror, but because these guys would almost surely undermine Fox Corp's case. "Tucker was going to trash Sidney Powell," a source said, "and he was going to undermine the other witnesses."

Shackelford was so confident that he took pains not to sound cocky. I asked what he was worried about, and he said he felt consternation that "people who watch Fox are never going to hear about this." (There would be no cameras permitted in the courtroom.) For all the money at stake—potentially life-changing money for some of the execs and investors and lawyers—he and his colleagues also wanted this trial to be the ultimate set-the-record-straight moment.

■

On Fox's side, Webb, at this point, still saw a wide pathway forward for his client. "I actually believed in and tested my theories with jury research," he said afterward, and "I had a compelling story to tell." In his opening statement, Webb would say that Trump's voter fraud claims were "the most newsworthy story of 2020," so extraordinary that "you had to cover it." And so Fox did, for a "short period of time," about thirty days, while Trump sought recourse from the courts. He would argue that Fox acted reasonably, not maliciously. And he would say a noun a verb and "the First Amendment" a lot.

Webb spent days preparing each Fox host for cross-examination. His plan was to portray them as innocent spectators who couldn't possibly know whether fraud was committed. "Tucker and Hannity and Maria and others, they were gonna basically explain, Fox was in a search for the truth," he explained.

To which Dominion responded: Bring it on. "We were very careful about the statements that we sued on," Clare said. The twenty at-bats were about wild claims that were *not* put forward by MAGA lawyers in court. For Dominion, Clare said, the issue "wasn't *why* Fox was talking about these allegations, but *how*." The jury would have to answer two big questions: whether Fox was guilty of actual malice and whether Dominion incurred any damages.

Once jury selection began on Thursday, Judge Davis privately urged Dominion and Fox to settle. He had been on the bench for a decade. He was a partner at Skadden, Arps earlier in his career. He knew that the sight of twelve jurors in a box was the supreme catalyst for settlements. At his behest, Nelson and Webb held several phone calls, but they were hundreds of millions of dollars apart. For a while Fox was only going as high as $550 million—which, in any other context, would be an earthshaking payout; but that was only a third of what Dominion demanded when it sued in 2021.

Shackelford, who spent the weekend in his ninth-floor suite at the Doubletree refining his opening argument, knew about the talks, "but honestly," he said, "I thought it was not going to lead to anything." He practiced his open, which was clocking in at a way-too-long one hour and forty-five minutes, in front of Hootan Yaghoobzadeh and a small group of colleagues, and figured out ways to streamline it.

In his open, Shackelford, with Yaghoobzadeh's encouragement, led with two powerful words from the summary judgment brief: "Fox knew." He made the case that people up and down the Fox chain of command knew the Dominion smears were false and often complete hogwash but let the lies air anyway. (When a liberal activist group drove a billboard truck around Wilmington with the words "FOX KNEW" in bold type, Shackelford cringed, because he didn't want the judge or jury "to think we had anything to do with that.") Then, in his open, he turned to Dominion, the company's role in upholding democracy, and why the company was so valuable heading into the 2020 election. He concluded with a short explanation to the jury about how to assess damages. He rehearsed and rehearsed, five or six times that weekend, knowing that Webb was doing the same over at the Du Pont.

On Sunday night, Judge Davis pushed the start of the trial from Monday to Tuesday. Shackelford knew this meant that Fox was trying hard to settle, but he used the extra day to further refine his opening statement, and he woke up Tuesday morning still believing he would get to deliver it. As he walked the two blocks from the hotel to the courthouse, distracted, he stepped clumsily off a curb and badly twisted his ankle. "Shack took all the break a leg advice a little too literally," an associate joked. He hobbled into court but barely noticed the injury at first because his adrenaline was flowing. It was finally happening: The jurors were seated, the court was in session, the feature presentation was about to begin. Curtain up; light the lights.

And then . . . everyone was excused for lunch. Shackelford ate at the Subway in the courthouse's basement. His ankle was starting to stiffen up, so he paced back and forth, trying to keep it loose, still ready to take one for the team. Court was supposed to resume at 1:30—but lawyers for both parties told Davis they needed more time. Davis knew why. "Having the jury in the box" was the deal-maker, Clare said.

Reporters at the courthouse sat and pre-wrote their stories about a settlement, deducing that one was imminent, but Shackelford held out hope until 3 p.m. By then, he was in serious pain, and he would have been limping while delivering his open. "I thought the jury would be sympathetic," he quipped.

One hour later, the deal was announced and Shackelford was on the courthouse steps with Nelson and Davida Brook. "Today's settlement of $787,500,000 represents vindication and accountability," Nelson said, revealing the price tag to the world.

"It was a flabbergasting figure," one of the people involved in the case told me, "and that was part of the point, to make jaws drop." To make a statement. And, of course, to make Fox shareholders wince. "We wanted them to feel the effects of what they had done," Clare said.

This, for Dominion, was the third and richest victory of all. In discovery, Fox had found a December 2020 text to a Staple Street Capital executive that said it "would be pretty unreal if you guys like 20x'ed your Dominion investment with these lawsuits." Staple Street didn't 20x—the law firms collectively netted well north of $100 million—but it posted an extraordinary return. This was the steepest known defamation award in the history of the American news media. And it was brokered by a man on a Danube River cruise.

■

At least three things happened on Sunday that helped trigger Tuesday's settlement:

First, Webb and Nelson emailed Jerry Roscoe, a veteran mediator who had worked with both their firms in the past, and Roscoe, though remote and afloat, immediately agreed to help.

Second, the Murdochs loosened up the company wallet and agreed to pay more than $550 million to make it all go away. Rupert was said to have soured on his defense team—"we have the wrong lawyers"—since, as you know by now, nothing could ever be his fault.

Third, the Fox Corp board of directors took action. "The untold story of this case," a Murdochworld source said, "is that the board grew a spine." Insiders who, in the past, insulted board members as "cronies" now noticed an independent streak, pointing to two directors in particular: Paul Ryan and hedge funder Anne Dias. Dominion published messages from the two of them in 2020 urging Fox to take a strong stand against the Big Lie. Both Ryan and Dias continued to agitate against Fox's extremist programming, I was told, and Ryan commented publicly in February 2023 about his distaste for Carlson. Of course, board members had to put shareholders' interests ahead of their own political preferences, but Fox's share price was likely to suffer during a trial. Fox's stock was down 20 percent in the four years since it became a standalone company; a more engaged board would be welcome news to mom-and-pop shareholders.

The first shareholder lawsuit relating to Dominion landed on April 11, six days before the expected trial. It exempted Ryan and Dias but roped in the other five people who were directors at the time of the defamation: Rupert; Lachlan; their longtime friend and former Fox Broadcasting CEO Chase Carey; former Telemundo boss Roland A. Hernandez; and former Ford Motor Co. CEO Jacques Nasser. The suit alleged that the board members consciously ignored "numerous red flags from reputable sources that Fox News' election fraud reporting was entirely false" and thereby breached their fiduciary duties.

The board knew that more of these missiles would be fired. Rabble-rousing investors were already using the Dominion case in Delaware as cover to demand internal records like board meeting minutes. It was as if the protesters who held anti-Fox signs outside the network's Manhattan HQ each Tuesday were now gathering on the well-manicured streets outside the directors' homes. It was getting personal.

Inevitably, some of the board members wanted to know: Just how exposed are we? According to a source, the directors asked to see the case exhibits that had been redacted from public view but could be presented at trial. The pile included Carlson's "not how white men fight" text and, at that point, unreported instances when he disparaged female Fox executives. Plus: sensitive messages between Rupert and Suzanne Scott; Sidney Powell's texts with Lou Dobbs, Jeanine Pirro, and Maria Bartiromo; and enough within-the-walls feuding to fuel a high school prom-planning committee.

I should make it abundantly clear that Ryan, Dias, and the rest of the board *could* have viewed these exhibits at any point in February or March, since they were attached to Dominion's summary judgment filings. The assertion that the board only exercised its powers on the eve of trial seemed awfully convenient—to say the least. But some directors may have opted to stay in the dark until the moment they absolutely had to drop the blindfold and see the light.

That moment was Sunday evening. The board—feeling like it needed some serious legal backup—met virtually and agreed to call in Wachtell, Lipton, Rosen & Katz, the same firm that had counseled the directors when Rupert wanted to re-merge the companies.

Four thousand five hundred miles away, Roscoe, the mediator, was hurriedly educating himself about Dominion and Fox. He was gliding down the Danube, aboard an AmaWaterways river cruise from Budapest, Hungary, to Bucharest, Romania, savoring vacation time with his wife. But he surely recognized this mediation gig would pay for a makeup cruise—and many more. Roscoe was seven time zones ahead of Wilmington, but way behind on the nuances of the case. All of a sudden "I was reading a thousand court transcripts and pleadings," he said, so he could impartially assess the situation.

Mediators like Roscoe position themselves as reliable, rigorous analysts who can help dueling parties see a case dispassionately. Think about it: After two years of litigation, Fox and Dominion were understood to be entrenched like warring parties on either side of no-man's-land. The principals and their lawyers had manifold reasons to be filled with emotion, not easily able to think objectively about a cease-fire—or an off-ramp. Roscoe brought an outsider POV while speaking an insider language both sides could comprehend.

Using his wife's iPad, he convened the two sides for a Zoom call on Monday. He talked in terms of risk aversion and loss aversion, urging Dominion to see the downside of an unpredictable trial, and for Fox to see the upside of jury-free certainty. At one point he held negotiations from the back row of a Romanian tour bus. Dealing with those seven hours of time difference with Wilmington, he was compelled to stay awake until sunup local time Tuesday to get the parties closer to an agreement. The dispute wasn't just about the dollar figure; it was about whether Dominion could publicly trumpet the figure, and how it would be announced, and what Fox's statement would say. Observers speculated that Dominion wanted to force Fox to apologize on the air, but that was never a top priority. For one thing, it probably wouldn't seem genuine. ("I don't think a forced apology is worth a nickel," Shackelford remarked—and he was dealing with a whole hell of a lot of nickels.) But Dominion did want a public admission of wrongdoing. Teams of lawyers eventually came up with this weaselly sentence: "We acknowledge the Court's rulings finding certain claims about Dominion to be false." Fox followed it with a boast that made CNN's Jake Tapper laugh out loud as he read it on air: "This settlement reflects Fox's continued commitment to the highest journalistic standards."

Roscoe declined to discuss the back-and-forth with me. But other sources said that the two companies were nearing a deal, but were not quite there yet, when the sun rose in Wilmington. Judge Davis, aware of the mediator's involvement but not overly confident in it, completed jury selection and said opening arguments would begin after lunch break. "Once the jury sits down and you're looking at people who are going to decide your fate, it's an awakening experience," Roscoe told CNN.

At noon Wilmington time, a reporter for *Slate* said the jury "appeared to be five Black men, two Black women, three white women, a white man, and a Latino woman." Suffice it to say, not your standard Fox News crowd. (For every one hundred Fox viewers, only one was Black.) "Jury selection went very poorly," a Fox source understated. It was the final nudge the network needed. While the jurors ate catered wraps in a courthouse conference room and wasted their time getting to know each other, Lachlan opened the treasure chest containing $787.5 million. "It went down to the wire," Roscoe said. It was pitch-black in Romania and the nai flutes and accordions were playing a serenade by the time the judge announced the deal in Wilmington. Dominion's team celebrated at a nearby restaurant; Fox's team tried to lick their wounds and forget this ever happened; and Jerry Roscoe finally went to bed.

"Unexpectedly bad"

Now we find ourselves back inside the studio where Carlson hosted (unbeknownst to anyone) his final week of shows. Tucker being Tucker, he could not get through settlement day without alluding to the news coverage of Fox's loss and its Big Lie admission. "Ignore the noise," he said at the end of his broadcast on April 18, "because the people around you are way more important than the news media." For one thing, those people never told Carlson anything he didn't want to hear.

Months after he was fired, Carlson claimed to know for a fact that he was canceled due to Dominion. "They agreed to take me off the air, my show off the air, as a condition of the Dominion settlement," he told Chadwick Moore, a frequent guest on his show who published a flattering biography of Carlson in August 2023.

Carlson's camp also leaked this claim to the entertainment news site *Variety* in mid-May, with the added detail that an unnamed Fox board member told Carlson about it on April 26, two days after the cancellation. I felt like I was witnessing the live birth of a conspiracy theory: "Dominion was looking for the best way to maim the conservative news network," *Variety* wrote, "and forcing Fox News to cut ties with the most-watched personality in cable news" was the way to do it, "according to Carlson's understanding."

Presumably "understanding" was the going euphemism for "hurt feelings."

Dominion refuted this theory about as strongly as any company has ever denied anything. "As the Fox principals who negotiated the settlement well know, Dominion made no demands about Tucker Carlson's employment orally or in writing," the company said. "Any claims otherwise are categorically false and a thinly veiled effort to further damage Dominion. Fox should take every effort to stop these lies immediately." Indeed, Fox did, calling the claim "categorically false."

A conspiracy-addled brain would think *"they agreed to deny it."* Conspiracy theories are self-sealing in that way. But nothing about Carlson's "condition of the Dominion settlement" statement made sense. Dominion harbored no special ill will toward Carlson. Given his aggressive vituperation in the transcripts, he actually helped their case by lambasting Sidney Powell! His name did not come up at all during the negotiations, according to my sources who were involved in the talks.

But it made sense for Carlson to lash himself to the good ship Dominion's anchor and pretend that was why he drowned. Though he was still being paid—and handsomely—in "pay or play" status, he was stuck in a locker in Fox's corporate basement, unable to bloviate for any other network. So Carlson's attorney Bryan Freedman had ample reason to seek maximum leverage to get the contract dissolved. What better way to gain leverage—and make Fox miserable—than to invoke Dominion? The Murdochs had just paid $787.5 million to "buy peace," as one Fox lawyer put it; they paid to make the headache go away, and now Freedman was smashing a mallet named Dominion right up against their cranium. In a May 9 letter to Dinh, Freedman accused Fox of fraud and breach of contract because, he wrote, the network promised that it would not settle with Dominion "in a way which would indicate wrongdoing" by Carlson. The letter was immediately shared with *Axios*, ensuring widespread attention. "We just put Dominion back on the table," a Carlson friend bragged to me, asserting that this move would help win Carlson his freedom.

Making Dominion a bogeyman also fit neatly into Carlson's "us" versus "them" framing of the world. He told Moore, his biographer, that the lawsuit was "silly" and that the whole point of the case "was to emasculate Fox, take Fox out of the game because Fox was a huge vector for Donald Trump." Dominion "got it in front of some sort of partisan, low-IQ jury," Carlson continued, staying in character and demeaning the majority-Black jurors, and Fox "worried they were going to lose," he said, so they settled. "That's not justice, that's a scam."

■

Let's take off our Reynolds Wrap beanies and step away from the conspiracy cliff. Carlson was not a victim of the settlement. So why *was* he removed and what does it reveal about the network of lies?

On the morning of Monday, April 24, Carlson for sure felt under siege. Representative Alexandria Ocasio-Cortez was on MSNBC the day before saying that the Dominion case raised larger questions about "what is permissible on air," questions that lawmakers should take up, since Fox Corp's local TV stations were licensed by the FCC and subject to federal regulation. Fox News itself, a cable entity, was not licensed or regulated, but that nuance wasn't her point. Government's responsibility to protect the public was her point. She was channeling the views of her constituents and saying that government should do more. "When you look at what Tucker Carlson and some of these other folks on Fox do," AOC said, "it is very, very clearly incitement of violence."

Cue the Mediaite articles, cue the vitriolic comments on social media, and cue Carlson's acidic response. "Here's the lead I'm envisioning," he wrote to his staff Monday morning, sharing a draft of his monologue. He said AOC was demanding "that authorities pull our show off the air." (She wasn't, unless he agreed his show incited violence.) He planned to open Monday night's show by saying "members of Congress aren't allowed to talk like this." (They are.) Then he planned to pivot to one of his other favorite targets, Ray Epps.

Epps, a Marine veteran from Arizona, went to D.C. to protest the election results in 2021. "Tomorrow, we need to go into the Capitol!" he said at an impromptu pro-Trump rally on January 5. He approached the Capitol the next day, but never entered the building, and thus was never charged with doing so. Months later, Epps was baselessly singled out as an agent provocateur, a "fed," in the far-right circles that desperately wanted to absolve MAGA for the attack. It got really toxic after Carlson began to give oxygen to the conspiracy theory. But Epps had been there partly because of him!

Epps "was an avid and loyal Fox viewer and a fan of Mr. Carlson's," according to the lawsuit Epps filed in July 2023. "When Fox, through its on-air personalities and guests, told its audience that the 2020 election had been stolen, Epps was listening. He believed Fox. And when Epps kept hearing that Trump supporters should let their views be known on January 6th in Washington, D.C., Epps took that to heart." He flew across the country. He marched on Washington. And then a prime-time host he trusted turned him into a villain in front of millions of people. The Epps family was bombarded with so many threatening messages—"fucking traitor," "YOU WORTHLESS BITCH," "you better sleep with one eye open," "tick tock," "WE'RE COMING RAY"—that they sold their home, gave up their businesses, and fled to a different state. "After destroying Epps's reputation and livelihood," the suit stated, "Fox will move on to its next story, while Ray and Robyn live in a 350-square foot RV and face harassment and fear true harm. Fox must be held accountable."

Onlookers were predicting that Epps would sue Fox by the time *60 Minutes* profiled him in April. The segment pointed out that Carlson "focused on Epps more than 20 times on his top-rated show." Carlson was planning to run his rhetorical steamroller back over Epps one more time in his Monday monologue, charging that Epps went on "the Democratic Party's biggest television show, '60 Minutes' on CBS, to attack this show for asking questions about who he is."

But then Suzanne Scott called to tell him his show was kaput.

Shell-shocked, he composed a quick email to his Tuckertroop before his Fox email account was disabled. "I've never worked with better people in my life, and I don't expect I ever will," he wrote. "Every day I am grateful for you. I mean that.

"I'm a little unclear on what's going on right now," he continued, "but at this point it looks unexpectedly bad. I'm so sorry. Whatever happens next, please know that you have my undying gratitude for all you've done."

Unclear. Unexpected. I'm so sorry.

Carlson suspected (rightly) that the staff would be laid off, if not that day, then soon. Scott's deputy Meade Cooper met with Carlson's team later in the day for what she dubbed a "catch-up meeting," which stupefied the staffers who had never talked to her before. (They cited the lack of communication as evidence of how distant and indifferent Fox management was.) Cooper was noncommittal about the team's fate, and was so "insulting," one of the attendees said, that the staff held an impromptu "ketchup meeting" later in the week to mock her version of "catch-up." If Cooper had known about that, she would have cited it as another in the show's long line of examples of indiscipline.

The Tuckertroop suddenly had to produce an hour-long show for host TBD. They weren't told until early that afternoon that Brian Kilmeade was the first guy placed in the impossible position of sustaining Carlson's boffo ratings, upward of 3 million on a typical night. Fox registered a very specific ratings spike between 7:59 and 8:01 because, as so many grandpas said every evening to so many long-suffering spouses, "it's time for Tucker." This spike still happened on Monday, maybe because folks were curious to see what Fox would do or say at 8 p.m. Or maybe because word of Carlson's firing was still ricocheting outward. Kilmeade's Monday episode netted 2.59 million. But on Tuesday the average dropped to 1.70 million. Wednesday, 1.33 million. Thursday, 1.46 million. Instead of gaining viewers at eight o'clock, as it had routinely done with Carlson, Fox was shedding like a sheep with mange. In the twenty-five- to fifty-four-year-old demographic, Fox was sinking to pre-9/11-era lows.

The drop-off hurt Fox's later shows too, especially Sean Hannity's 9 p.m. hour. Hannity, however, privately celebrated Carlson's canning for at least two reasons, I was told: Their differences of opinion were getting increasingly stark, and Carlson's shadow blotted out Hannity's own star. Once the ratings recover, Hannity reassured his staffers, "this will be great for us."

As the news soaked in on Tuesday, paparazzi (one paparazzo, anyway) showed up on the Gulf Coast beach near the Carlson compound and photographed Susie walking their dogs. The presence of a news camera gave her newly unemployed husband a great opportunity. They dressed up for a dinner date and drove past the photographer with oversize smiles on their faces. "Retirement is going great so far," he quipped. Carlson "looks like a man without a care in the world," the *Daily Mail* wrote the next morning. The *Mail* said Carlson was "howling with laughter"—but he was closer to the Wolfman than a cuddly singing canine.

Carlson pals told me that he was going to ensure that Fox would come to regret this. He knew all the buttons to push. He claimed, naturally, that the other side had stuck the knife in first, right in his back. "Fox did start to attack me personally, which was uncalled for and unfair," he told his biographer.

On Wednesday evening *The New York Times* published a story titled "On Eve of Trial, Discovery of Carlson Texts Set Off Crisis Atop Fox." The story did not reveal the "white men fight" text, but it pointed in that direction, reporting that Dominion's redacted filings included "highly offensive and crude remarks" made by Carlson. This leak inflamed Carlson so much that he decided to grab his camera and start talking. He recorded a two-minute video from the wood-paneled studio Fox equipped for him in Florida, but did it straight from an iPhone, causing commenters to snicker about the woeful production values. He alluded to his "time off" (as if it were his choice) and promised he'd be back soon. The only real point of the video was to warn Fox that he wasn't going to stay silent.

A handful of Carlson diehards were laid off at the end of the week. Cooper's second-in-command Ron Mitchell assured the rest of the team that their jobs were safe. They knew enough about lying to know not to trust his pledge.

"Too big for his boots"

Think, for just a moment, about the worst relationship in your past. I won't ask you to dredge up any of the bitter details. But think about why the relationship ended. Odds are there wasn't just one reason, it wasn't one thing, it was everything: A book's worth of fights and slights and resentments and grievances. Maybe there was a final indignity—an affair, a betrayal, the discovery of a derogatory text— but even if one party was blindsided, the other could list a dozen long-gestating reasons for the breakup. Animosity accumulates like plaque stuck to the walls of an artery until, one day, there is a rupture, and the heart stops.

That's why Fox dumped Carlson. It wasn't one thing. It was *everything*.

Yes, he was in the gunsights of the Fox board. Yes, he was under scrutiny for his "cunt" texts. Yes, his "white men fight" message made matters worse. Yes, his show's climate was so hostile that Abby Grossberg had standing to sue. But there was so much more:

- Carlson repulsed large swaths of the company he worked for.
- He overextended himself on the Fox Nation streaming service.
- He created internal strife with conspiratorial commentaries.
- He exposed Fox to defamation suits from the likes of Ray Epps.
- He offended key executives and seemed to take delight in doing so.
- He caused constant headaches, to the point that managers believed he broke rules and norms just to show he could.
- He strained friendships, as Rupert's and Lachlan's chums repeatedly complained to them about his poisonous rhetoric.
- He triggered so many ad boycotts and turned off so many advertisers that his time slot was far less profitable for Fox than it should have been.
- And he committed the cardinal Fox sin of acting like he was bigger than the network he was on.

In short, Carlson huffed his own gas. "He got too big for his boots," Rupert told at least one confidant.

It was a tale as old as TV: Stardom is a potent and often destructive drug. Icarus flew too close to the sun; he got his wings melted. Carlson flapped away, higher and higher, thinking the sun (or in this case the father) couldn't touch him. Until one day the Murdochs just couldn't tolerate his flapping anymore. It called to mind what I quoted one of Rupert's former deputies saying at the beginning of this book: He "is loyal, loyal, loyal, loyal, loyal—until the minute you're dead." By pulling Carlson's plug, Lachlan showed the same trait. But by keeping the reasons a secret, he allowed conspiracy theories about the firing to fester. "It's Dominion all over again," one lawyer sighed.

Dominion deserved credit for dragging some of Carlson's intolerability out in the open. "It's one thing to know about abusive language and angry emails. It's another thing to have it all read back to you during a deposition," a source observed. And to have the Fox board retain lawyers to read through his deepest, darkest texts. "People were telling Rupert and Lachlan, 'this guy is not worth it,'" an insider said. That's why Dominion's wins were a tipping point, even though Carlson's termination was not part of the settlement.

So I drilled deeper, wanting to understand ALL of the reasons why Rupert and Lachlan broke it off with their biggest star. Some of these dynamics were underappreciated, or totally unknown, by Carlson's fans and foes alike, but I heard about them from numerous sources in and around Fox. The word "assholes" was thrown around a lot; people clearly felt disrespected by Carlson and his inner circle of producers. "Their arrogance destroyed them," one former exec commented.

Carlson was incredibly protective and supportive of his own staff—sending attaboys at all hours—and dismissive of everyone else. He complained about other Fox talent. (On the eve of the 2020 election, Meade Cooper emailed Jay Wallace a "heads up" that "Tucker has expressed concerns that one of our news anchors is attacking the president.") He groaned about Irena Briganti, smeared her in his usual vulgar way, and tried to get her fired. He made comments that recipients perceived as threats.

I noticed some of this firsthand. Carlson's camp had nothing nice to say about Jason Klarman, the former head of the female-focused Oxygen network and former head of marketing at Bravo who was put in charge of Fox Nation in early 2021, around the same time Scott invested in two new Carlson franchises, *Tucker Carlson Originals* documentaries and *Tucker Carlson Today* interviews. The shows were supposed to turn Carlson TV viewers into Fox Nation streaming subscribers, but the content "bombed," two of his allies admitted. I reviewed internal data that showed minuscule audiences for the interviews. "More people live in my neighborhood," one source cracked. Carlson blamed Klarman and ridiculed the site's functionality. "Nobody watches Fox Nation because the site sucks," he said in mid-2022 in a video clip that leaked later. "I don't know why they're not fixing it. It's driving me insane. And they're like making, like, Lifetime movies but they don't, they don't work on the infrastructure of the site? Like what? It's crazy. And it drives me crazy because it's like we're doing all this extra work and no one can find it. It's unbelievable, actually."

Carlson's dig at Lifetime reflected Klarman's move to add movies, comedy shows, and celebrity star power to Fox Nation, which steadily gained subscribers and was on track to top two million in 2023. Carlson felt "eclipsed" by A-listers like Kevin Costner, a source said. No one should have been surprised that more people wanted to stream the reboot of *Cops* than the performative hypermasculinity of Carlson's *The End of Men* documentary—even though Carlson went viral when a guest hyped dubious testicle-tanning therapy—but the underwhelming results for Carlson's streaming shows undercut the image he had fostered of an irreplaceable superstar. Plus, there was that pesky little fact that *The Five* was usually higher-rated than he was. I could see why the executive team thought they could do without this prima donna and his totally discordant, dissonant nightly opera. As one insider put it, "He was much more trouble than it was worth."

■

In fairness to the thrice-booted formerly bow-tied bomb thrower, I can also see why he had so many gripes about his third and final cable TV home. He really *was* undermined sometimes by various department heads and divisions at Fox. When Carlson's show broke news, or at least something his team thought was news, it tended to get buried on the website. Other shows were expressly told not to follow up on Carlson's segments about the sabotage of the Nord Stream pipelines, I was told. His January 6 tapes were also given the cold shoulder by colleagues. And for all the talk of Carlson leaking to other media outlets, other hosts leaked about him too. There was no denying his paranoid streak—a few weeks before his firing, in a chat with Adam Carolla, he invoked the amorphous "they" and said "they'll probably figure out a way to get me"—but some people really *were* out to get him. (Even paranoids have real enemies.)

When Carlson was ditched by Scott as abruptly as Rupert dumped Jerry Hall and Ann Lesley Smith, those inside the "Tucker bunker," as *Puck* perfectly described it, began to trade theories, some of a decidedly conspiratorial bent. There was the "Rupert fired Carlson to get even with his ex-fiancée" theory . . . the "Rupert objected to Tucker's religiosity" theory . . . and of course the "Dominion did it" theory. None of these explanations added up, but there was a broader hypothesis that had some merit. If Carlson represented the "New Right," Rupert was part of the "Old Right." You could even say he was king of the "Old, Old Right." Every time Carlson blasted the Republican establishment, he was blasting F.O.R. (friends of Rupert). Maybe that was tolerable, even perversely enjoyable, for a while, but Carlson's position on Ukraine wasn't as easy to stomach.

What's clear is that some of the nationalist, isolationist views Carlson espoused were in opposition to Rupert's and to some extent Lachlan's positions. Carlson talked about this on a podcast with a former Fox host in early March: He said "one of the top people" at the company had recently texted him and said "for the record, I really disagree with you on Ukraine." Carlson claimed that he replied, "I know you do, and I'm so grateful that you let me disagree with you in public."

Months later, Carlson told an interviewer that "as a general matter, not even about me, the war in Ukraine is a red line for a lot of people in business and politics." Privately, he was blunter, pointing to Ukraine as a factor in his firing. Someone (guess who) also leaked the intro he drafted for April 24, about AOC and Ray Epps, to a far-right character who headlined it "The Monologue That Got Tucker Carlson Fired." This claim didn't pass the laugh test but it was embraced by Carlson's fans no less eagerly. As Steve Bannon infamously said: "Flood the zone with shit." That's what the "Tucker bunker" did.

■

At the end of holy-crap-Fox-fired-Tucker-Carlson week, Fox's small crew of real reporters joined thousands of other D.C. denizens for the White House Correspondents' Dinner. Guests at the Fox tables stifled laughs while Biden—with the help of speechwriters—took full advantage of the recent run of bad press. "It's great the cable news networks are here tonight," Biden said. "MSNBC, owned by

NBCUniversal. Fox News, owned by Dominion Voting Systems."
Howls of laughter erupted in the ballroom. "Last year, your favorite
Fox News reporters were able to attend because they were fully vaccinated and boosted. This year, with that $787 million settlement,
they're here because they couldn't say no to a free meal." More howls.
"And hell, I'd call Fox honest, fair, and truthful, but then I could
be sued for defamation." The howls continued. "It ain't nothing
compared to what they do to me. Look, I hope the Fox News team
finds this funny. My goal is to make them laugh as hard as CNN
did when they read the settlement. But then again, CNN was like,
'Wow, they actually have $787 million?' Whoa." Finally, the Fox ta-
bles could crack a smile.

Per tradition, the dinner ended with a comedian, this year Roy
Wood Jr. of *The Daily Show*, who looked at Biden and said "We've
gotta get Tucker back on the air, Mr. President, because right now
there are millions of Americans who don't know why they hate you!"

It was a great joke, but it assigned far more influence to Carlson than he actually had. For all of the Sturm und Drang caused
by Carlson's cancellation, the decision was about to prove once and
for all that Fox was much bigger than any single egomaniacal host.
Another presidential election was around the corner, and Fox was
still the black widow at the center of a web of lies, all to the benefit
of one man.

PART FIVE

"Fox knew"

The word "settle" implies a lack of satisfaction, and that's certainly how it felt in Wilmington and beyond when Rupert and Lachlan paid big to avoid the witness stand. James Murdoch, for one, thought the settlement amount was obscene and was further proof of his father's and brother's fumbling. He hoped, one day, to drag Fox News back into the actual news business. James had detailed plans for doing so, according to an associate. Prominent Fox hosts talked openly about how they might reposition their own personal brands in the event of a James-led takeover. Some Fox personalities even tried to establish back-channel relationships with James, even though Lachlan was the boss for as long as Rupert was alive.

In the summer of 2023, Murdoch-obsessed news outlets reported that James was absent when the rest of the family gathered for a "European super-yacht holiday" on the Amalfi Coast. (As of mid-2024, James and Lachlan were still not on speaking terms.) Then again, James might have been better off on the outside; shares in Fox Corp remained stagnant during a year when Netflix, to pick one high-flying rival, saw its shares nearly double in value.

If the opportunity ever presented itself, James could make a strong case that he could right what was wrong about the family business. Emphasis on if. Maybe. *Someday.* And he would need the support of his sisters.

In the meantime, in the here and now, many liberal activists and writers wished Dominion had held out for even more money. What they really yearned for was a Fox bankruptcy, which wasn't within the realm of possibility, partly because much of the Dominion payout was covered by Fox's insurers. Disinformation researcher Caroline Orr Bueno said it best: The settlement "is essentially a lying tax," simply the cost of doing business.

"Think of a bar that suddenly has to pay an alcohol tax for the first time," Bueno tweeted. "The bar owner is not going to be deterred from selling alcohol just because there's a tax on it. Bars are in the alcohol business; without alcohol, there is no bar. Fox is in the lying business."

Bueno had a point. The Dominion case, despite all its costs, did not cause any dramatic or immediate changes inside Murdoch-world. A few weeks after the settlement, in mid-May, Rupert's *New York Post* splashed a story titled "VETS KICKED OUT FOR MIGRANTS" across its front page. The subtitle said a group of New York hotels forced "20 homeless veterans to leave" to make room for illegal migrants bused in from Texas. The source of the story had not been sufficiently vetted. But Fox, always on the hunt for stories that fit its collection of grievance-guaranteed narratives, kicked into action anyway. Hosts like Harris Faulkner decried the "disgraceful treatment of our military veterans," while correspondents like Nate Foy used the word "confirm" to indicate that Fox had done its own due diligence. The outrage machine was in overdrive for five days.

In the non-Fox universe, actual reporters checking for actual facts were able to debunk the Murdoch media lie relatively quickly. A local paper, the *Mid Hudson News,* found that homeless men were offered money, food, and alcohol to pose as displaced veterans to further an anti-immigrant political agenda. Fox had once again run wild with an unchecked, unverified story because it pushed all of the audience's buttons—and, as with Dominion, it had blown up in the network's face. Laura Ingraham was tasked with the official cleanup-on-aisle-Fox when she ended her Friday night show—the perfect time to bury an embarrassing retraction—with what amounted to a "never mind" message: "Turns out, the group behind the claim made it up. We have no clue as to why anyone would do such a thing." Fox's breathless coverage was exactly the reason why.

So the network's misinformation machine was not crippled by the Dominion case, nor the parade of other lawsuits and scandals. But Dominion's lawyers at Susman Godfrey still felt successful, and for reasons beyond the firm's enormous windfall from Fox. Stephen Shackelford told me said the stratospheric settlement amount proved the lead of the opening argument he never got to give: "It's an enormous admission that Fox knew what it did was wrong. Fox knew."

Shackelford and his colleagues were only just beginning to achieve Big Lie accountability. Six other defamation cases were outstanding: five in Washington, D.C., against One America News, Mike Lindell, Rudy Giuliani, Sidney Powell, and former Overstock CEO Patrick Byrne; and one in Delaware, against Newsmax. "We're back at it," Shackelford told the *New York Law Journal.* "We've got a lot of work to do in holding these other parties accountable." Judge Eric Davis, who also refereed *Dominion v. Fox,* said that *Dominion v. Newsmax* would proceed to trial in the fall of 2024.

Fox still had lawsuits to fend off too. The biggest was the one initiated by the other voting machine company, Smartmatic, demanding more than twice what Dominion had settled for.

J. Erik Connolly, the lead attorney for Smartmatic, said on settlement day that "Dominion's litigation exposed some of the misconduct and damage caused by Fox's disinformation campaign" and "Smartmatic will expose the rest." His case against Fox was not expected to see the inside of a courtroom until 2025, but Connolly saw benefits to going second, like the foreknowledge of Fox hosts' earlier depositions. "We get a second bite of the apple," he remarked to colleagues. That's why, in the words of a Republican Party power broker, "Dominion was just the tip of the iceberg" for Fox. Connolly certainly believed so. "Smartmatic is a global company that was injured on a global scale," he told me. "The damages are much bigger." Fox countered by calling Smartmatic's damage claims "implausible, disconnected from reality, and on their face intended to chill First Amendment freedoms."

■

"At any other company," a Murdoch family friend told me days after the Dominion settlement, "Viet would have already been fired."

This was not stated with admiration for Rupert's and Lachlan's fervent loyalty. It was a condemnation of their wrongheaded faith in their top legal exec, Viet Dinh. Dinh came under harsh scrutiny for his "epic mismanagement" (the family friend's words) of the case. Dinh's associates trotted out a defense: His old friend Bill Barr, Trump's last attorney general, said Dinh was wise to pursue two paths at once—a courtroom defense that "I think would have eventually won at the appellate stage" and a settlement approach. Notably, no one at Fox repeated this talking point; executives like Scott uniformly blamed Dinh for underestimating Dominion and botching the response, so it was no surprise when, on a Friday in August primed for news-burying, Fox Corp said Dinh would be departing the company at year's end. It always seemed to work this way in Murdochworld: The mud splattered on everyone except, magically, the men who controlled one of the world's most indiscriminate splattering machines.

On his way out, Dinh won a $23 million severance package, and a two-year "advisory" role that would net him another $5 million, so it's little wonder why he said he had no regrets, Dominion-related or otherwise. In an appearance at Harvard Law School, his alma mater, he heaped blame on Judge Davis for hamstringing Fox's defenses at trial. "We knew we were right in the law," he insisted. But "the court lost control of the media circus, to our detriment," he said. And "the trial judge put us in a situation, increasingly, where it was very obvious that we were not able to win the trial, but we were very confident we would prevail on appeal."

Overdramatizing a tad, Dinh said trial attorney Dan Webb was "threatening to commit suicide in his hotel room because he [saw] no way to win this at trial," while the attorney tasked with the expected appeal, Paul Clement, was "doing cartwheels in his hotel room saying, 'Wow, I'm going to be the hero winning this case back for the company and for the First Amendment and for American democracy.'"

Dinh claimed that Fox was still, in late 2023, "confident in the legal arguments," which was a legally convenient position to take, since Fox Corp was battling multiple shareholder lawsuits. He said "the business decision was made" (by Lachlan) to settle in order to "save the organization from the cultural and reputational cost" of a hard-fought trial.

And then, curiously, Dinh brought up the presidential election calendar. "Especially, especially," he said, suggesting this timing was an important factor, while smiling at his lecture hall audience of students and faculty members. "We are walking into an early primary season of another hotly contested and very exciting electoral process. . . . And who do we have as the leading Republican candidate? The same guy who was contesting the 2020 election."

So Trump's return to center stage was a factor. "The business decision," Dinh said, interlocking his fingers in his hands, was "to take the pain so that we can do our job in the next cycle to cover the newly launched presidential election of 2024."

As I listened to Dinh rationalize the settlement at Harvard, it all began to make sense. The embarrassing disclosures in the pretrial paperwork damaged Fox's relationship with both Trump and its core audience. An actual trial was bound to dredge up even more discomfiting details. So Fox decided to "take the pain" (cut the check) in order to "do our job" (keep the Trump-loving audience happily tuned in) and satisfy investors.

By mid-2023, Fox's bill for the Big Lie exceeded even the $787.5 million that Dominion won: The company reported a total of $894 million in legal settlement costs, which included a secret settlement with a Venezuelan businessman who was smeared on Lou Dobbs's show. But to hear Dinh tell it, this was just the cost of doing business, when the business involved the next presidential campaign.

I concluded that the network learned a very narrow lesson from the Big Lie litigation: Be extra-careful about making spurious claims against specific, otherwise mostly obscure companies. And maybe think twice before airing Trump's voter fraud lies completely live and uncut. Networks "will put in tape delays," Dinh said, alluding to the former president, "just in order to protect themselves—and not just protect themselves legally, [but] protect the integrity of the product. Because that ultimately is what we're responsible for." But even the no-live-Trump rule was repealed in early 2024. When Trump wanted to bigfoot a GOP debate on CNN by holding a town hall on Fox instead, the network eagerly said yes, and even let him pick the time slot. "We offered a number of different times," Bret Baier said, and the Trump campaign stipulated the town hall would be at 9 p.m. to overshadow CNN's debate at the same hour. When

I shared this anecdote with an executive at a rival TV network, the person exclaimed, "It's their air! Who is in control?"

"We want no lawsuits"

Tucker Carlson was desperate. He wanted to get back on camera somewhere, anywhere, ASAP. His initial embrace of "retirement" was just for show. He once told an interviewer that he feared being "too happy" at rest and alluded to his alcoholic past: "If I had to sit outside a Sandals beach resort for a week with an open tab, I don't know what I would do. I would hurt myself." So in May of 2023 he plotted a comeback on Twitter, the platform owned by the man he'd promoted on Fox a few weeks earlier, Elon Musk. He wondered if Fox would try to stop him. He candidly welcomed the fight.

Carlson's defenders suspected that Fox wanted to keep him on the "pay or play" bench, and thus off any rival outlets, for several months at a minimum, to give the network time to repair the ratings damage caused by the cancellation. But "Team Tucker" also believed there was no way Fox would file an injunction or take other actions to stop him from posting videos on Twitter, because the MAGA audience would take the star's side—and because his contract did not expressly list Twitter as off-limits. This was like a loophole that doubled as a middle finger.

So Carlson got back to work, with the help of a growing number of his former producers, some of whom flew to Maine to set up a new TV studio after a repo crew trucked away the Fox-owned lights and cameras. He started to upload videos to Twitter while he strategized a long-term business plan. His first posts garnered more attention for where they were posted (on a social network not at all hospitable to binge-viewing) than for what he said. He looked like a shell of his former self. Still, his hard-core fans ate it up. And Fox gave him the fight he wanted by sending a cease-and-desist letter in early June, citing his still-in-force contract. His camp promptly went public with the threat and depicted Fox as corporate and censorious, maybe even, heaven forbid, "elitist"—precisely how Fox caricatured the rest of the media.

In June, when Trump was indicted for a second time, a Carlson loyalist who was still producing the in-limbo 8 p.m. hour, Alex McCaskill, put an on-screen banner below Biden that said "WANNABE DICTATOR SPEAKS AT THE WHITE HOUSE AFTER HAVING HIS POLITICAL RIVAL ARRESTED." Histrionic banners were a staple of *Tucker Carlson Tonight,* but that show was supposed to be dead, buried, and forgotten. Fox exec Meade Cooper erupted at the control room when she saw the banner. Carlson then reveled in the fallout from his lackey's pot-stirring; he told his Twitter viewers, with a wink of misogyny, that "the women who run the network panicked" about the banner and "scolded" McCaskill. When McCaskill resigned and offered two weeks' notice, "Fox told him to clear out his desk and leave immediately," Carlson said. McCaskill soon joined Carlson in Maine. It was time for a new show.

But as hundreds, nay, thousands of personalities and musicians and comedians have learned the hard way, it is painful to play in front of a mostly empty hall, even if the front rows are full. Without Fox, Carlson couldn't fill the theater. Fox-haters on the far right pretended otherwise, and claimed that Carlson was reaching more people online than he ever could on cable, but that was just wishful thinking and number fudging. Twitter said that it counted a "view" whenever "a user watches a video for at least 2 seconds and sees at least 50% of the video player in-view." In other words, a Carlson hater who ever-so-briefly clicked on one of his videos counted as a view, even though the interaction wasn't worth anything at all. Nielsen's flawed but fully vetted TV ratings system worked the opposite way—it reported average-per-minute audiences, a unit of measurement that was orders of magnitude larger than Twitter's. Thus, to exploit a phrase from the early days of the digital advertising wars, Nielsen was measuring analog dollars while Twitter was measuring digital pennies. Carlson was like the incredible shrinking man, reduced to ranting on Twitter like so many of the former guests on his former show. Fox was in the S&P 500, while Carlson was a penny stock.

■

Without TV ratings or believable web view counts to track, Carlson's currency was a more amorphous form of attention, which he gained through hosting forums like the Family Leadership Summit in Iowa. He interviewed six GOP presidential candidates onstage and pressured them to adopt his isolationist position toward Ukraine. The next day he spoke at a pro-Trump student activist conference in Florida and defended his pro-Russia leanings, saying, "If you're an American, you have the right to decide who you hate." Judging by the months of anti-Fox agitprop fomented by Carlson sympathizers, he wanted them to hate Fox and never watch the network again.

Yet Fox remained shockingly steady, almost in spite of itself. On a conference call for Wall Street analysts, Lachlan dubiously claimed all was well and said "there's no change to our programming strategy at Fox News," even though a move away from Tucker's burn-it-all-down populism was a major shift in strategy. Lachlan projected calm and it worked: While the Carlson-triggered exodus was stressful—"my fans are furious right now," one host told me in May—there was no Arizona-scale panic. "They say they'll never watch Fox again," the host said, but "I've seen this movie before." Newsmax and other wannabe rivals exaggerated Fox's post-Carlson ratings collapse, but 2020 had proved that the audience would trickle back over time, and it did.

That's why stories about Fox's weakened stature spurred C-suite laughter. One morning in May, Axios declared that "Elon Musk has displaced Rupert Murdoch and Fox News as the king of conservative media," and the very same day, Ron DeSantis tried to launch his campaign on Twitter in a live audio chat with Musk. Fox staffers were told to "avoid talking up Twitter" and ignore the DeSantis announcement; one producer told me that the edict emitted "major insecurity and jealousy vibes." But Twitter's servers couldn't handle even a fraction of a Fox-size audience, and the rollout, a cacophony of feedback and garbled audio, was a De-saster, leading Lachlan's inner circle to ridicule the Axios headline. Thankfully for DeSantis, he had a real TV appearance scheduled on Fox later in the evening. "Fox News will not crash during this interview," guest host Trey Gowdy cracked cheerfully.

"Don't crash" was a useful summation of Fox Corp's strategy, as seen in July's introduction of a new prime-time lineup, which had Laura Ingraham move up to 7 p.m., Jesse Watters slide down to 8, and Greg Gutfeld shift to 10. Carlson's remaining producers were laid off. Live hours at midnight and 4 a.m. were replaced by repeats to save money. As the cable TV ship continued to take on water, Fox had to shed weight and steer carefully through the prime-time seas. "Lachlan is protecting profits and minimizing headaches," an insider observed; and it worked. Watters at 8 didn't have anyone grasping for Tylenol like Carlson did. Sponsors like T-Mobile, which memorably had said "bye-bye, Tucker Carlson!" and stopped advertising at 8, came back to the time slot, along with heavy hitters like Procter & Gamble, General Motors, and Allstate. Fox PR finally had a good story to tell about 8 p.m. "We have seen new advertisers come in, and new demand," Fox News ad sales boss Jeff Collins told *Variety*.

Watters, who liked to read texts from his very liberal mother Anne on *The Five,* invited her to call in to review his first prime-time episode. "You've worked so hard" to get there, Anne said. "Now, let's aim to have you keep your job." Her first bit of advice: "Do not tumble into any conspiracy rabbit holes. We do not want to lose you and we want no lawsuits. Okay?" By the time she said to "do no harm" and "use your voice responsibly," Watters quipped, "I knew this was a bad idea."

Watters failed to heed his mom's advice. He routinely hosted segments that were grossly irresponsible. One day he even suggested that Taylor Swift could be part of a "psyop," a psychological operation designed to hurt Trump's re-election chances. "It's real," he said. (It wasn't.) "The Pentagon psy-op unit pitched NATO on turning Taylor Swift into an asset for combating misinformation online." (They didn't.) His on-screen banner said "IS TAYLOR SWIFT A PENTAGON ASSET?" (She wasn't.) Conspiracy thinking permeated his show night after night. And it hurt ordinary people—men like Joe Black, a Colorado resident who drove a pickup truck with a huge "TRUMP 2024" bumper sticker that said Trump's re-election would "MAKE LIBERALS CRY AGAIN." When CNN's Donie O'Sullivan interviewed Black about his media consumption habits, Black pointed to posts in his social media feed about the "psyop" stupidity. "I don't know what to believe about Taylor Swift," Black said.

Responsible media outlets tried to help people discern fact from fiction, but Fox operated the opposite way—airing lots of fictions, a few facts, and topping it off with a shrug of the shoulders. Watters could go even further whenever a segment went awry, and claim that he was just joking around. But crucially, Watters, unlike Carlson, usually stayed in a standard-issue GOP lane, with fewer of the heterodox and sometimes downright hateful segments that caused so much trouble for Fox. Watters was the "safe" choice for the time slot. *The Washington Post,* citing Watters's associates, said he was "more interested in making good TV than remaking American society." And the median Fox fan thought that what he made was good enough: In the spring of 2024, one year after Carlson's firing, Watters was averaging 2.5 to 3 million viewers a night. His total haul was 10 to 20 percent lower than Carlson's had been, and there were a few different reasons why: Ongoing cord-cutting meant fewer people were able to watch cable; Watters was still new to the time slot; and a core group of Carlson disciples had sworn off Fox altogether. But the major takeaway was that Fox had rebounded after the April 2023 ratings collapse. Watters was tolerable; Carlson wasn't. And everything Carlson did in his post-Fox life demonstrated why.

■

"I just want to keep doing what I'm doing," Carlson said, as a way of explaining why he immediately began making videos for Twitter (which became X) after being fired by Fox. By the fall of 2023, he had published a couple dozen episodes of "Tucker on X" and he had chatted with several potential investors and advertisers. He envisioned a "Tucker Carlson Network," to be run by his best friend Neil Patel and his producing partner Justin Wells, with subscription videos and live events and a gift shop and all the other components of a hyperpartisan digital media company. Strangely, though, he didn't replicate what made his Fox show so compelling (and so destructive). He didn't deliver straight-to-camera monologues or attempt to set the right-wing agenda in any way. Instead, he hosted in-depth, podcast-style interviews with allies like Robert F. Kennedy Jr. and Viktor Orbán, but also with fringe characters that even Fox wouldn't have welcomed. The best, meaning worst, example was his sit-down with a con man who made outlandish sex-and-drug allegations about Barack Obama during Obama's presidential campaign. Carlson dredged up the old smear and acted like it was a Very Serious Accusation, seemingly just for the scandalous attention he would get. The interview "was full of racist dog whistles (at one point, for example, Carlson claimed nobody could pronounce Obama's name despite it being really very easy to pronounce) and barely veiled homophobia," *The Guardian* reported.

It was around this time when several of Carlson's former Fox producers confided that they felt embarrassed for him. This feeling intensified after some of his other off-the-deep-end interviews, and then his softball session with Vladimir Putin in February 2024, which reviewers called "sycophantic," "shameless," and "pathetic." (Even Putin said he'd expected a tougher interview.) Carlson was ridiculed even more intensely for filming himself inside a Moscow grocery store, gushing about the food prices, and saying the visit "radicalized" him against American leaders.

The mockery of the Russia trip showed that Carlson still had first-name status, but unlike, say, Oprah, "Tucker" wasn't invoked with admiration or reverence. Instead I heard dismay: "What happened to Tucker?" Even one of his highest-profile critics, Kat Abu of Media Matters, said, "I didn't expect him to fall this hard this fast." Carlson, she said, had been reduced to "interviewing unhinged lunatics on a dying web site." Suzanne Scott and her C-suite executives ate up the bad press about Carlson; what they wanted to say out loud, but never could, was "now the rest of you know what we were dealing with."

One of Carlson's longtime confidants went public with the critiques that other former staffers whispered to each other. Gregg Re, who was Carlson's head writer at the time the show was canceled, was no fan of the network that fired him. He quipped that Fox News doesn't "really run a newsroom. More of a student paper." He said Fox's website was a "content mill" with "no standards at all, other than how many hits you can get for your section (for editors), and what story count quota you can meet (for reporters)." He wanted Carlson to be better than Fox—but he sensed that the newly launched subscription video service was a bust. "A year ago," Re tweeted, "Tucker could demand that every GOP candidate complete a homework assignment for him on foreign affairs. And they did it!" But "now no one would care."

Carlson still had *some* amount of sway; Donald Trump Jr. remarked on Newsmax that Carlson would "certainly be a contender" for vice president. But even Carlson admirers, like the anti-left crusader, Christopher Rufo knew something had changed. In prime time, Rufo wrote, Carlson "coordinated the whole movement" of the right, "offline and online, with the prestige and production of a cable news network behind it. Tucker on X is too fragmented, lacks the nightly rhythm, and the topics have been all over the place, with some serious missteps." Re replied to Rufo and said Carlson's programming had been "tough to watch at times." He had a theory for why: The host was surrounded by yes-men. What's "missing is someone to be extremely critical, internally," in a way that would make the finished product stronger, Re wrote. "Tucker's show had that before and I think it's missing now. That's the only way I can explain what's going on."

By the summer of 2024, founding president Justin Wells and hotshot producer Alex McCaskill were out at "Tucker Carlson Network." Wells reportedly stayed in the loop as an adviser of some sort. But there's "no real good way to spin losing two top producers in a year," a Carlson aide remarked.

In one moment of clarity after his Fox show was canceled, Carlson jovially said, "this is the third time I've been fired as an adult, and I would really recommend it to anybody." He said getting the boot is great "because it keeps you from being a truly horrible person." Otherwise, successful men "start to think they're Jesus," and "getting fired reminds you that, no, you're just like everybody else." When I read Carlson's comments, I agreed wholeheartedly, but I wondered what that insight portended for his future. By launching his own subscription service, he was becoming his own boss, accountable only to his paying customers. He was finally making himself unfireable. How long before he'd start to think he was the second coming of Christ?

"Cloud of confusion"

For once, Donald Trump was right. His hyperbolic claims about Fox opposing him were, for a long while, not a conspiracy theory but an actual plan. In 2021 Rupert really did try to make him a "non person." But eventually the Murdochs capitulated to the base; as the base warmed back up to Trump, so did Fox. Trump once more became Fox's biggest star, even in absentia.

"They are servants. They simply serve the audience," a Trump White House veteran said of Fox. "When Trump was considered a joke" during the early campaign days of 2015, "they were against him. The second they noticed that Republican voters liked him, they embraced him." And so it was, again, nearly a decade later: Trump was leading and Fox was merely following. "Rupert hates Trump," a Murdoch family friend told me in the summer of 2023. "He can't believe we're going to end up back with Trump."

Rupert, by then, had given up any semblance of control or influence. Like everyone else, he saw that each indictment of Trump solidified the former president's hold on his fan base. Trump kept saying "they're not coming after me, they're coming after you," and his rallygoers believed him. An investment banker might say that Fox had a fiduciary responsibility to stop standing in Trump's way. More than one Fox insider did say to me, on condition of anonymity, that once GOP primary voters made up their collective mind, Fox did too.

The network portrayed itself as Switzerland during the primaries, and pointed as proof to the GOP debates it produced despite Trump's boycott, but hosts and guests felt tremendous pressure from the audience to sing from the Trump song sheet. Any stray criticism or gentle pushback on Fox's air was met by a torrent of social media taunting ("RINO!" "Trump hater!" "Piece of shit!"). Ron DeSantis perceived this feedback loop too, and in the closing days of his campaign, he called out the "Praetorian Guard of the conservative media" for wrapping Trump in a warm fuzzy blanket. "Fox News, the web sites, all the stuff—they just don't hold him accountable because they're worried about losing viewers," DeSantis said. The commentator class stays silent, he said at another campaign pit stop, because "they're so concerned that someone might yell at them."

The fight within Fox mirrored the fight within the GOP. Centrist types at the network viewed the Trump thaw as "a pathetic surrender," a staffer told me in early January. "Meanwhile the Trump fans think it's one one-hundredth of what Fox should be doing" and assumed the feckless executives were "all sitting secretly praying for a Nikki Haley miracle in New Hampshire."

By the time Trump won the Iowa caucuses in mid-January and DeSantis dropped out of the race, leaving Haley, the former U.N. ambassador, as the last major challenger, Haley felt like she was running against both Fox and Trump. She visited the cast of *Fox*

& Friends on the morning of the New Hampshire primary and let rip, implying Fox was putting its thumb on the scale of the primary process, and saying "I don't know if y'all will tell the truth." One of those truths, she said, was that "70 percent of Americans don't want a Trump-Biden rematch." She was right! But that frustrated, fed-up supermajority wasn't showing up at the primary polls. Trump die-hards were. The *Friends* cohosts got defensive; "We try to cover it all," Ainsley Earhardt said, "but we only have X amount of time. So we try." Haley then went even harder: "I don't care how much you all want to coronate Donald Trump. . . . Americans want a choice, and we're going to give them one." Brian Kilmeade acted hurt by Haley's criticism: "I'm really wondering why you think we're the enemy."

"Because I've looked at the media," Haley responded. "Look at the media saying, 'Oh, this is Donald Trump's to have.' Look at the political class all coalescing and saying everybody needs to get out. That's not democracy. That's not who we are."

Haley's campaign puttered to an end in March. Her aides felt the same way that DeSantis's campaign manager James Uthmeier did in January: "Fox has turned into full blown Trump TV, honesty thrown to the wind," Uthmeier tweeted. As if honesty had ever been a prior-ity at all. *The Bulwark's* Charlie Sykes explained Fox's stance this way back before the primary even began in earnest: "They're in the busi-ness of fan service, and right now conservative politics is all the Trump show. If the show is back in town, Fox can either try to counterpro-gram or buy into it. Right now, what is the counterprogramming?"

■

Trump was able to reconsolidate control over the party, and its media wing, by exploiting what attorney Kenneth Chesebro called the "cloud of confusion."

Chesebro kept a relatively low profile for most of his career, but in 2020 he was one of the architects of the so-called fake electors plot. The idea, according to Jack Smith's conspiracy indictment of Trump, was to have Republican electors submit bogus Electoral College certificates claiming that the loser of the election was actually the winner. The indictment called it "a corrupt plan to subvert the federal government function by stopping Biden electors' votes from being counted and certified." And Chesebro, according to one of his own emails, knew exactly what he was doing.

On November 8, 2020, the same day Biden became president-elect, Chesebro emailed a fellow attorney, Jim Troupis, and volunteered to help Trump challenge the results in his native Wisconsin. Chesebro asserted that Wisconsin's Republican-controlled legislature could bigfoot the Democratic governor and declare Trump to be the winner of the state's electoral votes. He imagined "systemic abuses" and alternative slates of electors and wrote that "at minimum, with such a cloud of confusion, no votes from WI (and perhaps also MI and PA) should be counted, perhaps enough to throw the election to the House."

The hope—the prayer—was that VP Mike Pence, in his ceremonial role overseeing the certification, would accept the bogus certificates and overturn Biden's victory; or that the "cloud of confusion" would cast such a shadow that Congress would vote for president by state delegation instead, thereby tipping the election to Trump, since twenty-six states were GOP-controlled at the time. Chesebro's memos about so-called "alternate electors" were incredibly influential inside Trumpworld in the weeks leading up to January 6, but the public knew almost nothing about the scheme as it was happening. The House's January 6 committee used its legal powers to obtain some of the memos in 2022, and its final report said Chesebro was "central to the creation of the plan." But his November 8 email about sowing confusion did not see the light of day until a group of Democrats in Wisconsin sued Chesebro, Troupis, and the election posers. As part of a settlement deal, more than fourteen hundred pages of documents relating to the fake electors plot were released in March 2024. In other words, the public was still learning key details about the extent of the MAGA coup attempt more than three years after it occurred. The legal system was still achieving accountability.

"Cloud of confusion" was the perfect, succinct summary of the right's strategy. Candidates like Donald Trump, attorneys like Kenneth Chesebro, TV stars like Sean Hannity, and streaming shit-stirrers like Tucker Carlson sowed so much chaos and confusion that voters and viewers couldn't tell what was true anymore. Every time Trump wanted to disarm a damaging story about him, he called it a "hoax." Every time Hannity wanted to defend Trump from real but critical news coverage, he called the news "fake." I came to view the "cloud of confusion" as a key part of Trump's re-election toolkit. The results were evident in the right-wing media's blame-shifting about the border crisis, in polls showing that many voters didn't connect Trump to the repeal of *Roe v. Wade,* and in the GOP's denialism about the January 6 attack.

The cloud hovered over the White House during the four years of Trump's presidency. Hillary Clinton campaign chairman John Podesta identified it early on, in February 2017, when he warned that "Trump is deploying a strategy, used by autocrats, designed to completely disorient public perception." Trump, he warned, "is attempting to build a hall of mirrors where even our most basic sensory perceptions are shrouded in confusion. He is emulating the successful strategy of Vladimir Putin."

Unlike the border wall Trump promised to implement, a reality-compromising hall of mirrors was fully built in MAGA America by the time Biden took office. Clinton, on the political sidelines, felt she could speak out about it much more forcefully than Biden, who still fielded Fox correspondent Peter Doocy's questions on occasion. In October 2023, as Trump surged ahead in GOP primary polls, Clinton said of the "MAGA extremists" who took marching orders from Trump, "maybe there needs to be a formal deprogramming of the cult members." The comment sparked days of how-dare-she? uproar on Fox, but, in one very narrow way, "deprogramming" was already happening: through the January 6 prosecutions.

One defense attorney said an accused rioter suffered from "Foxitis." Another attorney said his client had "been watching a lot of Fox News at the time." In guilty plea after guilty plea, January 6 rioters admitted that they'd been snookered by Trump and the MAGA media. At least two of the convicted felons met with cult deprogramming specialists.

The "cloud of confusion" clearly affected some of the people who stormed the Capitol. Take "Rally Runner." The Missouri man, Daniel Donnelly Jr., earned his name by running around Busch Stadium during St. Louis Cardinals games in red clothes and paint. His social media footprint showed how he was radicalized—and how he trusted both Trump and Carlson over reliable sources of news. "This is so true!" he wrote on Facebook while sharing a Carlson clip. "Tucker nails it again!" he wrote on another Fox video. On January 6, he used a stolen police shield to help the mob push past the police. He fessed up to the crime in a Facebook video the night of the attack. But in December 2021, Carlson turned on his big fan, showing video of Donnelly in red face paint and expressing doubt that Donnelly was truly a Trump fan. Carlson welcomed a guest who said Donnelly was "clearly a law enforcement officer" and an "agent provocateur." This deeply offended Donnelly, who said he "believed Carlson was a responsible reporter focused on stopping 'fake news' "—until Carlson's show lied about *him.*

In March 2024 Donnelly pleaded guilty to a felony, civil disorder, for his part in the attack. With that, another Carlson lie disintegrated. But the courts could only accomplish so much in terms of truth-telling: On the day when another victim of Carlson's conspiratorial imagination, Ray Epps, pleaded guilty to a misdemeanor count, "baseless and fact-free conspiracy theories about him continued to spread," NBC reported. Epps's defamation suit against Fox was still active, and he was still in hiding due to merciless threats from fascistic Trump fans.

Remarkably, one of Fox's longtime personalities said he supported Epps's lawsuit! But his comments came after he had parted ways with the network. "Fox left me," Geraldo Rivera said, by way of explaining why his twenty-year relationship with the network ended in 2023. It all started when management removed Rivera from *The Five,* the top-rated show where he'd been a regular host and an equally regular pain in the ass, with an eye toward letting his pricey contract expire. But Rivera still had a year and a half left on his deal, so he was offered some pity prizes, like a streaming series on Fox Nation. He said no thanks and decided to leave the network altogether. And that's when he began to dish about the madness inside Fox. He confirmed (in an interview on his soon-to-be employer NewsNation) that he was reprimanded for speaking out against Carlson's inside-job inanity: "I got a call as soon as that was published . . . from Fox executives who said 'You're suspended. You're not supposed to speak to the press unless you clear it with us,' which of course is Catch-22 because they never clear it." Rivera didn't regret his decision, though, because "everyone knows that it was Donald Trump inciting an insurrection. . . . And I think that for Fox to pretend that there was an honest debate about January 6, or the 2020 election, I think, was obscene."

In other interviews, Rivera said he detected a climate of "fear" at the network due to the pileup of defamation lawsuits. But the lawsuits had merit, he said, agreeing with Epps's decision to sue, and calling the 2020 period an embarrassment that will be hard for Fox to live down.

Yes, except that some of the players seemed incapable of embarrassment anymore. While the "cloud of confusion" was real, it was also fair to say that a vocal minority of Americans, the type that flew "TRUMP OR DEATH" flags, really, truly wanted the most extreme form of Trumpism. They wanted their perceived enemies to feel intimidated. They wanted "patriots" to ransack the Capitol to stop the opposing party from taking power. They wanted their fellow Americans to suffer. They loved it when Trump talked about "retribution," deporting millions of people, and replacing government civil servants with MAGA loyalists. Trump's second-term pledges proved that he was the leader of a "global fascist movement," Brian Schatz, the Democratic senior senator from Hawaii, told me.

Schatz recognized the weight of his words. "When you describe things exactly as they are, you sound a little nuts," he said. "And that's the problem. If you want to sound like you're a thoughtful, moderate, deal-making pragmatist, then you're not supposed to say what is true, which is that there is now a—not even a loose alliance—a pretty explicit alliance between fascists all over the planet that includes Donald Trump." He cited, among other pieces of evidence, Trump's embrace of Hungarian prime minister Viktor Orbán at Mar-a-Lago. Trump praised the strongman at length, claiming Orbán is "a noncontroversial figure because he says, 'This is the way it's going to be,' and that's the end of it. Right? He's the boss."

Trump wanted the same powers. And some voters were inclined to give them to him because political sectarianism ruled all. "What we saw on January 6 was the tip of an iceberg," former Homeland Security secretary Jeh Johnson said on CNN. "More and more Americans are becoming detached from reality. More and more Americans are becoming prone to violence." Some of Fox's most popular shows played footsie with this extremist crowd even as Fox's ad sales execs promoted the network's bipartisan audience. (It was true—lots of Democrats and moderates hate-watched Fox and some even liked it.) This was Fox's version of "bothsidesism," flirting with the antidemocratic forces within the GOP while remaining attractive to a wider audience. By burying some stories, and overdramatizing others, Fox could have it both ways.

The network's shows never dwelled on Trump's appalling use of the phrase "January 6 hostages" to describe people facing charges for the insurrection. In fact, it barely ever came up at all. Hosts didn't call him out for glossing over the violence (a key tactic of fascist leaders) or whitewashing the riot by promoting an alternative national anthem sung by a group of prison inmates. Experts warned that Trump was borrowing from well-worn authoritarian playbooks. But pointing out his unfitness for office was "bad for business," to borrow Suzanne Scott's words from 2020. Thus Fox even downplayed its own major-league scoops when the storylines were hurtful to the Trump cause. Mike Pence decided to use a March 2024 interview on Fox to declare for the first time that he would not endorse Trump's reelection bid. In a normal political world it would have been jaw-dropping news; Biden exploited it in speeches, saying with a smile, "*My* vice president actually endorses me." But Fox ignored its own scoop. Pence's refusal to support his former running mate was barely mentioned on the network at all after the initial interview. "Pence provided a permission structure for Fox viewers to join him in declining to support Trump," Matt Gertz of Media Matters noted. "But Fox is in the tank for Trump's campaign, so the network shielded its viewers from the news."

Biden chose to call out Fox by name twice while marking the third anniversary of January 6, which he dubbed the day "that we nearly lost America." He referred to Fox's "record" payout to Dominion, and he said that the network's commentators quickly condemned the attack but later "changed their tune."

"Politics, fear, money—all have intervened," Biden said. "And now these MAGA voices who know the truth about Trump on January 6 have abandoned the truth and abandoned democracy." How did Fox's Martha MacCallum sum up the president's searing critiques? She said "he took a couple of pot shots at this network."

■

As the 2024 election calcified into the repeat episode that so many people dreaded, and the Trump indictments piled up, so did the excuses. Going back in time a bit, to the day when the former president was charged with thirty-seven criminal counts of illegally retaining classified documents and obstructing justice by refusing to return the documents to the government, Mark Levin went on Hannity's show and began a litany of berserk accusations by saying the Justice Department wanted Trump to die in federal prison. He claimed the case amounted to "war on the Republican party" and screamed, "You wanna talk about an insurrection? This is an insurrection!"

Fox elevated Levin and a small number of other legal "experts" (but really right-wing hard-liners) who condemned the indictment. They largely ignored the much greater number of experts who said the indictment was persuasive and devastating in its detail. Former

Fox commentator Jonah Goldberg pointed out that the network was, in its own twisted way, "respecting the audience." Carlson was doing the same thing off in the Twitterverse, adding a soupçon of religiosity, claiming that "yes, Donald Trump is a flawed man, but his sins are minor compared to those of his persecutors."

Then came the special counsel's indictment relating to January 6. And the RICO case in Georgia. And multiple state-level prosecutions of fake electors that IDed Trump as an "unindicted co-conspirator." A staggering mountain of evidence piled up, one case on top of another, portending serious consequences for election deniers. Trump "may be center stage but his story is being told by a chorus of prosecutors," liberal commentator David Rothkopf observed. "The NY hush money case depicts the sleaze. The Mar-a-Lago case depicts the national security threat. The E. Jean Carroll case depicts his misogyny and lies. The Jack Smith January 6 case cuts to his role at the center of an attack on our democracy."

And yet, in polling by *The New York Times* and Siena College, 91 percent of people who relied on Fox for information said they did not believe Trump had committed any serious crimes. The fact that the pollsters still asked specifically about Fox, and no other outlets, showed its outsize role. This was the age of "viewers as voters," as *Times* writer Jonathan Mahler put it, and "each new poll confirming the resilience of Trump's popularity—despite four indictments and 91 criminal charges—is a testament to Murdoch's impact."

At the Iowa State Fair, an NBC reporter approached one Jeff Lenderink, a school custodian from Pella, Iowa, and asked, "Do you care that he's been indicted four times?" No, Lenderink said, "it just makes me want to vote for him more."

"Why?"

"Because whoever the Democrats hate is who I like."

Whether unable or unwilling to tell the truth to a fully propagandized audience of men like Lenderink, Fox found itself in a prison of its own design. Trump and his fans were fully in charge of the MAGA media universe now. Ergo, helpful fictions were hyped while harmful facts were discarded. When the hush money cover-up trial began in New York, Trump's lawyers asked for court to be adjourned on the day of Barron Trump's high school graduation. Judge Juan M. Merchan did not immediately rule one way or another, but Trump came outside to a bank of live TV cameras and lied about it, claiming "I can't go to my son's graduation." He repeated the lies on his Truth Social platform. Reliable news outlets fact-checked his drivel, but Fox stars like Jesse Watters treated it like gospel. "If he tries to go" to graduation "the judge will throw him in jail," Watters claimed, because it sounded good, even though it was garbage. (Merchan later ruled that Trump could attend graduation, and Trump did, just as every normal person expected he would.)

Did management care about the effects of this never-ending misinformation pipeline? Evidently not. The execs underneath Rupert and Lachlan Murdoch "are mechanical, not ideological," as one host put it to me. Scott and her deputies weren't having lively off-air conversations about economic populism versus free market conservatism. They weren't secretly plotting whether to promote J. D. Vance or Tulsi Gabbard on-air as Trump VP options. They weren't interested in flaunting their power over the American right the way Roger Ailes was. No, in the Scott era, the executives were just trying to hit their ratings and profit targets. They weren't leading—they were following.

The same assessment applied to Rupert too. He was following his heart, or some body part, as he sailed the Mediterranean with another new gal pal, Elena Zhukova, a retired molecular biologist. In

June 2024, the couple exchanged vows at Rupert's Bel Air vineyard. He was still in an emeritus role at Fox; his semiretirement announcement was accompanied by the promise that he would still be roaming the company's halls on Friday afternoons, and that was generally true, if you substituted Zoom meetings for halls. He popped up there and here, still making his presence known, though with little substantive involvement. He wasn't plotting how to remove Trump's grip on the Republican Party, he was planning his next honeymoon.

But far too many people thought otherwise. People like Republican members of the House of Representatives, and MAGA-fluent school board members, and your neighbor who wore "I miss the America I grew up in" T-shirts, and your uncle who posted "own the libs" memes on Facebook. These people saw Fox as the commanding general of the army. And they were eager to salute and follow orders.

Fox was less like General George Patton and more like the bearded guy who gets out of his Ford F-150 at a traffic-choked intersection and starts directing drivers this way and that way, not with any special knowledge or experience, but just out of his own desire to get home faster. Yes, some individual Fox hosts knew how to wield influence. But Fox as an institution was not equipped or empowered—or even motivated—to lead. When Rupert was asked in his deposition, "Do you think that fair-minded people can conclude that Fox News bears some responsibility for the polarized divisions in our country?" his answer was "no."

That's what a passenger would say, not a leader.

What happens when the driver of a car thinks he's the passenger, just along for the ride? With no one at the wheel, most likely the car crashes in spectacular fashion, hurts innocent people, and causes more damage than the "driver" may ever comprehend.

AFTERWORD

The 2020 election was a storm that unleashed the darkest forces in America since the Civil War, and certainly the darkest moments in the history of Fox News: punishing losses from defamation lawsuits; embarrassing claims from employees; and ever more vocal condemnation in Washington, in columns by critical journalists, in the streets around its headquarters, in the halls of the same building—even inside its own boardroom.

Exposed in the courts and before the public for its willingness to traffic in lies that even its own most prominent messengers didn't believe, all to serve an audience it had conditioned to reject any visitation by the truth, Fox was finally stripped to its skin—shorn even of the real-journalism ("Fair & Balanced") fig leaf that it had hidden behind since its inception in 1996.

There was an ominous symmetry to the MAGA media's descent into rage-filled chaos. The country was battered month after month by a torrent of lies from a deposed political leader lacking in ethics and decency, and a party either in his thrall, or so cowardly it shrank from confronting him. The Trump-era war on truth mutated, in the Biden years, into an all-consuming war on trust.

Around every corner, down every social media feed, propagandists and grifters warned people not to believe old-line, established, peer-reviewed institutions. The message was "they're corrupt," "they're lying," so "do your own research." But the Fox stars who fashioned themselves as brave new truth-tellers, as replacements for the hollowed-out media of yore, demonstrated, over and over again, that they were unworthy of trust.

Thanks in large part to what Rupert started with Fox News nearly three decades earlier, the network of lies truly was a constellation now, with streaming upstarts like Steve Bannon's War Room and Right Side Broadcasting and Real America's Voice. What they lacked in scale, they added in intensity; the volume was pure *Spinal Tap*, amped up to 11, all the time, creating all sorts of newfound competition for Fox. But none of the noise rated or profited or warped public perception quite like the original; people who tried to write off Fox News were wrong in 1996 and they were wrong again now. Even Dominion's quest for justice and Carlson's quest for revenge were not fatal blows. Newsmax was still a JV operation. OAN was still a joke. Fox was still the beating heart of the Trumpified GOP.

Trump's never-ending all-caps complaints about Fox distracted from the far more relevant fact that Fox's targets were his targets. They shared an enemies list. Biden was at the top, since the surest way to produce a successful Fox segment was to cast Biden as a crook, a dementia patient, a wannabe dictator—or, ideally, somehow, all of the above. The sheer volume of Biden hatred was bewildering to anyone not fully steeped in the Fox cinematic universe. One day Watters gave up the game: "Do I feel sorry for Joe Biden? No!" he said on air. "I work at Fox! I want to see disarray on the left! It's good for America! It's good for our ratings!"

Day after day, year after year, in ways big and small, Fox viewers heard that Biden and his allies were destroying America. Fox hyped a nonexistent "crime wave" for months. (FBI data showed the crime rate was dropping.) Fox falsely claimed that Biden was "mandating" production of electric vehicles. (His administration encouraged them but didn't ban conventional cars.) A Fox story wrongly acted as though the Biden White House had banned religious themes in an Easter egg art contest. (Those nonpartisan guidelines dated back to the 1970s and had nothing to do with Biden.) White House deputy press secretary Andrew Bates hit back by saying "the only 'news' outlet in U.S. history to pay almost $1 billion for lying to their viewers/readers has egg on their faces again."

Clever statements were no match for the fire hose of falsehood. On Fox, the House GOP's shambolic Biden impeachment inquiry was a virtuous probe into a capital-S scandal, when the actual scandal was the GOP's decision to waste time on a political vendetta mission that inevitably fell apart. On Fox, Biden's handling of the post-pandemic economy was catastrophic, when the truth was that America's economy was the envy of the world. Whenever political analysts assessed the reasons for Biden's low approval ratings, rightwing media propaganda had to be near the top of the list. Plus, Trump watched it all and spit it back at rallies, hardening the audience's views into cement.

As the 2024 election season ramped up, Fox ran multiple Trump campaign ads disguised as interviews; at the end of February, for instance, Fox erected an entire studio along the U.S. southern border at Eagle Pass, Texas, and welcomed Trump for an hour of fearmongering with Sean Hannity. "Our country is being poisoned," Trump declared. "Millions of people from lots of bad places" are "pouring into our country." He mentioned "mental institutions" and "insane asylums." And he said he'd been listening to Hannity's warnings about terrorists crossing the border. "As somebody who watches your show a lot," Trump said, "I think you do a fantastic job." The dark days of January 2021, when Rupert said Hannity was "in despair" about Trump, and Suzanne Scott said Hannity "wants to help lead the 75 million forward away from Trump," were entirely forgotten. *The New Yorker* called it "Trump's amnesia advantage."

The Big Lie lawsuits were a crucial way to remember. As I absorbed thousands of pages of emails, texts, and Dominion deposition transcripts, I found myself thinking that the people in charge of the Fox machine should take their own advice. As Rupert said to Suzanne Scott on February 5, 2021, in an apparent rebuke of newly minted GOP congresswoman Marjorie Taylor Greene of Georgia, "Fox News and shows like *Hannity* should not champion public figures who appear mad." (As in nuts.)

As Scott said in editorial meetings, shows should "focus on the facts."

As Lachlan said in his deposition, "You never want to knowingly report a falsehood."

And as Hannity said in his deposition, "If you can't prove it, you better not say it."

Most powerfully, when Rupert was asked "Does Fox have a responsibility to tell the truth, even when its viewers don't want to hear it?" he said yes.

Imagine if Fox actually lived up to that responsibility.

Instead, Fox whispered the truth and shouted the lies.

But there are ways to resist. Ways to recognize and reject the brainwashing that right-wing media transmits. Ways to ensure accountability. Here are a few:

- *Journalists are helping people see through the "cloud of confusion."*

In early 2024 *The New York Times* analyzed a week's worth of Trump interviews, speeches, and social media posts and put together a guide to his "recurring rhetorical moves." It was like a cheat sheet for the entire election season. "He grossly distorts his opponents' records and proposals to make them sound unreasonable," the *Times* said. He "exaggerates and twists the facts to make his record sound better than it is." He "relies on both well-worn and fresh claims of election rigging to suggest he can lose only if his opponents cheat." He "has turned his criminal cases into a rallying cry, baselessly asserting that he is being persecuted by his successor." He "makes unverifiable claims about what the world would have been like had he secured a second term." He "describes the United States as a nation in ruins." Once the tricks are outlined, readers and viewers can call foul.

- *Media veterans, including former Fox executives, are challenging Fox's fitness.*

Preston Padden, a key executive in the Murdochs' assemblage of broadcasting stations to build and expand the Fox broadcasting network in the nineties, publicly turned on Rupert over what he considered egregious violations of the public's trust by Fox News. "In my opinion, Fox News does not actually present news because that is not what their core viewers want," Padden told me. "Those viewers want anger/resentment confirmation, and that is what the channel serves up." In 2023 Padden organized an effort to stop the FCC from rubber-stamping the renewal of Fox's broadcast license in Philadelphia. Other former Fox bigwigs joined him. Although the broadcast TV business is declining, challenges to license renewals could still be a potent tool for making change.

- *Former Fox personalities are speaking out about the network's tactics.*

Geraldo Rivera's resignation freed him up to testify in public about Carlson's "unforgivable" January 6 propaganda. Rivera said Carlson engaged in it because "that's what the audience wants. In other words, it wasn't the malevolent media leading the audience. It was the audience leading the malevolent media." The more clearly this dynamic is understood, the more thoroughly it can be defeated.

- *A new generation of elected officials is approaching hyperpartisan media with more savvy.*

Some Democrats, such as California governor Gavin Newsom and transportation secretary Pete Buttigieg, choose to go on Fox from time to time, specifically to puncture the filter bubble. Others study the network to understand how it operates and distorts political outcomes. "People think Fox News is just about indoctrinating right-wingers, but it's also about conditioning Dems on what to run away from," New York congresswoman Alexandria Ocasio-Cortez told her allies. She cautioned them not to indulge made-up "controversy" frames.

- *Average voters are rejecting the dehumanization of political opponents.*

The country's divisions are all too often exaggerated and exploited by brands like Fox. As Monica Guzman, author of *I Never Thought of It That Way,* put it, "Whoever is underrepresented in your life will be overrepresented in your imagination." We have all experienced a version of this. "Instead of people," she said, "you'll see monsters. Instead of possibilities, you'll see disasters. That's the challenge of a polarized world." Organizations like More in Common and Braver Angels exist to counter this phenomenon. Filmmaker Jen Senko, who made the documentary *The Brainwashing of My Dad,* collects personal stories from people who feel they've lost loved ones to a cult. Reading the stories can be gut-wrenching, but also reassuring, because so many families are facing the same challenges.

- *Even some Murdoch family members are funding antidotes to Fox's poison.*

Many of James and Kathryn Murdoch's investments are meant to address what they see as right-wing media damage, particularly around climate issues. Most recently, in the summer of 2023, they started a production studio to encourage "more protopian stories—protopian being realistic, better futures," Kathryn said, to counter the dystopian narratives around every corner. Kathryn also served on the Aspen Institute's Commission on Information Disorder, which proposes solutions like new platforms "that are designed to bridge divides, build empathy, and strengthen trust among communities," rather than tear it all down; the promotion of new "accountability norms" so that lie "superspreaders" aren't let off the hook; and a Public Restoration Fund to counter misinformation.

- *Lawyers are making it more costly to sow disinformation.*

   Dominion and Smartmatic are just the highest-profile examples. Multiple individuals have also sued Fox and other hard-right outlets. In July 2024, Hunter Biden took a novel approach by accusing Fox of allegedly violating New York's revenge-porn statute. He wanted to expose Fox for exposing him.

   ■

No single investment or indictment or congressional committee could cure what ailed American politics. No single lawsuit or exposé or petition could heal its sickened information streams. But, all together, in combination, the steps toward accountability were powerful and persuasive. All across America new ideas and initiatives were being imagined and enacted in a widely shared determination to uproot the network of lies with seeds of truth. Could Americans of all ages and backgrounds and beliefs come together to speak more loudly than the liars? Yes, they could, and they did, knowing that fictions aided autocracy while facts nourished democracy. Most people just want to know what is true, not what trolls want them to think. The network of reality will, in the end, triumph.

ACKNOWLEDGMENTS

When I pitched this book to my editor, Julia Cheiffetz, I also proposed an impossible timeline. "This is a story about American politics and media circa 2020 to 2023," I wrote. "A story about what's broken, who broke it, and how to fix it." We should publish before the 2024 election begins in earnest, I continued, because the revelations from the Big Lie lawsuits and the January 6 investigations should be widely accessible to the public, not buried in court filings and government databases.

Cheiffetz made it happen. I'm still not sure how, but she did. She also challenged me in all the best ways. Thank you, Julia, and thanks to editorial assistant Hannah Frankel; assistant editor Abby Mohr; executive editor Nick Ciani; production editor Mark LaFlaur; copy editor Fred Chase; and Alessandra Bastagli, Libby McGuire, Jonathan Karp, Adam Rothberg, David Brown, and Falon Kirby.

To hit the deadlines, I reunited with a former colleague from *The New York Times*, and a four-time author of must-read tales about must-see TV, Bill Carter. Bill scrutinized every word and helped me see what was missing from the story. Getting to work with him again was one of the highlights of my professional life. Thank you, Bill.

I incubated this project while on a fellowship at Harvard Kennedy School's Shorenstein Center on Media, Politics and Public Policy and am grateful to Nancy Gibbs, Laura Manley, and the entire Shorenstein team. I am also indebted to intrepid researchers Scott Nover and Natalie Korach; to my unstoppable book agent Pilar Queen; and to the many executives and spokespeople who facilitated interviews and meetings for this book. Several online tools were indispensable, namely the Internet Archive's TV news database; SnapStream; and TVEyes.

Spending nearly a decade on TV honed my understanding of how networks do and don't work. Thank you to Jeff Zucker, Amy Entelis, and Andrew Morse for giving me a chance behind the anchor desk; and to friends like Oliver Darcy, Emily Kuhn, and Jonathan Auerbach for making every day at CNN meaningful.

Post-CNN, I was fortunate to take on a new assignment: stay-at-home-dad. The shift in perspective was valuable beyond belief. Thank you to my mother, Donna, for teaching me the difference between fact and fiction at a very young age. Thank you to my in-laws Helen and Neil for being my biggest fans. And thanks, most of all, to my wife of ten years, Jamie, who believed in this project even when I did not believe I could finish it in time.

One day last spring my six-year-old, Sunny, came home from school and gave me a quiz she'd taken in class. "Fact or opinion?" she asked before imagining examples of each. I aced the quiz (whew) and then proposed a more nuanced version: "Fact, opinion, or lie?" My four-year-old, Story, soon joined in. The kids found it fantastically easy to ferret out lies and distinguish between feelings and facts. If they can do it, there's hope for the rest of us.

NOTES

Most quotations that are not otherwise specifically attributed are from direct communications between a source and the author or from legal filings in the *Dominion Voting Systems v. Fox News Network* lawsuit (settled April 2023).

PROLOGUE

1   *special counsel Jack Smith alleged:* United States v. Donald J. Trump, Case 1:23-cr-00257-TSC, hereinafter *United States v. Donald J. Trump.*

2   *the two executives asked:* Jonathan Swan and Maggie Haberman, "Trump Dines with Fox News Executives After Learning of Third Indictment," *New York Times*, August 2, 2023, https://www.nytimes.com/2023/08/02/us /politics/trump-fox-news-indictment.html.

2   *"it would be foolish":* Trump interview with *Breitbart News*, published August 2, 2023.

2   *"You're 90 percent good":* Rupert Murdoch's deposition in *Dominion v. Fox News*, N21C-03-257 EMD, hereinafter *Dominion v. Fox.*

3   *"we want to make Trump a non person":* Ibid.

3   *"dozens of specific claims":* United States v. Donald J. Trump.

4   *Lachlan sued the site:* Jeremy Barr, "Lachlan Murdoch Sues Site over Article Linking Family to Capitol Riot," *Washington Post*, August 23, 2022, https: //www.washingtonpost.com/media/2022/08/23/lachland-murdoch-sues -crikey-defamation/.

4   *"it's a slam-dunk First Amendment case":* Abby Grossberg, *Deadline: White House*, MSNBC, April 25, 2023.

7   *"sometimes the point"*: Anne Applebaum, "History Will Judge the Complicit," *The Atlantic*, July/August 2020 , https://www.theatlantic.com/magazine/archive/2020/07/trumps-collaborators/612250/.

7   *"flood the zone with shit"*: Michael Lewis, "Has Anyone Seen the President?," Bloomberg, February 9, 2018, https://www.bloomberg.com/view/articles/2018-02-09/has-anyone-seen-the-president.

7   *"the American Right has"*: Jon Meacham, *The 11th Hour*, MSNBC, August 4, 2023.

PART ONE

"The purge"

11   *"Abby Grossberg's lawsuits"*: *Abby Grossberg v. Fox Corporation et al.*, Case No.: 1:23-cv-02368, hereinafter *Abby Grossberg v. Fox.*

11   *"going to any means possible"*: Ray Epps, *60 Minutes*, CBS, April 23, 2023.

12   *"antagonistic conduct"*: Lydia O'Connor, "Ex-Fox News Reporter Says Network Fired Him For Opposing Its Jan. 6 Coverage," *HuffPost*, November 13, 2023, https://www.huffpost.com/entry/fox-news-reporter-lawsuit-capitol-riot_n_6552ac62e4b0373d70b351f3.

12   *"Fox News wanted to purge"*: *Jason Donner v. Fox News Network*, Case No.: 2023-CAB-006055, hereinafter *Jason Donner v. Fox.*

13   *"To win back"*: *Jason Donner v. Fox.*

13   *"Be safe"*: Jason Donner, "Reporter's Notebook: Inside the US Capitol during the Jan. 6 riot," FoxNews.com, January 10, 2021, https://www.foxnews.com/politics/reporters-notebook-capitol-riot.

14   *"Then the video feed"*: Ibid.

14   *plan an escape route*: *Jason Donner v. Fox.*

17   *"More than just"*: Edward-Isaac Dovere, Steve Contorno, and Annie Grayer, "Why does Biden keep mentioning January 6? Because Trump won't stop talking about it," CNN.com, March 16, 2024, https://www.cnn.com/2024/03/16/politics/biden-trump-january-6/index.html.

"Hurting America"

19   *"I had financial demands"*: Kelefa Sanneh, "Tucker Carlson's Fighting Words," *The New Yorker*, April 3, 2017, https://www.newyorker.com/magazine /2017/04/10/tucker-carlsons-fighting-words.

19 *he told a biographer:* Chadwick Moore, *Tucker* (Fort Lauderdale: All Seasons Press, 2023).

20 *Stewart had been reluctant:* Josh Cowen, "My Profane, Revealing Year Working for Tucker Carlson," *Slate*, April 25, 2023, https://slate.com/business/2023/04/tucker-carlson-fired-crossfire-cnn-fox-news-offensive-jokes.html.

21 *"I was long gone from CNN":* Lyz Lenz, "The Mystery of Tucker Carlson," *Columbia Journalism Review*, September 5, 2018, https://www.cjr.org/the_profile/tucker-carlson.php.

21 *"It took me twenty years":* Brian Stelter, "Still a Conservative Provocateur, Carlson Angles for Clicks, Not Fights," *New York Times*, October 7, 2012, https://www.nytimes.com/2012/10/08/business/media/tucker-carlson-angles-for-daily-caller-clicks-not-fights.html.

22 *After only six weeks:* Brian Stelter, "Carlson's Situation Moves to Late-Night," *TVNewser*, July 29, 2005, https://www.adweek.com/tvnewser/carlsons-situation-moves-to-late-night/7069/.

23 *"You're a loser":* Jason Zengerle, "Fox News Gambled, but Tucker Can Still Take Down the House," *New York Times*, April 28, 2023, https://www.nytimes.com/2023/04/28/opinion/tucker-carlson-fox.html.

24 *"whatever they want me to do":* Brian Stelter, "Tucker Carlson Turns 40, Moves to Fox News," *New York Times*, May 15, 2009, https://nyti.ms/3QENG9c.

26 *"effective populists are":* Carlson's interview on *Stay Free with Russell Brand*, July 7, 2023.

26 *who emailed his neighbor Hunter Biden:* Martin Pengelly, "Tucker Carlson Tried to Use Hunter Biden to Get His Son into Georgetown," *The Guardian*, May 20, 2022, https://www.theguardian.com/us-news/2022/may/19/tucker-carlson-hunter-biden-georgetown-emails.

26 *"last night in Sweden":* Peter Baker and Sewell Chan, "From an Anchor's Lips to Trump's Ears to Sweden's Disbelief," *New York Times*, February 20, 2017, https://www.nytimes.com/2017/02/20/world/europe/trump-pursues-his-attack-on-sweden-with-scant-evidence.html.

"You are not crazy"

29 *The government called it:* "Cesar Sayoc Pleads Guilty to 65 Felonies," Department of Justice press release, March 21, 2019, https://www.justice.gov

/opa/pr/cesar-sayoc-pleads-guilty-65-felonies-mailing-16-improvised-explo
sive-devices-connection.

29 *Carlson felt attacked*: Allyson Chiu, "Tucker Carlson's Home Targeted by
Protesters," *Washington Post*, November 8, 2018, https://www.washington
post.com/nation/2018/11/08/they-were-threatening-me-my-family-tucker
-carlsons-home-targeted-by-protesters/.

29 *police observed no damage*: Brian Stelter, "Tucker Carlson Claimed His
Door Was 'Cracked' by Antifa Protesters. The Police Saw No Sign of
That," CNN, November 16, 2018, https://www.cnn.com/2018/11/16/media
/tucker-carlson-cracked-door/index.html.

30 *"we're good"*: Nicholas Confessore, "How Tucker Carlson Stoked White
Fear to Conquer Cable," *New York Times*, April 30, 2022, https://www.ny
times.com/2022/04/30/us/tucker-carlson-gop-republican-party.html.

30 *"You couldn't ask"*: Sarah Ellison, "Fox News Host Tucker Carlson Is
Loudly Ignoring Impeachment," *Washington Post*, November 12, 2019,
https://wapo.st/3YrmpZP.

31 *"more in tune"*: Michael Anton, "Tucker's Right," *Claremont Review of
Books*, Spring 2019, https://claremontreviewofbooks.com/tuckers-right1/.

31 *"My family watches"*: Derek Black, The Van Jones Show, CNN, March 30,
2019.

31 *When surveyed*: "Summer Unrest over Racial Injustice Moves the Country,
but Not Republicans or White Evangelicals," August 21, 2020, https://
www.prri.org/research/racial-justice-2020-george-floyd/.

32 *When a young Fox producer*: Nicholas Confessore, "What to Know About
Tucker Carlson's Rise," *New York Times*, April 30, 2022, https://www.nytimes
.com/2022/04/30/business/media/tucker-carlson-fox-news-takeaways.html.

33 *"treated his audience with contempt"*: Jennifer Mercieca, "Tucker Carlson's Show
Was Bad for America," *Resolute Square*, April 27, 2023, https://bit.ly/45oYb4Z.

34 *"I want to live in a world"*: Tucker Carlson, *Tucker Carlson Tonight*, Fox
News, January 16, 2020.

35 *"you are not alone"*: Tucker Carlson, *Tucker Carlson Tonight*, Fox News,
June 16, 2020.

"That cunt"

35 *"I'll die here"*: Rosemary Rossi, "Tucker Carlson Felt Trapped at Fox News,
Newly-Released Texts Reveal," *TheWrap*, May 9, 2023, https://www.the
wrap.com/tucker-carlson-fox-news-ill-die-here-texts/.

35 *"I'm stuck with Fox":* Ibid.

36 *"I hate him passionately":* Dominion Voting Systems v. Fox News Network.

36 *"You are the worst human":* Daniel Politi, "Watch Montana Man Confront Tucker Carlson," Slate, July 24, 2021, https://slate.com/news-and-politics /2021/07/video-dan-bailey-confronts-tucker-carlson-montana.html.

37 *Trump got Carlson on the phone:* Sravasti Dasgupta, "Tucker Carlson Tells 'Wounded' Trump That He Loves Him," *The Independent*, March 22, 2023, https://www.independent.co.uk/news/world/americas/us-politics /tucker-carlson-dominion-texts-donald-trump-b2305597.html.

38 *"Carlson would have been better off":* Nikki McCann Ramirez, "Trump Steamrolls Tucker Carlson on His Own Show," *Rolling Stone*, April 11, 2023, https://www.rollingstone.com/politics/politics-news/trump-tucker -carlson-fox-news-arraignment-interview-1234713349/.

38 *he drove a golf cart:* Chadwick Moore, *Tucker* (Fort Lauderdale: All Seasons Press, 2023).

38 *"We're taking you off":* Ibid.

41 *"actually mind-blowing":* Julia Mueller, "Trump Jr. Slams Fox News over Carlson Exit," *The Hill*, April 24, 2023, https://thehill.com/homenews /media/3966850-trump-jr-slams-fox-news-over-carlson-exit-this-changes -things -permanently/.

41 *"He's a very good person":* Dominick Mastrangelo, "Trump 'Shocked' to HEAR of Tucker Carlson's Departure from Fox News," *The Hill*, April 24, 2023, https://thehill.com/homenews/3969592-trump-shocked-to-hear-of -tucker-carlsons-departure-from-fox-news/.

41 *Grossberg said she was hauled:* Abby Grossberg v. Fox.

42 *"a full-blown nut case":* Carlson's interview on *The Adam Carolla Show*, April 2, 2023.

42 *"so overused":* Moore, Tucker.

43 *"a movement":* Moore, Tucker.

44 *"more time for fishing?":* Shawn Cohen, "Tucker Carlson's Shocked Neighbors in His Quaint Maine Town Rally Round the Firebrand," Daily Mail, April 28, 2023, https://www.dailymail.co.uk/news/article-12025347/Tucker-Carlsons -shock-firing-set-outpouring-support-locals-quaint-Maine-town.html.

"Messenger from God"

44 *By one account:* Neil Chenoweth, *Rupert Murdoch: The Untold Story of the World's Media Wizard* (Crown Business, 2002).

44 *"I thought she was"*: William Shawcross, *Rupert Murdoch: Ringmaster of the Information Circus* (London: Pan Books, 1993).

44 *"He was like a whirlwind"*: Ibid.

45 *"I think that Rupert's affair"*: David Leser, "Anna and Her Kingdom," *The Australian Women's Weekly,* February 2000.

45 *"You didn't know you were poor"*: Rob Haskell, "Wendi Murdoch Is Nothing Less than a Force of Nature," *Vogue,* July 20, 2016, https://www.vogue.com /article/businesswoman-wendi-murdoch-career-profile.

45 *Deng befriended a California couple:* John Lippman, Leslie Chang, and Robert Frank, "Rupert Murdoch's Wife Wendi Wields Influence at News Corp," *Wall Street Journal,* October 31, 2000, https://www.wsj.com/articles /SB973040597961471219.

45 *They only lived together:* Ibid.

46 *"die pretty quickly"*: Erich Boehm, "Real Rupe Revealed," *Variety,* November 9, 1998.

46 *"If he marries Deng"*: Emily Bell and Mark Honigsbaum, "Dynasty in Distress," *The Guardian,* March 27, 1999.

47 *The couple nearly broke up:* Amy Chozick, "After 14 Years, Murdoch Files for Divorce from Third Wife," *New York Times,* June 13, 2013, https://www .nytimes.com/2013/06/14/business/media/rupert-murdoch-files-for-divorce -after-14-years-of-marriage.html.

48 *Reason number one:* Mark Seal, "Seduced and Abandoned," *Vanity Fair,* March 2014, https://archive.vanityfair.com/article/2014/3/seduced-and-abandoned.

48 *"verbal abuse"*: Ibid.

48 *"Rupert's never retiring"*: Matthew Belloni, "James and Lachlan Murdoch in First Interview Atop Fox," *Hollywood Reporter,* October 21, 2015, https: //www.hollywoodreporter.com/movies/movie-features/james-lachlan-murdoch -first-interview-833194/.

49 *he viewed Lachlan:* Jonathan Mahler and Jim Rutenberg, "How Rupert Murdoch's Empire of Influence Remade the World," *New York Times,* April 3, 2019, https://www.nytimes.com/interactive/2019/04/03/magazine /james-murdoch-lachlan-succession.html.

49 *"Why the fuck"*: Ibid.

49 *"an American political project"*: Ibid.

51 *He reportedly groused:* Maggie Haberman, *Confidence Man: The Making of Donald Trump and the Breaking of America* (New York: Penguin Press, 2022).

51 *"Jerry, sadly I've decided"*: Gabriel Sherman, "Inside Rupert Murdoch's Suc-

cession Drama," *Vanity Fair*, April 12, 2023, https://www.vanityfair.com
/news/2023/04/rupert-murdoch-cover-story.

53 *Bankers and analysts:* Lauren Hirsch, Maureen Farrell, and Benjamin Mullin, "Major Shareholder Raises Concerns About News Corp's Merger with Fox," *New York Times*, November 25, 2022, https://www.nytimes.com/2022 /11/25/business/dealbook/news-corps-fox-merger.html.

53 *Carlson met Smith:* Gabriel Sherman, "Tucker Carlson's Prayer Talk May Have Led to Fox News Ouster," *Vanity Fair*, April 25, 2023, https://www .vanityfair.com/news/2023/04/tucker-carlson-fox-news-rupert-murdoch.

55 *"He's trying to position himself":* Claire Atkinson, "Insiders Say Tucker Carlson Overplayed His Hand at Fox," *Insider*, April 25, 2023, https: //www.businessinsider.com/tucker-carlson-overplayed-hand-at-fox-where -he-could-go-2023-4.

56 *The Fox board retained:* Jim Rutenberg, Michael S. Schmidt, and Jeremy W. Peters, "Inside Fox's Legal and Business Debacle," *New York Times*, May 27, 2023, https://www.nytimes.com/2023/05/27/business/media/fox-news -dominion-voting.html..

"Pain sponge"

58 *"a laid-back executive":* Ben Smith, "Rupert Murdoch Put His Son in Charge of Fox. It Was a Dangerous Mistake," *New York Times*, March 22, 2020, https://www.nytimes.com/2020/03/22/business/coronavirus-fox-news -lachlan-murdoch.html.

60 *"one little piece of real estate":* Marisa Guthrie, "I Sleep Well at Night: Suzanne Scott on Running Fox News," *Hollywood Reporter*, October 7, 2021, https://www.hollywoodreporter.com/tv/tv-features/suzanne-scott-fox-news -25th-anniversary-1235025880/.

61 *Lindell propped up Carlson:* iSpot.TV data of estimated ad spending, January 1–June 30, 2020.

62 *"Two women approach Donald Trump":* Tucker Carlson, *Tucker Carlson Tonight*, Fox News, December 10, 2018.

PART TWO

"They will cheat big"

69 *"we're in for":* Josh Dawsey and Yasmeen Abutaleb, "Fauci warns of covid-19 surge, offers blunt assessment of Trump's response," *Washington Post*, Octo-

ber, 31, 2020, https://www.washingtonpost.com/politics/fauci-covid-win
ter-forecast/2020/10/31/e3970eb0-1b8b-11eb-bb35-2dcfdab0a345_story.html.

70 *"the single biggest threat to our democracy"*: Jeffrey Goldberg, "Why Obama
Fears for Our Democracy," *The Atlantic*, November 16, 2020, https://www
.theatlantic.com/ideas/archive/2020/11/why-obama-fears-for-our-democracy
/617087/.

71 *"you're not gonna have"*: Emily Goodin, "Barack Obama mocks Donald
Trump's 'superspreader' rallies," *Daily Mail*, October 31, 2020, https://bit.ly
/3P4351J.

72 *Longtime friends said:* William D. Cohan, "Maria Bartiromo Was a Gener-
ational Icon for Financial Television. What Happened?," *Institutional Inves-
tor*, January 15, 2019, https://bit.ly/3DMCeko.

"We love competition"

73 *He told aides:* Jonathan Swan, "Scoop: Trump's Plan to Declare Premature
Victory," *Axios*, November 1, 2020, https://www.axios.com/2020/11/01
/trump-claim-election-victory-ballots.

73 *"It was commonly understood"*: Chris Stirewalt's deposition in *Dominion v. Fox*.

73 *"when the most powerful person"*: Ibid.

77 *Newsmax averaged 50,000:* Brian Stelter, "Fox News Staffers Thought Newsmax Was a Joke. But They're Not Laughing Anymore," CNN, November 25,
2020, https://www.cnn.com/2020/11/25/media/fox-news-newsmax/index.html.

"Call Rupert"

78 *Sean Hannity wrote:* A trove of text messages to and from Mark Meadows
was obtained by the House Select Committee to Investigate the January 6th
Attack on the United States Capitol (hereinafter House's January 6 committee) and shared with news outlets.

78 *Lachlan was texting:* Messages from inside Fox were obtained by Dominion
during the discovery process in *Dominion v. Fox*.

83 *the president shouted:* Carol Leonnig and Phil Rucker, *I Alone Can Fix It*
(New York: Penguin, 2021).

84 *"You better be careful"*: Rupert Murdoch's deposition in *Dominion v. Fox*.

84 *"outlandish"*: Dr. Anthony Fauci, *Reliable Sources*, CNN, September 29, 2020.

85 *He was about to be offered:* Peter Baker, "Inside the Panic at Fox News After
the 2020 Election," *New York Times*, March 4, 2023, https://www.nytimes
.com/2023/03/04/us/politics/panic-fox-news-2020-election.html.

86 *election forecasters still debate:* Nate Cohn, "Why Fox's Call on Arizona, Which Was Right, Was Still Wrong," *New York Times*, March 13, 2023, https://www.nytimes.com/2023/03/13/upshot/fox-arizona-election-call.html.

87 *"way too soon":* Bill Sammon's deposition in *Dominion v. Fox.*

89 *Fox stop making any further projections:* Peter Baker and Susan Glasser, *The Divider* (New York: Doubleday, 2022).

"Those fuckers"

92 *"When I defended":* Chris Stirewalt, "Op-Ed: I Called Arizona for Biden on Fox News. Here's What I Learned," *Los Angeles Times*, January 28, 2021, https://www.latimes.com/opinion/story/2021-01-28/fox-news-chris-stirewalt-firing-arizona.

"Sore loser"

99 *an internal RNC memo:* David Folkenflik, "With Trump's Loss, Murdoch's Fox News Faces Wrath and Tough Choices," NPR, November 7, 2020, https://www.npr.org/2020/11/07/932203022/as-trumps-chances-fade-murdoch-s-fox-news-faces-wrath-and-tough-choices.

100 *"had a closer relationship":* Rupert Murdoch's deposition in *Dominion v. Fox.*

"A Trump explosion"

100 *"I'm not there yet":* Peter Baker, "Inside the Panic at Fox News After the 2020 Election," *New York Times*, March 4, 2023, https://www.nytimes.com/2023/03/04/us/politics/panic-fox-news-2020-election.html.

101 *"still tied up":* Jon Favreau, Twitter post, November 7, 2020, 11:33 a.m., https://twitter.com/jonfavs/status/1325114137085583360.

105 *They ignored Biden's call:* "Biden Pledges to Unify, Not Divide US in Address to Nation," Voice of America, November 7, 2020, https://www.voanews.com/a/2020-usa-votes_biden-pledges-unify-not-divide-us-address-nation/6198097.html.

"The network is being rejected"

107 *Bartiromo thought Rudy Giuliani:* Abby Grossberg's deposition in *Dominion v. Fox.*

107 *"after being impressed":* Maggie Haberman, *Confidence Man: The Making of Donald Trump and the Breaking of America* (New York: Penguin Press, 2022).

110 *Rupert's view:* Rupert Murdoch's deposition in *Dominion v. Fox.*

116 *Separately on Monday:* J. Clara Chan, "Fox News' Sandra Smith Caught on

Hot Mic Scoffing at Guest Who Denied Biden Win," *TheWrap*, November 9, 2020, https://www.thewrap.com/fox-news-sandra-smith-americans-newsroom-guest-deny-biden-victory/.

117 *"Fox News earns the trust":* Philip Bump, "The 'Trust' Fox News Seeks from Its Viewers Isn't About Truth," Philip Bump, *Washington Post*, March 1, 2023, https://www.washingtonpost.com/politics/2023/03/01/fox-news-trump-defamation-lawsuit/.

"Respect the audience"

121 *"What is the downside":* Amy Gardner, Ashley Parker, Josh Dawsey, and Emma Brown, "Top Republicans Back Trump's Efforts to Challenge Election Results," *Washington Post*, November 9, 2020, https://www.washingtonpost.com/politics/trump-republicans-election-challenges/2020/11/09/49e2c238-22c4-11eb-952e-0c475972cfc0_story.html.

127 *"We needed to create":* Interview with the author.

129 *"once the defamation happened":* Dan Primack, "Dominion Voting Systems Tells Its Fox News Lawsuit Story," *Axios*, May 1, 2023, https://www.axios.com/2023/05/01/fox-news-dominion-lawsuit-history.

"Everything at stake here"

132 *"One thing I can't comprehend":* Veronica Stracqualursi, "Republican Election Official in Philadelphia Says He's Seen No Evidence of Widespread Fraud," CNN, November 11, 2020, https://www.cnn.com/2020/11/11/politics/philadelphia-city-commissioner-2020-election-cnntv/index.html.

132 *the crowd's mood changed:* "After Thousands of Trump Supporters Rally in D.C., Violence Erupts When Night Falls," *Washington Post*, November 14, 2020, https://www.washingtonpost.com/dc-md-va/2020/11/14/million-maga-march-dc-protests/.

133 *"if we hadn't called Arizona":* Peter Baker, "Inside the Panic at Fox News After the 2020 Election," *New York Times*, March 4, 2023, https://www.nytimes.com/2023/03/04/us/politics/panic-fox-news-2020-election.html.

133 *"In a Trump environment":* Ibid.

134 *he talked with Lachlan:* Rupert Murdoch's deposition in *Dominion v. Fox.*

135 *"present all the evidence":* Jason Miller's testimony to the House's January 6 committee, February 3, 2022.

140 *snapped at Powell:* Hope Hicks's testimony to the House's January 6 committee, October 25, 2022.

140 *"This does sound crazy"*: Ibid.

141 *The* Examine*r story worked:* Jerry Dunleavy, "Trump Legal Team Shuns Sidney Powell," *Washington Examiner*, November 22, 2020, https://www .washingtonexaminer.com/news/trump-legal-team-shuns-sidney-powell -as-insiders-and-national-security-officials-see-no-evidence-supporting -her-voting-machine-claims.

"No one can tell me differently"

145 *"while we were preparing Thanksgiving"*: First Amendment Salon with Lee Levine, Tom Clare, and Dan Webb, published by the *So to Speak* podcast, May 15, 2023, https://www.thefire.org/research-learn/so-speak-podcast -transcript-first-amendment-salon-lee-levine-tom-clare-and-dan-webb.

145 *"When we got the call"*: Ibid.

146 *According to Dominion:* Motion for Summary Judgment in *Dominion v. Fox*, filed on January 17, 2023, https://bit.ly/3PllRXP.

146 *back in October:* Joe DePaolo, "Fox's Decker Repeatedly Confronts McEnany on Trump Claim Ballots Were Dumped in a River," Mediaite, October 1, 2020, https://www.mediaite.com/news/white-house-briefing-ignites-after-mcenany -scolds-reporter-for-lack-of-journalistic-curiosity-while-dodging-his-question/.

149 *pushed Attorney General:* William Barr's testimony to the House's January 6 committee, June 2, 2022.

150 *he noticed the TV:* Ibid.

153 *The idea had been suggested:* Maggie Haberman and Luke Broadwater, "Emails Shed Light on Trump Fake Electors Plan," *New York Times*, July 26, 2022, https://www.nytimes.com/2022/07/26/us/politics/trump-fake-electors-emails .html.

153 *When Chris Wallace interviewed:* Alex Azar, *Fox News Sunday*, Fox News, December 6, 2020.

"Slipping away"

156 *On December 14, she texted him:* Kayleigh McEnany's testimony to the House's January 6 committee, January 12, 2022.

157 *"this is an* extraordinary *case"*: Adam Klasfeld, "Another Trump-Appointed Judge Rejects Another of the President's Meritless Post-Election Lawsuits," *Law & Crime*, December 12, 2020, https://lawandcrime.com/2020-election /another-trump-appointed-judge-rejects-another-one-of-the-presidents -meritless-post-election-lawsuits/.

PART THREE

"Destroying everything"

161 *"he was in a fantastic mood"*: Sarah Matthews's testimony to the House's January 6 committee, February 8, 2022.

161 *"It was so loud"*: Ibid.

161 *"do the right thing"*: Ibid.

162 *"willing to battle"*: Jeanine Pirro, *Justice with Judge Jeanine*, Fox News, January 3, 2021.

163 *"who doesn't stand up"*: Mark Levin, *Life, Liberty & Levin*, Fox News, January 3, 2021.

163 *"constitutional tinderbox"*: Pete Hegseth, *Fox & Friends*, Fox News, January 6, 2021.

165 *"I'm watching my people getting slammed"*: "Outgoing Capitol Police Chief: House, Senate Security Officials Hamstrung Efforts to Call in National Guard," *Washington Post*, January 10, 2021, https://www.washingtonpost.com/politics/sund-riot-national-guard/2021/01/10/fc2ce7d4-5384-11eb-a817-e5e7f8a406d6_story.html.

165 *"came with riot helmets"*: Ibid.

167 *"Oh, boy"*: Hope Hicks's testimony to the House's January 6 committee, October 25, 2022.

167 *Fox's John Roberts wrote*: Kayleigh McEnany's testimony to the House's January 6 committee, January 12, 2022.

169 *"should call into Fox"*: Ben Williamson's testimony to the House's January 6 committee, January 25, 2022.

170 *"If we ever make it to sentencing"*: Ryan Reilly, "Tucker Carlson's Capitol Videos Are Giving Jan. 6 Defendants False Hope," NBC News, March 13, 2023, https://www.nbcnews.com/politics/justice-department/tucker-carlsons-capitol-videos-are-giving-jan-6-defendants-false-hope-rcna74672.

170 *Trump aide Jason Miller texted*: Ja'han Jones, "Reported Texts Show Just How Far Team Trump Went to Push Lies," MSNBC, April 26, 2022, https://www.msnbc.com/the-reidout/reidout-blog/mark-meadows-texts-jason-miller-rcna26034.

"It is not your fault"

172 *"save the lives"*: "Officer Who Shot Ashli Babbitt During Capitol Riot Breaks Silence," NBC News, August 26, 2021, https://www.nbcnews.com

/news/us-news/officer-who-shot-ashli-babbitt-during-capitol-riot-breaks
-silence-n1277736.

173   *a Trump dead-ender:* Azmi Haroun, "Slain Trump Supporter Tweeted
Conspiracy Theories and Her Devotion to Trump in Days Before Her
Death," *Insider,* January 7, 2021, https://www.businessinsider.com/ashli
-babbitt-tweeted-qanon-and-trump-conspiracies-before-capitol-death-2021-1.

173   *"You are my fave":* Bellingcat Investigation Team, "The Journey of Ashli
Babbitt," *Bellingcat,* January 8, 2021, https://www.bellingcat.com/news/2021
/01/08/the-journey-of-ashli-babbitt/.

173   *She went full-QAnon in 2020:* Ibid.

173   *"When do we start winning?":* Ibid.

175   *"the fantasy-industrial complex":* Sean Illing, "The Fantasy-Industrial Complex Gave Us the Capitol Hill Insurrection," *Vox,* January 8, 2021, https:
//bit.ly/3YsukX1.

176   *"The mob that stormed":* Margaret Sullivan, "The Pro-Trump Media World
Peddled the Lies That Fueled the Capitol Mob. Fox News Led the Way,"
Washington Post, January 7, 2021, https://wapo.st/454nNUL.

177   *"elderly and retiring":* Tucker Carlson, *Tucker Carlson Tonight,* Fox News,
January 13, 2021.

177   *"a dead duck politically":* Brit Hume, *Tucker Carlson Tonight,* Fox News,
January 13, 2021.

179   *On January 12, Ryan forwarded Rupert and Lachlan an article:* "The Morning Dispatch: The Alternate Reality Machine," *The Dispatch,* January 12,
2021, https://thedispatch.com/newsletter/morning/the-morning-dispatch
-the-alternate/.

180   *numerous polls in 2021 and 2022:* Philip Bump, "Nearly 700 Days Later,
Most Republicans Still Believe Trump's Big Lie," *Washington Post,* September 28, 2022, https://www.washingtonpost.com/politics/2022/09/28/nearly
-700-days-later-most-republicans-still-believe-trumps-big-lie/.

"Uncontrollable forces"

182   *Sean Hannity ended 2020:* Brian Flood, "Fox News Finishes 2020 as Most-
Watched Cable News Channel in History," Fox News, December 16, 2020,
https://www.foxnews.com/media/fox-news-finishes-2020-as-most-watched
-cable-news-channel-in-history.

182   *Carlson pressured Mitch McConnell:* Tucker Carlson, *Tucker Carlson Tonight,*
January 13, 2021.

184 *"Some things are simply impervious":* Tucker Carlson, *Politicians, Partisans, and Parasites: My Adventures in Cable News* (New York: Grand Central Publishing, 2003).

185 *Gutfeld hesitated at first:* Greg Gutfeld, *The King of Late Night* (New York: Threshold Editions, 2023).

186 *who had been convicted:* David W. Chen, "Pirro Sentenced to 29 Months in U.S. Prison," *New York Times,* November 2, 2000, https://www.nytimes.com /2000/11/02/nyregion/pirro-sentenced-to-29-months-in-us-prison.html.

"A semi conscious corpse"

188 *Ailes's old rule:* Keach Hagey, "Beck to Leave Fox News Show," *Politico,* April 4, 2011, https://www.politico.com/story/2011/04/beck-to-leave-fox -news-show-052666.

188 *By 2023, six in ten:* Gary Langer, "Broad Doubts About Biden's Age and Acuity Spell Republican Opportunity in 2024," ABC News, May 7, 2023, https://abcnews.go.com/Politics/broad-doubts-bidens-age-acuity-spell -republican-opportunity/story?id=99109308.

189 *Before the election:* Josh Feldman, "Tucker Carlson: Liberals Want to Scare People into Obedience," Mediaite, July 8, 2020, https://bit.ly/47tl09h.

190 *"dripping in bad faith":* Brian Tyler Cohen, Twitter post, January 25, 2021, 4:24 p.m., https://twitter.com/briantylercohen/status/135381599467480 2688.

190 *"one of the most destructive forces in the United States":* Jonathan Martin and Alexander Burns, *This Will Not Pass: Trump, Biden, and the Battle for America's Future* (New York: Simon & Schuster, 2022).

191 *the base gravitated back to Fox:* Brian Stelter, "Newsmax's Post-Election Ratings Bonanza Is Over. What Now?," CNN, March 11, 2021, https://www .cnn.com/2021/03/11/media/newsmax-ratings-decline/index.html.

191 *"further from the real":* Jay Rosen, Twitter post, June 21, 2021, 9:48 p.m., https://twitter.com/jayrosen_nyu/status/1407153469082017792.

"Seeking to kill us"

192 *at least $177 million:* "Disney Pays at Least $177 Million to Settle 'Pink Slime' Case," Reuters, August 9, 2017, https://reut.rs/45pr4xA.

192 *detailed lawsuit: Smartmatic v. Fox Corp et al.,* Case No.: 151136/2021.

193 *"one of the strangest":* Ben Smith, "The 'Red Slime' Lawsuit That Could Sink Right-Wing Media," *New York Times,* December 20, 2021, https:

//www.nytimes.com/2020/12/20/business/media/smartmatic-lawsuit-fox
-news-newsmax-oan.html.

194 *"an intel source telling me"*: Aidan McLaughlin, "Maria Bartiromo Claims
an 'Intel Source' Told Her Trump Did in Fact Win the Election," Mediaite,
December 15, 2020, https://www.mediaite.com/tv/maria-bartiromo-claims
-an-intel-source-told-her-trump-did-in-fact-win-the-election/.

195 *Scott later said:* Suzanne Scott's deposition in *Dominion v. Fox.*

196 *"Mr. Ailes was running"*: Rupert Murdoch's deposition in *Dominion v. Fox.*

197 *"It was clear"*: First Amendment Salon with Lee Levine, Tom Clare, and
Dan Webb, published by the *So to Speak* podcast, May 15, 2023, https://www
.thefire.org/research-learn/so-speak-podcast-transcript-first-amendment
-salon-lee-levine-tom-clare-and-dan-webb.

197 *The suit enumerated four categories of lies: Dominion v. Fox News*, N21C-03
-257 EMD.

198 *I put that to Shackelford: Reliable Sources*, CNN, March 28, 2021.

198 *He was once dubbed:* Anna Schneider-Mayerson, "Hewlett-Packard Lawyer
Dinh Gives Washington the 'Viet-Spin,'" *The Observer*, September 18, 2006,
https://observer.com/2006/09/hewlettpackard-lawyer-dinh-gives-washington
-the-vietspin-2/.

199 *Dinh said the aggrandizement was false:* David Lat, "Is Viet Dinh the Most
Powerful Lawyer In America?," *Original Jurisdiction*, March 17, 2021,
https://davidlat.substack.com/p/is-viet-dinh-the-most-powerful-lawyer.

199 *"They've wasted no time"*: Andrew Hornery, "Murdoch Thrilled to Be Back
in Sydney, While Packer Only Reminded of Failures," *Sydney Morning
Herald*, May 2, 2021, https://bit.ly/3KwE8t1.

199 *"a kind of regent"*: Ben Smith, "Fox Settled a Lawsuit over Its Lies. But It
Insisted on One Unusual Condition," *New York Times*, January 17, 2021,
https://www.nytimes.com/2021/01/17/business/media/fox-news-seth-rich
-settlement.html.

"New war on terror"

201 *"one day in January"*: Chris Cillizza, "Mike Pence Just Said Something
Absolutely Ridiculous About January 6," CNN, October 5, 2021, https:
//www.cnn.com/2021/10/05/politics/mike-pence-january-6-sean-hannity
/index.html.

202 *"We still don't know"*: Tucker Carlson, *Tucker Carlson Tonight*, Fox News,
September 23, 2021.

202 *"We believe that it answers"*: Tucker Carlson, *Tucker Carlson Tonight*, Fox News, October 27, 2021.

203 *most of the people swept up:* "The Jan. 6 Attack: The Cases Behind the Biggest Criminal Investigation in U.S. History," NPR, https://www.npr.org /2021/02/09/965472049/the-capitol-siege-the-arrested-and-their-stories.

204 *"Tucker's wonderful"*: Michael Grynbaum, "Geraldo Rivera Criticizes His Fox News Colleague Tucker Carlson," *New York Times*, October 28, 2021, https://www.nytimes.com/2021/10/28/business/media/tucker-carlson-geraldo -rivera-fox.html.

204 *"I'm tempted just to quit Fox"*: Ben Smith, "Two Fox News Contributors Quit in Protest of Tucker Carlson's Jan. 6 Special," *New York Times*, November 21, 2021, https://www.nytimes.com/2021/11/21/business/jonah-goldberg-steve -hayes-quit-fox-tucker-carlson.html.

205 *"Great news"*: Ibid.

205 *Wallace said later:* Michael Grynbaum, "Chris Wallace Says Life at Fox News Became Unsustainable," *New York Times*, March 27, 2022, https:// www.nytimes.com/2022/03/27/business/media/chris-wallace-cnn-fox -news.html.

206 *"when organizations radicalize"*: Brian Klaas, Twitter post, December 12, 2021, 10:03 a.m., https://twitter.com/brianklaas/status/1470046577981075462.

207 *Fox was hyperventilating about Dr. Seuss:* Aaron Rupar, "Why Fox News Is Having a Day-long Meltdown over Dr. Seuss," *Vox*, March 2, 2021, https: //www.vox.com/2021/3/2/22309176/fox-news-dr-seuss-cancel-culture-fox -news-biden.

208 *"The fundamental dividing line"*: Ron Brownstein, *Reliable Sources* podcast, CNN, January 24, 2021, https://www.cnn.com/audio/podcasts/reliable -sources.

208 *Hannity refused:* Caleb Ecarma, "Sean Hannity Wants the January 6 Committee to Believe He's a Journalist," *Vanity Fair*, January 5, 2022, https:// www.vanityfair.com/news/2022/01/sean-hannity-january-6-committee -journalist.

209 *"You don't want to deal"*: Josephine Harvey, "Juan Williams Accuses Fox News Co-Hosts of 'Ignoring' Impeachment Trial," *HuffPost*, February 10, 2021, https://www.huffpost.com/entry/juan-williams-fox-news-fight _n_6024620bc5b6ddb358159167.

209 *Williams was off:* Brian Steinberg, "Juan Williams Leaving Fox News' The

Five," *Variety*, May 26, 2021, https://variety.com/2021/tv/news/juan-williams
-fox-news-exits-the-five-1234982579/.

209 *"We wanted both"*: Interview with the author.

"Hire some Trump people"

210 *"Need some fresh blood"*: Corbin Bolies and Justin Baragona, "What Else
Do Tucker Carlson's Unredacted Texts Reveal?," *Daily Beast*, May 8, 2023,
https://www.thedailybeast.com/what-else-do-tucker-carlsons-unredacted
-texts-reveal.

211 *"knew we lost the election"*: Alyssa Farah's testimony to the House's January 6
committee, April 15, 2022.

211 *"the arc of Fox News"*: Charlie Sykes, *Deadline: White House*, MSNBC, January 10, 2022.

212 *Growing up at Fox:* Brian Stelter, "Gotcha TV: Crews Stalk Bill O'Reilly's
Targets," *New York Times*, April 15, 2009, https://www.nytimes.com/2009
/04/16/arts/television/16ambush.html.

213 *Most of the statement:* John Haltiwanger, "Trump Plagiarized His Endorsement of Fox News' Jesse Watters Book by Cribbing a Full Sentence from
HarperCollins," *Insider*, July 14, 2021, https://bit.ly/3OUpHC0.

213 *Newsmax was lucky:* Brian Stelter, Twitter post, January 30, 2022,
12:43 p.m., https://twitter.com/brianstelter/status/1487843909820633090.

213 *"lost steam in legacy media"*: Alyssa Farah, Reliable Sources, CNN, January 16,
2022.

214 *Babbitt represented:* Roseann M. Mandziuk, "Memory and Martyrdom:
The Transmogrification of Ashli Babbitt," *Journal of Contemporary Rhetoric*, Vol. 12, No. 3 (2022).

215 *"It was definitely not"*: Tucker Carlson, *Tucker Carlson Tonight*, Fox News,
January 5, 2022.

218 *"You shouldn't be saying that"*: Igor Derysh, "Laura Ingraham Corrects Trump
After He Mistakenly Thinks US Troops, Not Russians, Stormed Ukraine,"
Salon, February 24, 2022, https://www.salon.com/2022/02/24/corrects-after
-he-mistakenly-thinks-us-troops-not-russians-stormed-ukraine/.

219 *Their car came under fire:* Benjamin Hall, *Saved* (New York: HarperCollins,
2023).

220 *Carlson's open disdain:* Aaron Blake, "Tucker Carlson Goes Full Blame-America
on Russia's Ukraine Invasion," *Washington Post*, March 8, 2022, https://www

.washingtonpost.com/politics/2022/03/08/tucker-carlson-goes-full-blame
-america-russias-ukraine-invasion/.

"They are lying"

222 *Every time the committee:* Brian Stelter, Twitter post, July 14, 2022, 10:16 a.m., https://twitter.com/brianstelter/status/1547585915983257600.

222 *"We cannot abandon the truth":* Monica Hesse, "Liz Cheney Understood the Assignment," *Washington Post*, July 22, 2022, https://www.washingtonpost .com/lifestyle/2022/07/22/liz-cheney-hearings-monica-hesse/.

224 *"On our side of the aisle":* First Amendment Salon with Lee Levine, Tom Clare, and Dan Webb, published by the *So to Speak* podcast, May 15, 2023, https://www.thefire.org/research-learn/so-speak-podcast-transcript-first -amendment-salon-lee-levine-tom-clare-and-dan-webb.

224 *said "settlement" was a curse word:* Sarah Krouse, "How Dominion's Owner Turned a $38 Million Investment into a Windfall Settlement with Fox News," *Wall Street Journal*, April 20, 2023, https://on.wsj.com/47tDNkJ.

225 *Carlson said of the lawyer:* Sam Levine, "New Video Reveals Tucker Carlson's Coarse Remark About Dominion Lawyer," *The Guardian*, May 3, 2023, https://www.theguardian.com/media/2023/may/03/tucker-carlson-video -fox-news-dominion-lawyer.

236 *The governor's office staged:* James Call, "Florida Gov. DeSantis Brings 100-Year-Old on FOX & Friends for COVID Vaccination Milestone," *Tallahassee Democrat*, January 22, 2021, https://bit.ly/3s0ElhM.

228 *"That show has been terrible":* Dominick Mastrangelo, "Trump: 'Fox & Friends' Has Gone to the 'Dark Side,'" *The Hill*, July 25, 2022, https: //thehill.com/homenews/media/3572831-trump-fox-friends-has-gone-to -the-dark-side/.

228 *As CNN media analyst:* David Zurawik, "We Thought Murdoch's News Outlets Were Abandoning Trump. Then the FBI Searched Mar-a-Lago," CNN, August 12, 2022, https://www.cnn.com/2022/08/12/media/fox-news -coverage-fbi-mar-a-lago-search/index.html.

228 *"I'm angry":* Jesse Watters, *The Five*, Fox News, August 9, 2022.

"They must be stopped"

228 *which was starting to eclipse:* Stephen Battaglio, "Fox News' 'The Five' Topples 'Tucker Carlson Tonight' to Become New Cable News Ratings Leader," *Los Angeles Times*, December 19, 2022, https://lat.ms/47pU3Dx.

229 *"If I wasted any time"*: "I Sleep Well at Night: Suzanne Scott on Running Fox News," *Hollywood Reporter*, October 7, 2021, https://www.hollywoodreporter .com/tv/tv-features/suzanne-scott-fox-news-25th-anniversary-1235025880/.

229 *Orbán praised Carlson:* Sarah Polus, "Hungary's Orban Says Shows Like Tucker Carlson's Should Be Broadcast 24/7," *The Hill*, May 22, 2022, https: //thehill.com/policy/international/3497575-hungarys-orban-says-shows-like -tucker-carlsons-should-be-broadcast-24-7/.

230 *"Donald Trump and the MAGA Republicans"*: Remarks by President Biden on the Continued Battle for the Soul of the Nation, September 1, 2022, https://www.whitehouse.gov/briefing-room/speeches-remarks/2022/09/01 /remarks-by-president-bidenon-the-continued-battle-for-the-soul-of-the -nation/.

231 *In October James:* Remarks by President Biden at Democratic Senatorial Campaign Committee Reception, October 6, 2022, https://www.whitehouse .gov/briefing-room/speeches-remarks/2022/10/06/remarks-by-president -biden-at-democratic-senatorial-campaign-committee-reception/.

"Wackadoodle"

232 *Bourne wrote:* Cheryl Teh and Jacob Shamsian, "Sidney Powell Cited Woman Who Claimed to Be Headless, Time-Traveling Entity in Email Pushing Election Conspiracy Theories," *Insider*, February 17, 2023, https: //www.businessinsider.com/sidney-powell-voter-fraud-claims-headless -time-travel-dominion-fox-2023-2.

233 *If any of them:* Will Sommer, "Meet the 'Ghost' Woman Fox Relied on for Voter Fraud Claims," *Daily Beast*, March 9, 2023, https://www.thedailybeast .com/meet-the-ghost-minnesota-artist-fox-relied-on-for-voter-fraud-claims.

234 *"I also see reports"*: Maria Bartiromo, *Sunday Morning Futures*, Fox News, November 8, 2020.

234 *To make matters even worse:* Motion for Summary Judgment in *Dominion v. Fox*, filed on January 17, 2023, https://bit.ly/3P1lRXP.

234 *"coerced, intimidated, and misinformed"*: Abby Grossberg v. Fox Corp et al., Case No.: 1:23-cv-02368.

235 *"I tried hard"*: Ibid.

235 *She said the office:* Ibid.

236 *"When I went into the office"*: Abby Grossberg, *Deadline: White House*, MSNBC, April 25, 2023.

237 *"it was our show"*: Maria Bartiromo's deposition in *Dominion v. Fox*.

"I have no freaking idea"

238 *explicitly endorsed:* Nikki McCann Ramirez, "Tucker Carlson Tried to Play Election Kingmaker. It Went Terribly," *Rolling Stone*, November 12, 2022, https://www.rollingstone.com/politics/politics-features/tucker-carlson -election-senate-jd-vance-blake-masters-1234629984/.

238 *"Being able to get on Tucker":* Charles Homans, "Without Tucker Carlson, Far Right Loses a Foothold in the Mainstream," *New York Times*, May 16, 2023, https://www.nytimes.com/2023/05/16/us/politics/tucker-carlson-far-right.html.

239 *"got it wrong":* Tucker Carlson on *The Charlie Kirk Show* podcast, April 28, 2023.

239 *"They have run this country":* Tucker Carlson, *Tucker Carlson Tonight*, Fox News, November 2, 2022.

240 *"no one is going to":* Jesse Watters, *Jesse Watters Primetime*, Fox News, November 2, 2022.

241 *"I was huffing my own gas":* Tucker Carlson on *The Charlie Kirk Show* podcast, April 28, 2023.

242 *"Most of the voices":* Trey Gowdy, *America's News Headquarters*, Fox News, January 7, 2021.

242 *semantically bleached:* Brandon Tensley, "How 'Woke' Went from a Social Justice Term to a Pejorative Favored by Some Conservatives," CNN, July 10, 2022, https://www.cnn.com/2022/07/10/us/woke-race-deconstructed -newsletter-reaj/index.html.

242 *"leaned into so-called":* Aaron Rupar, "Why Fox News Is Having a Day-Long Meltdown over Dr. Seuss," *Vox*, March 2, 2021, https://www.vox.com /2021/3/2/22309176/fox-news-dr-seuss-cancel-culture-fox-news-biden.

243 *part of a backlash to gay and transgender rights:* Trip Gabriel, "After Roe, Republicans Sharpen Attacks on Gay and Transgender Rights," *New York Times*, July 22, 2022, https://www.nytimes.com/2022/07/22/us/politics/after -roe-republicans-sharpen-attacks-on-gay-and-transgender-rights.html.

243 *A transgender teacher:* Claire Goforth, "Trans Teacher Reveals How Fox News' Coverage of Their TikTok Led to Bomb, Death Threats," *Daily Dot*, March 29, 2023, https://www.dailydot.com/debug/fox-news-trans-teachers/.

244 *Trump actually seemed taken aback:* Ewan Palmer, "Trump Says Supporters More Concerned About Transgender Issues than Taxes," *Newsweek*, June 11, 2023, https://www.newsweek.com/trump-transgender-supporters -north-carolina-1805783.

244 *When liberal stalwart:* Robert Reich, Twitter post, July 30, 2023, 9:21 p.m., https://twitter.com/RBReich/status/1685822840044482560.

244 *His 2021 polemic:* Dominick Mastrangelo, "Tucker Carlson Targets McCarthy over Ties to GOP Pollster Frank Luntz," *The Hill*, May 4, 2021, https://bit.ly/440uOEZ.

245 *"release the January 6 files":* Tucker Carlson, *Tucker Carlson Tonight*, Fox News, January 3, 2023.

245 *Carlson told Grossberg: Abby Grossberg v. Fox Corp et al.*, Case No.: 1:23-cv-02368.

246 *Grossberg said later:* Abby Grossberg, *Anderson Cooper 360*, CNN, May 2, 2023.

246 *"You gotta feed":* Matt Fuller, Twitter post, May 23, 2023, 8:55 a.m., https://twitter.com/MEPFuller/status/1660992904301510656.

246 *"The Republican party exists":* Andrew Lawrence, "Hate-Watching Fox News so You Don't Have to," the Offline with Jon Favreau podcast, May 30, 2023.

PART FOUR

"They endorsed"

249 *"make sure the truth got exposed":* Dan Primack, "Dominion Voting Systems Tells Its Fox News Lawsuit Story," *Axios*, May 1, 2023, https://www.axios.com/2023/05/01/fox-news-dominion-lawsuit-history.

250 *Days before his deposition:* Roisin O'Connor, "Rupert Murdoch Spotted in Barbados with New Girlfriend Ann-Lesley Smith," *The Independent*, January 16, 2023, https://yhoo.it/3OUKZ2l.

260 *"I go back and forth":* Kevin Robillard, "Fox News Refuses to Run Snarky White House Comment in Story Criticizing Biden's Age," *HuffPost*, June 5, 2023, https://www.huffpost.com/entry/fox-news-white-house-joe-biden-age_n_647de965e4b0a7554f45c0c2.

"Tell Tucker to stop"

261 *news outlets had been petitioning:* Zoe Richards, "News Outlets Request McCarthy Share Jan. 6 Footage That Tucker Carlson Says He Has Access to," NBC News, February 24, 2023, https://nbcnews.to/44WtN1T.

262 *"mistake":* "Senator McConnell Calls Tucker Carlson's Depiction of January 6 Attack a 'Mistake,'" C-SPAN, March 7, 2023, https://www.c-span.org/video/?c5060662/senator-mcconnell-calls-tucker-carlsons-depiction-january-6-attack-mistake.

262 *"Tucker was very set":* Abby Grossberg, *Deadline: White House*, MSNBC, April 25, 2023.

263 *Chansley watched Carlson's show:* Kyle Cheney, "DOJ Counters Qanon Shaman's Bid to Toss His Jan. 6 Sentence," *Politico*, June 6, 2023, https://www.politico.com/news/2023/06/06/qanon-shaman-sentencing-appeal-jan6-00100684.

264 *Kristin Fisher said:* David Bauder, "Records in Fox Defamation Case Show Pressures on Reporters," Associated Press, March 11, 2023, https://apnews.com/article/fox-news-journalism-election-dominion-defamation-9b33fc9ca1e11fc0b49e2f437fc60007.

265 *libel law training sessions:* Brian Stelter, "Inside Fox News as Dominion Revelations Rattle the Network," *Vanity Fair*, March 8, 2023, https://www.vanityfair.com/news/2023/03/fox-news-dominion-lawsuit-tucker-carlson-rupert-murdoch.

266 *"Our bosses are acting":* Ibid.

267 *"There seems to be a Dobbs problem":* Marshall Cohen, "Judge in Dominion Defamation Case Skeptical of Fox's Arguments, as Both Sides Seek a Pre-trial Win," CNN, March 21, 2023, https://www.cnn.com/2023/03/21/business/fox-news-dominion-summary-judgment/index.html.

"I am your retribution"

269 *"JUST TELL THE TRUTH":* Marina Pitofsky, "Trump Calls on Rupert Murdoch to Back False 2020 Election Fraud Claims Ahead of Dominion Trial," *USA Today*, April 17, 2023, https://www.usatoday.com/story/news/politics/2023/04/17/donald-trump-murdoch-fox-false-2020-election/11684375002/.

271 *"Fox primary":* David Bauder, "Debate Line-up Illustrates Power of Fox News in GOP Campaign," Associated Press, August 4, 2015, https://apnews.com/article/——-7e92fefd7782467db38d8be54c68a408.

271 *slavering promotion:* Michael Grynbaum, "Ron DeSantis Usually Avoids the Press. For Murdoch, He'll Make an Exception," *New York Times*, March 2, 2023, https://www.nytimes.com/2023/03/02/business/media/ron-desantis-murdoch-media.html.

271 *winding up like Nikki Haley:* Charles Mahtesian and Calder McHugh, "How Tucker Carlson's Exit Reshapes the Republican Primary," *Politico*, April 24, 2023, https://www.politico.com/newsletters/politico-nightly/2023/04/24/how-tucker-carlsons-exit-reshapes-the-republican-primary-00093590.

272 *"kind of presumptuous":* Tucker Carlson, *Tucker Carlson Tonight*, Fox News, March 13, 2023.

272 *headline and head-shaking news:* Peter Wehner, "Vengeance Is Trump's,"

The Atlantic, March 13, 2023, https://www.theatlantic.com/ideas/archive
/2023/03/donald-trump-cpac-republican-primary-retribution/673373/.

273   *"feel protected by him"*: Ruth Ben-Ghiat, *Velshi*, MSNBC, March 26, 2023.

"Search for the truth"

276   *Dan Webb said:* First Amendment Salon with Lee Levine, Tom Clare, and
Dan Webb, published by the *So to Speak* podcast, May 15, 2023, https://
www.thefire.org/research-learn/so-speak-podcast-transcript-first
-amendment-salon-lee-levine-tom-clare-and-dan-webb.

276   *Tom Clare said:* Ibid.

277   *"could have been the card":* Ibid.

278   *belatedly disclosed to Dominion:* Ted Johnson, "Judge Considers Next Steps
After Disclosure That Rupert Murdoch Is an Officer," *Deadline*, April 12, 2023,
https://deadline.com/2023/04/fox-dominion-defamation-trial-1235321771/.

279   *"it was Maria's responsibility"*: Nina Golgowski, "Fox News Producer Says
She Was Fired After Correcting Dominion Deposition," *HuffPost*, March 27,
2023, https://bit.ly/3OT3Omo.

279   *"I thought I could just"*: Abby Grossberg, *NBC Nightly News with Lester
Holt*, NBC, March 30, 2023.

280   *"That's a little harder"*: Justin Baragona, "Ex-Fox Producer: There Are Secret Rudy Giuliani Recordings About Dominion," *Daily Beast*, April 11,
2023, https://bit.ly/3OVPnhC.

280   *At the end of June:* Helen Coster and Jonathan Stempel, "Fox Settles Lawsuit with Fired Former Producer for $12 Million," Reuters, June 30, 2023,
https://www.reuters.com/legal/fox-settles-lawsuit-with-fired-former-producer
-grossberg-12-million-2023-06-30/.

280   *"You don't pay"*: Gretchen Carlson, Twitter post, June 30, 2023, 3:16 p.m.,
https://twitter.com/GretchenCarlson/status/1674859487990095873.

281   *"Roger was too busy harassing"*: Brian Stelter, "Inside Fox News as Dominion
Revelations Rattle the Network," *Vanity Fair*, March 8, 2023, https://www
.vanityfair.com/news/2023/03/fox-news-dominion-lawsuit-tucker-carlson
-rupert-murdoch.

285   *Webb and Nelson emailed Jerry Roscoe:* Sarah Ellison, Josh Dawsey, and
Rosalind S. Helderman, "Fox Was Resigned to a Tough Trial. Then, a Secret
Mediator Stepped in," *Washington Post*, April 19, 2023, https://www.wash
ingtonpost.com/media/2023/04/19/mediator-fox-news-dominion-settlement/.

286   *The first shareholder lawsuit:* Julia Malleck, "A Fox Shareholder Sued Rupert

Murdoch over the Network's 2020 Election Coverage," *Quartz*, April 12, 2023, https://qz.com/fox-shareholder-rupert-murdoch-2020-election-coverage-1850326635.

288 *"I was reading a thousand"*: Joe Flint, "The Man Who Settled the Fox-Dominion Defamation Case from a Romanian Tour Bus," *Wall Street Journal*, April 19, 2023, https://www.wsj.com/articles/the-man-who-settled-the-fox-dominion-defamation-case-from-a-romanian-tour-bus-b3abf87f.

288 *wife's iPad:* Ibid.

288 *"I don't think a forced apology"*: David Bauder, "Last Minute Brinkmanship and Overseas Assist End Fox Case," Associated Press, April 19, 2023, https://bit.ly/3KApyRi.

289 *"It went down to the wire"*: Marshall Cohen and Oliver Darcy, "Inside the historic Settlement Talks Between Fox News and Dominion," CNN, April 19, 2023, https://www.cnn.com/2023/04/19/media/fox-dominion-how-it-happened/index.html.

"Unexpectedly bad"

290 *"They agreed to take me"*: Chadwick Moore, *Tucker* (Fort Lauderdale: All Seasons Press, 2023).

290 *"Dominion was looking"*: Tatiana Siegel, "Inside Tucker Carlson's Battle to Trade His $20 Million Fox News Salary for a Twitter Show," *Variety*, May 16, 2023, https://variety.com/2023/tv/news/tucker-carlson-fox-news-exit-dominion-lawsuit-twitter-show-1235613404/.

290 *"As the Fox principals"*: Ibid.

291 *calling the claim "categorically false"*: Ibid.

291 *in a May 9 letter*: Mike Allen and Sara Fischer, "Tucker Carlson Accuses Fox of Fraud, Contract Breach," *Axios*, May 9, 2023, https://www.axios.com/2023/05/09/tucker-carlson-fox-news-letter-fraud.

292 *"what is permissible on air"*: Alexandria Ocasio-Cortez, *Inside with Jen Psaki*, MSNBC, April 23, 2023.

293 *"an avid and loyal Fox viewer"*: *James Ray Epps v. Fox News*, Case No.: 1:23-cv-00761-UNA.

293 *The segment pointed out: 60 Minutes*, CBS News, April 23, 2023.

295 *upward of 3 million*: A. J. Katz, "These Are the Top-Rated Cable News Shows for March 2023," *TVNewser*, March 29, 2023, https://www.adweek.com/tvnewser/these-are-the-top-rated-cable-news-shows-for-march-2023/527004/.

295 *Fox was shedding*: Stephen Battaglio, "Fox News Prime-time Ratings Plummet

After Tucker Carlson Firing as Newsmax Sees Boost," *Los Angeles Times*, April 26, 2023, https://www.latimes.com/entertainment-arts/business/story/2023-04-26/fox-news-ratings-plummet-without-tucker-carlson.

"Too big for his boots"

297 *He triggered so many ad boycotts:* Oliver Darcy, "Tucker Carlson's Show Has Been Hit by an Advertiser Boycott, and It's Having a Visible Effect," CNN, December 20, 2018, https://www.cnn.com/2018/12/20/media/tucker-carlson-fox-news-ad-boycott/index.html.

299 *"Nobody watches Fox Nation":* Ryan Bort, "Tucker Carlson Bashes Fox Nation in Leaked Video," *Rolling Stone*, May 1, 2023, https://www.rollingstone.com/politics/politics-news/tucker-carlson-bashes-fox-nation-leaked-video-1234726800/.

300 *"Tucker bunker":* Tina Nguyen, "Murmurs from the Tucker Bunker," *Puck*, April 27, 2023, https://puck.news/murmurs-from-the-tucker-bunker/.

301 *"one of the top people":* Tucker Carlson on *Redacted* with Clayton Morris, March 11, 2023, https://www.youtube.com/watch?v=SI9OdnyvQew.

301 *Months later:* Carlson's interview on *Stay Free with Russell Brand*, July 7, 2023.

301 *took full advantage:* Remarks by President Biden at the White House Correspondents' Dinner, April 29, 2023, https://www.whitehouse.gov/briefing-room/speeches-remarks/2023/04/30/remarks-by-president-biden-at-the-white-house-correspondents-dinner/.

PART FIVE

"Fox knew"

305 *"European super-yacht holiday":* Andrew Hornery, "All the Murdochs gather for a European super-yacht holiday, except one," *Sydney Morning Herald,* July 15, 2023, https://bit.ly/3XjoJ3s.

306 *"is essentially a lying tax":* Caroline Orr Bueno, Twitter post, April 18, 2023, 10:22 p.m., https://twitter.com/RVAwonk/status/1648512445303115777.

306 *The outrage machine:* Justin Baragona, "Fox News Stoked Outrage Over Migrants Displacing Homeless Vets. It Was a Hoax," *Daily Beast,* May 19, 2023, https://www.thedailybeast.com/fox-news-stoked-outrage-over-migrants-displacing-homeless-vets-it-was-a-hoax.

306 *blown up in the network's face:* Gabriel Hays, "No evidence supporting claim that New York hotels kicked out veterans to make room for migrants," Fox News, May 21, 2023, https://fxn.ws/3ssHHKB.

308 *"I think would have eventually won":* Jim Rutenberg, Michael S. Schmidt, and Jeremy W. Peters, "Inside Fox's Legal and Business Debacle," *New York Times,* May 27, 2023.

309 *In an appearance:* YouTube, "A Conversation with Viet D. Dinh '93," https://www.youtube.com/watch?v=EJ4KKvcLtFk.

310 *"We offered a number":* Jennifer Graham, "Q&A: Fox's Bret Baier on going head-to-head with Trump," *Deseret News,* January 8, 2024, https://www.deseret.com/2024/1/8/24027148/bret-baier-fox-town-hall-desantis-haley-trump/.

"We want no lawsuits"

311 *he plotted a comeback:* Oliver Darcy, "Tucker Carlson Announces Plans to Relaunch His Show on Twitter," CNN, May 9, 2023, https://www.cnn.com/2023/05/09/media/tucker-carlson-twitter/index.html.

314 *came back to the time slot:* Brian Steinberg, "After Tucker Carlson Exits Fox News, Advertisers Start to Return," *Variety,* May 8, 2023, https://bit.ly/4aTDQHb.

315 *"We have seen":* Ibid.

315 *"You've worked so hard":* Jesse Watters, *Jesse Watters Primetime,* Fox News, July 17, 2023.

315 *When CNN's Donie O'Sullivan:* "Misinformation, The Trump Faithful," CNN, April 28, 2024.

316 *"I just want":* Lex Fridman Podcast #414 with Tucker Carlson, https://bit.ly/4aQo4N9.

317 *"was full of racist dog whistles":* Arwa Mahdawi, "Even for Tucker Carlson, his supposed Obama sex exposé was ridiculous," *The Guardian,* September 7, 2023, https://bit.ly/3Xd1sTY.

317 *Even Putin said:* Sarah Gray and Kelsey Vlamis, "Putin says he thought Tucker Carlson would ask tougher questions," *Business Insider,* February 14, 2024, https://bit.ly/4bM6E5v.

318 *"really run a newsroom":* Gregg Re, X, March 23, 2024, https://twitter.com/gregg_re/status/1771576497217626194.

318 *"coordinated the whole movement":* Christopher Rufo, X, March 26, 2024, https://twitter.com/realchrisrufo/status/1772758018922553455.

318 *By the summer of 2024:* Max Tani and Shelby Talcott, "Top executive departs Tucker Carlson's new company," *Semafor,* May 15, 2024, https://bit.ly/3x88G0R.

319 *"this is the third time":* Aila Slisco, "Tucker Carlson Grateful for Fox News Humiliation," *Newsweek,* August 28, 2023, https://bit.ly/3VvvtNt.

"Cloud of confusion"

320 *"Praetorian Guard":* A. G. Gancarski, "Ron DeSantis rips the conservative media that propelled him to a national level," *Florida Politics,* January 13, 2024, https://bit.ly/3VaBVZ6.

321 *"They're in the business of fan service":* David Bauder, "Look who's back: Donald Trump's big return to Fox News," Associated Press, April 12, 2023, https://apnews.com/article/fox-news-dominion-trial-trump-carlson-election-f580413e13d1bfaea1e94827a4f35dc1.

322 *Chesebro emailed a fellow attorney:* Rich Kremer, "Documents suggest Wisconsin was genesis of Trump false elector plot," Wisconsin Public Radio, March 8, 2024, https://www.wpr.org/politics/documents-suggest-wisconsin-was-genesis-of-trump-false-elector-plot.

323 *As part of a settlement deal:* Ibid.

323 *"Trump is deploying a strategy":* John Podesta, "Trump's dangerous strategy to undermine reality," *Washington Post,* February 16, 2017, https://wapo.st/3xcVrvO.

324 *One defense attorney said:* Jaclyn Peiser, "Accused Capitol Rioter Had 'Foxitis,' His Attorney Says," *Washington Post,* May 7, 2021, https://www.washingtonpost.com/nation/2021/05/07/fox-news-anthony-antonio-capitol-riot/.

324 *"Tucker nails it again!":* Ryan J. Reilly, "Tucker Carlson's Jan. 6 'Agent Provocateur' Is a Big Tucker Fan and an Amateur Cardinals Mascot," *HuffPost,* December 9, 2021, https://bit.ly/4c8c3nl.

324 *This deeply offended:* Ryan J. Reilly, "Jan. 6 Rioter Who Tucker Carlson Guest Said Was a Fed Is Arrested by the FBI," NBC News, August 2, 2023, https://nbcnews.to/3KucMDA.

326 *Schatz recognized the weight:* Brian Stelter, "Senator Brian Schatz Explains What Donald Trump's 'Fascism' Would Mean for America," *Vanity Fair,* March 7, 2024, https://www.vanityfair.com/news/brian-schatz-donald-trump-fascism.

327 *"What we saw on January 6":* Jeh Johnson, *Anderson Cooper 360,* CNN, August 22, 2023.

328 *"Pence provided":* Matt Gertz, X, March 19, 2024, https://twitter.com/Matt Gertz/status/1770117627421098167.

329 *"may be center stage":* David Rothkopf, Twitter post, August 17, 2023, 9:42 a.m., https://twitter.com/djrothkopf/status/1692169984808730669.

329 *91 percent of people:* Greg Sargent, "Trump has 'my Kevin' trapped. New data on Fox News viewers shows why," *Washington Post,* July 31, 2023, https://www.washingtonpost.com/opinions/2023/07/31/fox-trump-indict ment-poll-desantis/.

329 *At the Iowa State Fair:* Shawn Reynolds, Twitter post, August 15, 2023, 6:10 p.m., https://twitter.com/ShawnReynolds_/status/16915729840691 32560.

AFTERWORD

334 *"Do I feel sorry":* Jesse Watters, *The Five,* Fox News, January 3, 2022.

335 *"egg on their faces again":* Andrew Bates, X, March 30, 2024, https://twitter .com/AndrewJBates46/status/1774201605530800496.

335 *"Our country is being poisoned":* Donald Trump, *Hannity,* Fox News, February 29, 2024.

338 *"People think Fox News":* Alexandria Ocasio-Cortez, Twitter post, November 7, 2021, 8:54 p.m., https://twitter.com/AOC/status/145752687986 7506696.

339 *"Whoever is underrepresented":* Monica Guzman, Twitter post, March 3, 2022, 12:01 p.m., https://twitter.com/moniguzman/status/1499429749566816 258?lang=en.

339 *"more protopian stories":* Joe Pompeo, "Kathryn Murdoch Wants to Flip the Dystopian Script With New 'Protopian' Production Studio," *Vanity Fair,* July 21, 2023, https://www.vanityfair.com/news/2023/07/kathryn-murdoch -james-murdoch-production-studio-protopian.

ABOUT THE AUTHOR

Brian Stelter has covered television and politics for twenty years as founder of *TVNewser*, media reporter at *The New York Times*, chief media correspondent for CNN Worldwide, and anchor of *Reliable Sources* on CNN. He has also been a Walter Shorenstein Fellow at Harvard Kennedy School's Shorenstein Center on Media, Politics and Public Policy. He is currently a special correspondent for *Vanity Fair* and host of *Inside the Hive*. Stelter is also a producer on the Apple TV+ series *The Morning Show*, which was inspired by his first book, *Top of the Morning*, and he executive-produced the HBO documentary *After Truth: Disinformation and the Cost of Fake News* (2020). He lives in New Jersey with his wife and two children. Follow him across social media @BrianStelter.